Wright, Benjamin G.
(Benjamin Givins)

No small difference.

DATE			

NO SMALL DIFFERENCE

SOCIETY OF BIBLICAL LITERATURE
SEPTUAGINT AND COGNATE STUDIES SERIES

Edited by
Claude E. Cox

Number 26

NO SMALL DIFFERENCE
Sirach's Relationship to Its Hebrew Parent Text

Benjamin G. Wright

NO SMALL DIFFERENCE
Sirach's Relationship to Its Hebrew Parent Text

Benjamin G. Wright

Scholars Press
Atlanta, Georgia

NO SMALL DIFFERENCE
Sirach's Relationship to Its Hebrew Parent Text

Benjamin G. Wright

Library of Congress Cataloging-in-Publication Data

Wright, Benjamin G. (Benjamin Givins)
 No small difference : Sirach's relationship to its Hebrew parent
text / Benjamin G. Wright.
  p. cm. -- (Septuagint and cognate studies series ; no. 26)
  Originally presented as the author's thesis (Ph. D.)
  Bibliography: p.
  Includes indexes.
  ISBN 1-55540-374-3 (alk. paper). -- ISBN 1-55540-375-1 (pbk. :
alk. paper)
  1. Bible. O.T. Apocrypha. Ecclesiasticus. Hebrew. 2. Bible.
O.T. Apocrypha. Ecclesiasticus--Translating. I. Title
II. Series.
BS1762.W75 1989
229'.4044-dc20   89-10371
                                                  CIP

Printed in the United States of America
on acid-free paper

DEDICATION

To my wife, Ann,
whose love is a "pillar of support."

To my daughter, Rachel,
who has never been a "treasure of sleeplessness"
for her father.

To my grandparents, Chris and Hilda Schwarz,
who like Ben Sira acquired much wisdom and did
not keep it to themselves.

TABLE OF CONTENTS

LIST OF TABLES

TABLES CONTAINED IN CHAPTER 2

WORD ORDER

SEGMENTATION

QUANTITATIVE REPRESENTATION

LEXICAL REPRESENTATION

TABLES CONTAINED IN CHAPTER 3

LIST OF ABBREVIATIONS

(The abbreviations of books of the Bible, Apocrypha, and Pseudepigrapha conform to those of the Society of Biblical Literature "Instructions to Contributors," in the Members' Handbook [1980].)

AASF - Annales Academiae Scientiarum Fennicae
AnBib - Analecta biblica
APOT - R. H. Charles, ed., The Apocrypha and Pseudepigrapha of the Old Testament.
ASOR - American Schools of Oriental Research
ATAbh - Alttestamentliche Abhandlungen
Barr - The Typology of Literalism in Ancient Biblical Translations
BASOR - Bulletin of the American Schools of Oriental Research
BBB - Bonner biblische Beiträge
BDB - F. Brown, S. R. Driver, and C. A. Briggs. A Hebrew and English Lexicon of the Old Testament.
BETL - Bibliotheca ephemeridum theologicarum lovaniensium
Bib - Biblica
BibOr - Biblica et orientalia
BIOSCS - Bulletin of the International Organization for Septuagint and Cognate Studies
BLE - Bulletin de littérature ecclésiastique
Box and Oesterley - G. H. Box and W. O. E. Oesterley, "Sirach," in APOT.
BTFT - Bijdragen: Tijdschrift voor Filosofie en Theologie
BVC - Bible et vie chrétienne
BZ - Biblische Zeitschrift
BZAW - Beihefte zur Zeitschrift für die alttestamentliche Wissenschaft
CATSS - Computer Assisted Tools for Septuagint Studies
CBQ - Catholic Biblical Quarterly
Cox - Claude E. Cox, VIth Congress of the International Organization for Septuagint and Cognate Studies - Jerusalem
DJD - Discoveries in the Judean Desert
EBib - Études bibliques
EHAT - Exegetisches Handbuch zum Alten Testament
EstBib - Estudios Bíblicos
EstEcl - Estudios Eclesiásticos
EvT - Evangelische Theologie
ExpTim - The Expository Times
GKI - The Greek translation of Ben Sira's grandson
GKII - The later expanded Greek translation of Ben Sira

GRBS - Greek, Roman, and Byzantine Studies
HR   - E. Hatch and Henry A. Redpath. A Concordance
        to the Septuagint and the Other Versions of
        the Old Testament.
HTR   - Harvard Theological Review
HUCA - Hebrew Union College Annual
IsrOrSt - Israel Oriental Studies
Jastrow - M. Jastrow. A Dictionary of the Targumim,
        The Talmud Babli and Yerushalmi, and the
        Midrashic Literature.
JBL   - Journal of Biblical Literature
JETS - Journal of the Evangelical Theological Society
JJS   - Journal of Jewish Studies
JNES - Journal of Near Eastern Studies
JQR   - Jewish Quarterly Review
JSJ   - Journal for the Study of Judaism in the
        Persian, Hellenistic, and Roman Periods
JTS   - Journal of Theological Studies
Lévi - I. Lévi. L'Ecclésiastique ou la Sagesse de
        Jésus, fils de Sira.
Liddell and Scott - H. G. Liddell and Robert Scott.
        A Greek-English Lexicon.
LXX   - The earliest recoverable translation of the
        Greek Pentateuch.
Middendorp - Th. Middendorp. Die Stellung Jesus Ben
        Siras zwischen Judentum und Hellenismus.
MS A, B, B(mg) C, D, E, F - The Geniza Hebrew
        manuscripts of Ben Sira
MS M - The Hebrew scroll of Ben Sira from Masada
MT   - Masoretic Text
NAWG, I. phil.-hist. Kl. - Nachrichten der Akademie
        der Wissenschaften in Göttingen I.
        philologisch-historische Klasse
NTS   - New Testament Studies
OBO   - Orbis biblicus et Orientalis
OG   - The earliest recoverable Greek translations of
        the Hebrew scriptures and their subsequent
        textual traditions.
OTS   - Oudtestamentische Studien
PAAJR - Proceedings of the American Academy for
        Jewish Research
Peters - Norbert Peters. Das Buch Jesus Sirach oder
        Ecclesiasticus.
Peters, Text - Norbert Peters. Der jüngst
        wiederaufgefundene hebräische Text des Buches
        Ecclesiasticus untersucht, herausgegeben,
        übersetzt und mit kritischen Noten versehen.
RBén - Revue Bénédictine
Reiterer - Franz Vinzenz Reiterer. "Urtext" und
        Übersetzungen: Sprachstudie über Sir 44,16-
        45,26 als Beitrag zur Siraforschung.
RevQ - Revue de Qumrân

REJ   - Revue des études juives
RBén - Revue bénédictine
RTL   - Revue théologique de Louvain
SBL   - Society of Biblical Literature
SBLDS - Society of Biblical Literature Dissertation
        Series
Schechter and Taylor - Solomon Schechter and C.
        Taylor. The Wisdom of Ben Sira: Portions of
        the Book of Ecclesiasticus from the Hebrew
        Manuscripts in the Cairo Geniza Collections
        Presented to the University of Cambridge by
        the Editors.
SCS   - Septuagint and Cognate Studies Series
Segal - M. H. Segal, ‎ספר בן-סירא השלם.
Sir   - The Wisdom of Ben Sira, also called Sirach
Skehan and Di Lella - Patrick Skehan and A. A. Di
        Lella. The Wisdom of Ben Sira.
Smend - Rudolph Smend. Die Weisheit des Jesus Sirach
        erklärt.
SSS   - Semitic Studies Series
SVTP - Studia in Vetus Testamentum Pseudepigrapha
Syr   - Syriac translation of Ben Sira
Tov, Text-Critical Use of the Septuagint - E. Tov.
        The Text-Critical Use of the Septuagint in
        Biblical Research.
TLG   - Thesaurus Linguae Graecae
TLZ   - Theologische Literaturzeitung
Tov and Wright - E. Tov and Benjamin G. Wright. "A
        Computer-Assisted Study of the Criteria for
        Assessing the Literalness of Translation
        Units in the LXX."
TRu   - Theologische Rundschau
TU   - Texte und Untersuchungen zur Geschichte der
        altchristlichen Literatur
TZ   - Theologische Zeitschrift
VD   - Verbum Domini
VT   - Vetus Testamentum
VTSup - Vetus Testamentum (Supplement)
WDienst - Wort und Dienst
ZAW   - Zeitschrift für die alttestamentliche
        Wissenschaft
ZKT   - Zeitschrift für katholische Theologie

PREFACE

This book is essentially an unrevised version of my Ph.D. dissertation. The only changes that have been made are typographical errors and some matters of clarification. The idea for this study of the Book of Ben Sira came while I was taking my Ph.D. field examination in Septuagint Studies. One of the questions focused on the characterizations of Greek biblical translations as literal or free. As I thought about the translations that were available to modern scholars, the reality struck home that virtually nothing is known about the people who translated the Hebrew scriptures, as well as when and where they worked. I realized that the only translator about whom we know anything and whose translation was transmitted relatively intact was Ben Sira's grandson, who had the foresight to introduce his translation. In that introduction, he reveals some important information for those who study the Jewish-Greek translations. Not only is he aware of Greek translations of the Hebrew scriptures, but he knows that the translations do not always say the same thing as their Hebrew sources. He then requests the reader's forebearance for his own shortcomings.

Here is a translator about whom we know certain personal facts, who he was, when and where he worked, but in the prologue to his work we also find that he had thought about the problems of translating. This translation, I thought, should be an ideal case in which to study how a translator worked. He was aware of the difficulties; he knew other translations that he could use and from which he could learn.

In fact, the idea seemed so obvious that I
almost did not approach my advisor about the
subject, but after some research, I found that such
a study had not been undertaken. Only after I had
become absorbed in the work did I discover the real
pitfalls of working with this book. The primary
problem is the state of preservation of the Hebrew
texts. The Hebrew manuscripts of Ben Sira are
fragmentary, and the texts that they contain are
full of difficult textual problems. I felt,
however, that these problems could be overcome, or
at least that I could compensate somewhat for them.

As I read the literature on the book of Ben
Sira, I realized that two problems needed to be
addressed, if even in an outline fashion. The first
concerned the translation technique of the grandson. Since the sometimes overlapping Hebrew texts
were only extant for about two-thirds of the book,
a study of the translation technique, with the goal
of characterizing various facets of the grandson's
translation, might provide valuable data for
reconstructions of some elements of his Hebrew
parent text. Second, since he knew other Greek
translations, presumably of the Hebrew scriptures,
his possible dependence on those translations could
give a second and more specific avenue for information that would benefit the recovery of his
grandfather's Hebrew text.

Part of the difficulty in pursuing such a
study was the limitations of the available tools.
For such a long translation as Greek Sir, there
would be large amounts of data, particularly
because of the specific aspects of translation
technique that I planned to treat, and in addition,

the grandson's work would need to be compared to
other translations for the same issues. The answer
was provided by the computer data bank and
technical resources of the Computer Assisted Tools
for Septuagint Studies Project (CATSS). As a
consequence, the data for this study was excerpted
from computer data files by means of programs
developed at CATSS. Since this study is one of the
first to use this extensive data bank, there were
many technical hurdles, and I am much indebted to
those members of the project who assisted me in
solving what seemed like a mountain of difficulties.

Besides the complex textual problems that
accompany any study of Sir, a very practical
problem faces anyone who works with this book. It
is well known that all the extant Greek manuscripts
of Sir have suffered the displacement of a large
body of text, so that 30.25-33.13a comes after
33.13b-36.16a. This displacement is not found in
the Cairo Geniza Hebrew manuscripts. The two
different sequences engender two different systems
of chapter and verse numbering. Joseph Ziegler, in
his Göttingen edition of the Greek, records the
traditional Greek numbering in his chapter and
verse scheme and puts the Hebrew numbering in
parentheses. The Latin, with its numerous additions, as well as its retention of the Hebrew
order, has a different numbering system from the
Greek and Hebrew. To make matters worse, many of
the modern translations have chapter and verse
schemes that correspond neither to the Greek nor to
the Latin numbering systems. This state of confusion needs to be rectified. In accordance with A.
A. Di Lella's plea in the Preface to the Anchor

Bible commentary on Ben Sira for scholars to adopt
and use one numbering system for chapters and
verses in Sir, I have adopted the same system used
in that commentary. Ziegler's chapter and verse
numbers are followed throughout. In the displaced
chapters, I have followed Ziegler's numbers in
parentheses, which represent the Hebrew (non-
displaced) textual order. This method of denoting
chapters and verses has also been adopted for the
forthcoming New Revised Standard Version of the
Bible.

Although the present study is particularly
focused on the translation made by Ben Sira's
grandson, the research had secondary benefits.
Since the grandson's translation technique could
not be studied in a vacuum, large amounts of data
were compiled for a number of translations other
than Sir. The need to compare Sir to other
translations was clear from the beginning, and
therefore, the results of the chapter on translation technique go beyond Sir alone. The data
compiled for these other Greek translations have
the potential to reveal much about the respective
translation techniques of these works. Unfortunately, such issues could only be discussed here in
broad terms, but they merit further study. Also,
Chapter 3, concerning the grandson's use of other
translations, has implications not only for the
reconstruction of Ben Sira's Hebrew, but is
significant in its own right as an examination of
the grandson's use of biblical sources. Comparisons
between the way that the grandson and other Greek-
Jewish works of the Second Temple Period used the
biblical traditions may provide further insight

into the transmission and development of the
biblical text at that time and of the concept of a
"biblical" text.

At the completion of this study, I owe a debt
of gratitude to a number of people. Yet, a simple
thank-you seems insufficient to repay the assistance and support that I have received from them.

My greatest debt is to Robert A. Kraft, who
supervised this work. As well as a teacher, he has
been a valued counselor and friend throughout the
entire process, from his advice in defining an area
in which to work until his reading of the final
copy. Many thanks are also due to Emanuel Tov of
the Hebrew University of Jerusalem, who took an
early interest in this study, and who, as a reader,
made many invaluable suggestions. I would like to
express my appreciation to my other reader,
Alexander A. Di Lella of the Catholic University of
America, whose prompt and careful reading of the
dissertation served to strengthen it even more in
the final stages. I would like to thank my former
teachers, Glenn A. Koch and Thomas McDaniel of
Eastern Baptist Theological Seminary, who have been
a constant source of encouragement.

A special word of thanks goes to the staff of
the Computer Assisted Tools for Septuagint Studies
Project, both in Philadelphia and Jerusalem. Each
member of the staff has always been ready to help
me work through any difficulties that I might
encounter. Walter Mankowski and Jay Treat, in
particular, deserve much credit for the time they
spent programming. Much of the data gathering could
not have been done without their efforts.

An expression of appreciation also goes to

Claude Cox, the editor of the Septuagint side of
SBLSCS for his comments and his assistance in
seeing this manuscript through to its appearance.
At the University of Pennsylvania, I would
also like to thank the Penn-Mellon Graduate
Fellowship Committee, which provided funding during
the final year of my graduate work. I am also
indebted to Marie Michaels for her invaluable
administrative assistance. Thanks go as well to my
student colleagues in the Department of Religious
Studies for their encouragement and support. At
Eastern Baptist Theological Seminary, I owe much to
the library staff for their willingness to help me
find and acquire whatever I needed.

I am greatly indebted to my parents Terry and
Doris Weber, and to my friends, who have been there
when I needed them, especially to my mother-in-law,
Joan Phillips, Raeleen Maynard, and Barbara Bianco
for their willingness to babysit. Finally, and most
importantly, a loving thank-you to my wife, Ann,
and my daughter, Rachel. Seeing a husband and
father through a dissertation is certainly an act
of monumental endurance (ὑπομονή) and sacrificial
love.

                                        Benjamin Givens Wright III
                                        March 8, 1989

CHAPTER 1

INTRODUCTION

1.1 THE TEXT OF BEN SIRA

The Wisdom of Ben Sira (Sir) was composed in the first quarter of the second century BCE by a Jerusalemite named Yeshua, son of Eleazar, son of Sira (50.27).[1] According to his grandson, who translated the book into Greek some 65 to 70 years later, his grandfather,

> who had given himself for a long time to the reading of the Law and the prophets and the other books of the ancestors and having acquired considerable skill in them, determined also himself to write something of those things pertaining to instruction and wisdom so that those who are lovers of learning and who hold them fast might make even more progress through a life of subjection to the Law. (Prologue 7-14)[2]

The grandson goes on to say that he has translated his grandfather's work so that those who want to follow the Law but live "abroad" (ἐν τῇ παροικίᾳ) may also benefit by this wisdom.

The book is a collection of proverbial wisdom with much in common with the Book of Proverbs. The author utilizes different types of wisdom material in order to teach the reader what things lead to a "life of subjection to the Law."[3] He also has a long section at the end of his book (chaps. 44-50) that glorifies the heroes of Israel's past. The section culminates in chap. 50, which praises a contemporary of the author, the high priest Simeon II.[4] The book concludes in chap. 51 with an acrostic poem about the author's own search for wisdom.

1

1.1.1 THE HEBREW MANUSCRIPTS

The Hebrew text of the book subsequently seems
to have fallen into disuse, except in some peri-
pheral Jewish groups, and the grandson's Greek
translation became its primary means of transmission.[5] Consequently, the discovery in 1896 by
Solomon Schechter of a leaf of a medieval manuscript of the "lost" Hebrew of Ben Sira among a
cache of manuscripts brought to England by two
travelers, Mrs. Lewis and Mrs. Gibson, produced a
flurry of interest in Ben Sira's book of wisdom.[6]
The subsequent discoveries of fragments of five
other medieval Hebrew manuscripts from the Cairo
Geniza, of a portion of a first century BCE scroll
of Ben Sira at Masada, of some scraps of Ben Sira
at Qumran (2Q18), and of part of chap. 51 in a
Psalms scroll from cave 11 at Qumran (11QPs[a])
created wide additional interest in this important
book.[7]

After an initial period of confidence in which
the Hebrew Geniza texts of Sir were regarded as
substantially reflecting the author's Hebrew, a
number of scholars began to express doubts about
the authenticity of the Hebrew texts contained in
the Hebrew manuscripts. The major argument put
forward against the Geniza texts was that they were
actually a retranslation from the Syriac.[8]
Unfortunately, the Qumran discoveries were too
fragmentary to provide any decisive evidence
regarding the value of the Geniza texts, but the
discovery of the Masada scroll, whose text is
remarkably similar to Cairo Geniza MS B and its

marginal corrections (MS B[mg]), demonstrated that
the doubters were wrong.[9] A. A. Di Lella's 1966
book The Hebrew Texts of Sirach: A Text-Critical
and Historical Study gave further proof that the
Geniza Hebrew texts were largely authentic. Thus it
is that the doubts about the medieval Hebrew
manuscripts of Ben Sira have been put to rest, and
it can be held with confidence that despite
numerous errors and corruptions in the Geniza texts
they substantially reflect the Hebrew that Ben Sira
himself wrote.[10]

Some considerable textual problems remain,
despite the fact that the Geniza manuscripts have
been shown to reflect, in essence, Ben Sira's
Hebrew. They also contain evidence of a second
Hebrew recension of the book. Besides the
apparently original text of Ben Sira, there is a
later, expanded revision of the book, which
contains additional proverbs. This second text,
extant in some of the Geniza manuscripts, includes
a number of additional cola, as well as other
smaller editorial additions. Some of the second
Hebrew recension readings can be found in the
differences in the readings of Hebrew manuscripts
where they overlap.[11]

According to Patrick Skehan and A. A. Di Lella
in their Anchor Bible commentary on Ben Sira,
approximately 68 percent of the book is extant in
Hebrew in the following places:
The Manuscripts from the Cairo Geniza

The Discoveries of 1896-1900 and 1931

MS A - 3.6b-16.26.
MS B - written stichometrically, 30.11-33.3;
        35.11-38.27b; 39.15c-51.30(plus
        subscription).

MS C - This manuscript is a florilegium and
contains 4.23, 30, 31; 5.4-7, 9-13;
6.18b, 19, 28, 35; 7.1, 2, 4, 6, 17, 20,
21, 23-25; 18.31b-19.3b; 20.5-7; 37.19,
22, 24, 26; 20.13; 25.8, 13,
17-24; 26.1-2a.
MS D - 36.29-38.1a.
MS E - 32.16-34.1.

Schirmann's Material from MSS B and C

MS B - 10.19c-11.10; 15.1-16.7.
MS C - 3.14-18, 21-22; 41.16; 4.21; 20.22-23;
4.22-23b; 26.2b-3, 13, 15-17; 36.27-31.

Scheiber's Material from MSS C and F

MS C - 25.8, 20-21.
MS F - 31.24-32.7; 32.12-33.8.

The Masada Scroll

Usually denoted MS M, this manuscript is
written stichometrically and contains
portions of 39.27-44.17.

Qumran Cave 2

2Q18 - contains a few letters of 6.20-31 and
6.14-15 (this piece could possibly
belong to 1.19-20).

Qumran Cave 11

11QPs^a - 51.13-20, 30b.[12]

1.1.2 THE GREEK TEXT

The Greek text of the book has been transmitted in two forms, usually designated GKI and
GKII. GKI, which has been transmitted in the major
uncial manuscripts A B C S and the minuscules that
are allied with them, represents the translation of
Ben Sira's grandson. GKII, which is not contained
in any single manuscript, but can be reconstructed

in large part from Joseph Ziegler's Origenic and
Lucianic groups, is a later expanded Greek translation based primarily on the expanded second
Hebrew recension.[13] In the introduction to his
excellent Göttingen edition of the Greek, Ziegler
argues that GKII was not a completely separate
translation, as some have argued, but that it used
GKI as a base text. The translator of GKII then
translated the second Hebrew recension into Greek
only in those places where GKI would not suffice.[14]
The Greek tradition also has one unique
characteristic. All of the extant Greek manuscripts
have a textual displacement where 30.25-33.13a and
33.13b-36.16a have exchanged places. This is most
likely the result of the transposition of leaves of
a Greek manuscript, but it also means that every
Greek manuscript in existence derives ultimately
from this one exemplar.[15] Ziegler's chapter and
verse numbers follow the Greek order while he
places the Hebrew chapter and verse numbers for
these sections in parentheses.

1.1.3 THE LATIN TEXT

The Old Latin text, which was incorporated
into the Vulgate because Jerome did not make a new
translation of Sir, is a valuable witness to the
GKII text from which it was translated. The
translation was probably made in the second century
CE and lacked the Prologue of the grandson as well
as chaps. 44-50, the so-called Praise of the
Ancestors section.[16] The Old Latin is especially
valuable because it contains many GKII readings,
but it does not have the displacement found in all

the extant Greek manuscripts. As a result, it is of
great importance for studying GKII.[17] The translation itself presents a number of difficulties
since it often gives double and triple readings as
well as numerous additions and transpositions.[18]

1.1.4 THE SYRIAC TEXT

Although a number of theories have been
proposed concerning the origins of the Syriac
translation of Sir, it now seems probable that the
book was translated from Hebrew by Ebionite
Christians sometime before the early fourth century
CE. A later revision was undertaken in the latter
part of that century.[19] This version of Sir was
translated from a Hebrew text that had charac-
teristics of both Hebrew recensions, but the
translator was also frequently influenced by a
Greek version that had much in common with GKII.[20]
From a text-critical standpoint the Syriac is a
valuable witness to the Hebrew, although it is
generally acknowledged that the translation was
frequently not very carefully done and, given its
Christian origins, often changes the import of the
text deliberately.[21]

1.2 RECOVERING THE HEBREW TEXT OF BEN SIRA

Since about one-third of the Hebrew text of
Ben Sira has not yet been recovered, a great deal
of interest has been understandably directed toward
the textual criticism of the extant Hebrew texts
along with the reconstruction of the Hebrew for
those places where no Hebrew has come to light. The

Greek translation of Ben Sira's grandson is the
primary basis from which such reconstructions are
made, but the later Syriac translation, and to a
lesser extent the Old Latin, need to be consulted
as well. This focus on textual criticism and
reconstruction can be seen especially in the
commentaries by Israel Lévi, Norbert Peters, M. H.
Segal, the exceptional commentary of Rudolph Smend,
and in the critical apparatus to the translation of
Sir by G. H. Box and W. O. E. Oesterley in R. H.
Charles's Apocrypha and Pseudepigrapha of the Old
Testament.[22]

The basis for the textual criticism and
subsequent reconstruction of the Hebrew, however,
is often not explicit. The usefulness of a
translation as a witness for the text of its source
depends to a large degree on how clearly the
translator's approach to the source text is
understood. This attitude can be seen in the
translation technique, that is, the means by which
the translator rendered different facets of the
source text into the target language. The study of
translation technique in the Jewish-Greek translations has increased greatly in the past few
years, both in the examinations of particular
aspects of the translation techniques of the OG
translators and in the methodological problems
inherent in trying to isolate and study those
techniques.[23] One important aspect of this increase
in study of translation technique has been the
emphasis on the understanding that the translation
technique of any OG translation plays a large role
in the textual criticism of the Hebrew text of the
Bible. Only by having a clear understanding of

translation technique is one able to evaluate
clearly when a Greek translation can be used with
relative confidence to reconstruct its (sometimes
variant) Hebrew parent text, or when it reflects
the translator's exegesis of a parent text
identical with the preserved Hebrew, and thus, has
no text-critical import.

Unfortunately, all of the above mentioned
studies on Sir do little more than make certain
general assumptions about the ways in which the
grandson rendered his grandfather's Hebrew. In each
case, however, the Greek translation is expected to
provide important clues as to what the Hebrew of
Ben Sira looked like. Besides the inadequate
treatments in the aforementioned commentaries, very
little has been written specifically on the
translation technique of Ben Sira's grandson. One
study by Franz Vinzenz Reiterer, "Urtext" und
Übersetzungen: Sprachstudie über Sir 44,16-45,26
als Beitrag zur Siraforschung, attempts to examine
specific elements of translation technique for the
three major versions (Greek, Latin, Syriac) in the
beginning of the Praise of the Ancestors section.[24]
Although the study is an excellent treatment of
this brief chapter and a half, one cannot readily
generalize for the entire translation based on the
evaluation of such a small section, a section that
is of a different character from much of the rest
of the book.

Except for Reiterer's study, when any kind of
reconstruction of the Hebrew Sir is attempted, the
major emphasis usually centers on the lexical
elements in the translation. That is, the words
that the translator chose to render particular

Hebrew words form the main concern of the examination. The lexical choices made by the translator, however, only comprise a part of the activity of translation. Issues such as how closely the translator follows the Hebrew word order, or how consistently the translator renders into Greek such elements as pronominal suffixes or conjunctions are just as crucial for understanding the nature of the Hebrew parent text. To my knowledge, except for the brief section of Sir covered by Reiterer, none of these categories have been examined systematically for Sir.

A second important approach to recovering the Hebrew Sir has been the use of Greek translations of the Hebrew scriptures for identifying possible lexical equivalences between the Greek and Hebrew of Sir. This approach first assumes some dependence of the grandson on these translations, or at least a similar approach on his part to choosing lexical equivalents, primarily because it is clear that he was aware of Greek translations of the Hebrew scriptures (Prologue 8-10, 24-25). The assumption is then made that he would have used the same translation equivalents as those found in the available Greek translations, even though: (1) the validity of this assumption has not been demonstrated at all, and (2) the OG translations themselves are not always consistent among themselves. In fact, for the brief text that Reiterer studied, he concluded that the grandson showed little dependence at all on the Greek Pentateuch, and this conclusion was based on the study of a section of the book where this kind of dependence would be most likely.[25] Does this

conclusion hold for the remainder of the book as
well? Does the grandson depend on Greek translations outside of the Pentateuch for his work?
These are questions that for the Greek translation
of Sir still require answers.

1.3 THE APPROACH OF THIS STUDY

In the light of these questions, there is a
clear need to look systematically at the translation technique of the book, as well as at the
extent to which the grandson's translation reflects
dependence on Greek translations of the Hebrew
scriptures. These two foci should give a better
indication of the answer to what should be the
primary questions concerning the Greek translation:
Does the Greek translation of Ben Sira's grandson
provide adequate evidence for recovering his Hebrew
parent text, and from there, the Hebrew of Ben Sira
himself? If it does, in what areas of the grandson's translation activity does one find the best
possibilities for recovering his Hebrew parent
text?

Two basic areas will be treated in this study.
First, Chapter 2 deals with the translation
technique of the grandson. Recent discussions,
especially those by James Barr and Emanuel Tov,
concerning the nature of "literal" and "free"
translations are considered in order to ascertain
in what ways these adjectives can be useful as
general descriptions of translations. Can such
characterizations of translations help in trying to
understand the Hebrew parent text of a translation?
What do these terms communicate? In particular, the

grandson's approach to four features of translation
technique, word order, segmentation, quantitative
representation, and lexical representation, are
analyzed and compared with other Greek translations
in order to see how closely the grandson represented his Hebrew parent text in these matters. The
results of these analyses provide important indications of the extent to which his parent text can
be reconstructed based on these aspects of
translation technique.

The study of general features of translation
technique like those examined in Chapter 2 has
historically been very difficult because of the
large amounts of data required for a complete
analysis. Although some scholars have attempted to
base studies on the minutiae of translation, the
gathering of the data has consumed a great amount
of time, and organization of the data has been
hampered by technical inconveniences.[26] Consequently, only small portions of certain translations could be treated effectively, especially for
relatively long translations like Sir. The results
of these studies must then be generalized for the
entire work. Reiterer's examination of Sir 44.16-
45.26 is a good example. He is able to reach
certain conclusions regarding the translation
technique of this section, but the kind of
"historical" material contained in the Praise of
the Ancestors section is different from the more
proverbial passages found elsewhere in Sir, and
therefore, conclusions regarding this "history" may
not hold for those other sections.[27] As a result of
problems such as these, if an entire text is to be
examined, more specific, detailed aspects of

translation technique are usually chosen. This
comprehensive, but select approach has been well
utilized in the studies of I. Soisalon-Soininen and
his students on the Greek translations, especially
the Pentateuch.[28]

The analyses of word order, segmentation,
quantitative representation, and lexical
representation also depend on the ability to
examine certain minutiae of translation, and
therefore, depend on the gathering of large amounts
of data. The data, in these cases, have been
gathered with the assistance of a newly developing
tool for textual analysis, the computer. The
analyses of translation technique undertaken in
this study rely heavily on "machine readable" texts
and on the ability of the computer to gather and
organize data. As a result, I have examined entire
translations for the aspects of translation
technique listed above; and generalized conclusions
based on examinations of small sections of text
have been unnecessary.[29]

Next, in Chapter 3, since the grandson's
statements in the Prologue to his translation
clearly show his knowledge of Greek translations of
various parts of the Bible, the issue of the extent
of his dependence on those translations is
addressed. This issue relates directly to the
problem of reconstructing the grandson's Hebrew
parent text in two ways. First, if one can demonstrate that the grandson used Greek translations of
biblical materials to translate biblical passages
from his grandfather's Hebrew, the Hebrew and Greek
scriptures become fertile ground for use in
attempting reconstructions of the Hebrew Sir.

Second, concerning lexical equivalences, if the
grandson can be shown to fall into the same
tradition of translation as one or another of the
Greek scriptural translations, the lexical equivalences used in those translations supply additional
evidence for reconstructing the lexical elements of
the grandson's parent text. If, on the the other
hand, the grandson does not rely on the Greek
scriptural translations in either of these two
ways, their usefulness for reconstructions of the
Hebrew Sir is severely diminished. In a manner of
speaking, dependence by the grandson on the Greek
scriptural translations could be called a technique
of translation. To what degree does he actually
rely on these translations? Does he model his
translations after those that he knows?

Finally, Chapter 4 treats some of the
implications of these analyses. What do the results
of Chapters 2 and 3 tell about the possibility of
recovering Ben Sira's Hebrew based on the Greek
translation of his grandson? Is the grandson
consistent enough in his translation to warrant
confident reconstructions of particular elements of
the Hebrew? The initial answers to these questions
constitute the conclusions of this study.

1.4 THE IDEA OF FORMAL EQUIVALENCE

The basic principle by which comparisons of
the MT and the Greek scriptural translations, as
well as the Hebrew and Greek of Sir, are made is
called "formal equivalence" or "formal representation." Although this principle can be defined
succinctly, a number of difficulties attend it.

Formal equivalence is the arbitrary procedure of
comparing a Hebrew text and a Greek translation as
if the extant Hebrew were the parent text of the
Greek. It is, however, obvious that for both the OG
and the grandson's translation, the MT and the
extant Hebrew texts of Sir were not identical with
the Greek translations in many respects.[30] Thus, in
many instances what is compared is the word or
words in the Greek that do no more than mechanically or formally stand in the position of what is
in the Hebrew, although clearly not representing
semantically what is in the Hebrew.

The use of such a procedure of formal equivalence necessarily involves certain subjective
judgments. Decisions constantly have to be made as
to which elements of the Greek translation formally
parallel which elements of the Hebrew. These kinds
of decisions can be especially difficult in translations such as Proverbs or Job where the Greek and
Hebrew often differ dramatically from one another.
Thus, this procedure often produces difficult, even
bizarre equivalences due to the textual differences
between the presumed parent text of the translation
and the MT. The difficulties that arise in using
the idea of formal representation concern both
qualitative and quantitative differences between
the MT and OG. This is especially true of translations such as Proverbs, in which numerous strange
equivalences occur because, even though a particular equivalence might be unusual, there is
something in the Hebrew to which the Greek can
formally correspond, or because the translation
tends to be paraphrastic, entire phrases in Greek
may formally correspond to only one or two Hebrew

words. The problem, however, is certainly not
restricted to the more "free" translations. In Mic
4.5, for example, בשם אלהיו ("in the name of its
Lord") in the MT is the formal equivalent of τὴν
ὁδὸν αὐτοῦ ("his way") simply because the two
phrases stand in the same place in the verse. That
is, they formally (positionally) correspond to each
other.[31]

In Sir, the idea of formal equivalence
produces additional difficulty beyond what is true
of Hebrew biblical works. If, under more ideal
circumstances, strange equivalents are sometimes
produced, even more anomalies result from the
situation in Sir where there can be variant Hebrew
texts for the same passage, places where the Hebrew
is only partially preserved, and the recognition
that many corruptions have entered into the extant
Hebrew manuscripts. This increased susceptibility
to the problems of using a procedure of formal
equivalence must be considered constantly when one
compares the Hebrew and Greek texts of Sir, and
more careful attention must be paid to every
individual passage.

Even when such care is taken, the problems
present in the resulting textual base for Sir,
because of its partial and diverse state of
preservation, have serious implications for statistical analysis. In some instances, which are
discussed in Chapter 2, these difficulties raise
the possibility that the statistics given for Sir
are somewhat skewed due to either a variant parent
text or the second Hebrew recension. Despite these
problems, however, formal representation would
still seem to be the most controlled way to

approach the analysis of translation technique in
Sir.

The application of formal representation in
Sir leads to the question of what is to be used, on
a formal level, to represent the parent text of the
Greek. In the other books the answer is taken for
granted, the MT as represented in the Leningrad
Codex. Due to the fragmentary state of preservation
of all the extant Hebrew manuscripts of Sir, one
single manuscript cannot be chosen to fulfill this
function because no single extant Hebrew manuscript
includes all the passages in which Hebrew material
has been preserved. In some places, it might be MS
A or MS B or any of the others. Also, the manuscripts overlap in some sections, often giving two,
or even three, different readings for a given
passage. Frequently, in passages where more than
one manuscript is extant, the nature of the overlapping passages creates difficulties. The presence
of such variations in the Hebrew manuscripts as
synonymous words or word-order differences
complicates the use of formal representation as a
guiding principle. Fortunately, in many of these
cases, except for synonyms, one of the variant
Hebrew readings agrees more closely with the Greek
translation and can thus be considered as the
formal equivalent.

In addition, as noted above, the Hebrew
manuscripts have been subject to many corruptions
during the transmission of the text. This situation
can be demonstrated in many passages where variant
Hebrew texts have been preserved, and it is
extremely likely in many places where the extant
versional witnesses (Greek, Syriac, Latin, etc.)

attest similar textual confusions. In light of this
situation, the desire to recreate the "original"
Hebrew of Ben Sira has produced many emendations of
the extant Hebrew texts, but these emendations are
often made without adequate controls.

The approach to the problem adopted below is
somewhat different. Because one of the goals of
this study is to try to provide a more solid base
for making these kinds of editorial judgments about
the Hebrew Sir, I have not normally incorporated
such emendations into my base text, but have taken
a "minimalist" view of these issues. Thus, if only
one Hebrew manuscript exists in any given place, I
have treated it as formally representing the parent
text of the Greek, unless I cannot recreate any
reasonable exegetical path from which the translator could arrive at the Greek translation on the
basis of the extant Hebrew.

Where two or more Hebrew manuscripts exist and
deviate from one another, I accept the reading that
agrees most closely with the Greek as the formal
parent text. If none agrees with the Greek
translation, the problem becomes more difficult,
and only a provisional decision can be made, but
usually the word or phrase for which the clearest
exegetical route can be reconstructed is given the
initial preference.

Thus, although I do not rely absolutely on the
Hebrew texts of Sir in every case, but include a
few emended readings, particularly in those places
where the parent text of the Greek is absolutely
clear (such as the misreading by the translator of
a Hebrew letter) or where the readings of the
extant Hebrew manuscripts allow, the practical

result of this procedure at the outset is that I
rely on the formal equivalent of the extant Hebrew
manuscripts as the parent text of the Greek in much
the same way as would be done in the other biblical
books. The use of some emended readings is largely
due to the problem of the textual base for Sir.
When the MT is used as the formal parent text of
the OG translations, it is an arbitrary, but
necessary choice, since it is complete for all the
books. In Sir, where the texts are partial and
sometimes fragmentary, where they overlap and often
represent divergent textual traditions of the
Hebrew Sir, certain choices are made by necessity
that can be avoided when using the MT.[32] My
intention is that by proceeding in this manner,
especially for the study of translation technique,
the results will provide data that will help to
make a more confident and judicious use of
emendations to the preserved Hebrew texts than is
possible without this approach.

CHAPTER 2

ASPECTS OF TRANSLATION TECHNIQUE IN BEN SIRA: FREEDOM, LITERALNESS, AND THE RECONSTRUCTION OF THE HEBREW

2.1 INTRODUCTION

2.1.1 THE TRANSLATION TECHNIQUE OF THE GREEK SIR

Since the discovery of the Cairo Geniza fragments of Ben Sira and the subsequent unearthing of the Masada scroll, scholars who study the text of Ben Sira have been primarily concerned with two basic issues. First, despite initial misgivings by some scholars, the general consensus that the Hebrew manuscripts found in the Cairo Geniza and at Masada substantially reflect the Hebrew of Jesus Ben Sira naturally led to an investigation of the text-critical value of the extant texts. Although the available Hebrew texts probably represent the substance of Ben Sira's Hebrew, the more pressing question concerns the extent to which they contain what he actually wrote. This concern is overriding in the early commentaries written after the Geniza finds, and it plays a large role in Skehan and Di Lella's Anchor Bible Commentary.[1] Further, a large number of articles on Sir has appeared throughout this century that attempt to reconstruct individual passages or terms in the book.[2]

Second, since the extant Hebrew fragments only cover about two-thirds of the book, there has been a keen interest to attempt to reconstruct what the Hebrew of Ben Sira was in those portions of Sir for which no Hebrew is available. As was noted in Chapter 1, the process of reconstructing the Hebrew

has been based for the most part on the Greek,
along with a judicious use of the Syriac and Latin
translations. Scholars have tended, however, to
rely mostly on the Greek because it is complete for
the whole book and because it was translated within
sixty-five to seventy-five years of the original
composition. Even so, most of the attempts at
reconstructions of the Hebrew of Ben Sira have been
rather haphazard, and for the most part, they have
not been undertaken with a great deal of methodological self-consciousness.[3]

One of the reasons for the haphazard nature of
these reconstructions is that there has been no
systematic attempt to understand the translation
technique of Ben Sira's grandson, which results in
a consequent inability to make accurate assessments
concerning the closeness with which the grandson
follows the Hebrew. In fact, the commentators on
Sir only give the most summary descriptions of the
"literal" or "free" translation technique of the
grandson, and even then these characterizations are
most often confined to descriptions of the grandson's choice of words in the translation. Yet such
broad assessments of the grandson's translation
technique are used as a general basis for relying
on the Greek to reconstruct the Hebrew of Ben Sira.

The range of comments made about the
grandson's translation technique reveals the
general lack of certainty about the issue. Skehan
and Di Lella make only one remark about the
grandson's technique, saying that he usually
translated "quite literally, even on occasion
utilizing Semitisms."[4] Ziegler, in the introduction
to the Göttingen critical edition of the Greek Sir,

only remarks that one should use extreme caution
when using the adjective "free" about the two Greek
recensions, given the nature of the extant Hebrew
manuscripts.[5] Roy K. Patteson simply states that
the Greek is the best single text of Sir "due to
its fidelity to the Hebrew."[6] In his assessment of
the Greek translation, Th. Middendorp also assumes
that the Greek is a literal translation of its
Hebrew parent text.[7] In contrast to these
assessments of the grandson's fidelity to his
Hebrew, Smend, Peters, and Box and Oesterley all
emphasize the non-literal character of the Greek
translation. Box and Oesterley's comment provides a
good example of this evaluation of the grandson's
approach.

> Ben Sira's grandson clearly does not consider
> it the duty of the translator to give anything
> in the shape of a literal translation of his
> original; he seeks, rightly, to present as far
> as possible a well-constructed Greek
> interpretation rather than a slavish
> reproduction of what he translated. . . .

Box and Oesterley make this assessment of the
grandson's translation immediately after claiming
that it is invaluable for reconstructing the Hebrew
text. Similarly, both Smend and Peters argue that
the grandson did not intend a literal translation,
but that he produced a translation in good Greek
that would make his grandfather's wisdom accessible
to the Greek reader. Smend goes on to suggest that
Ben Sira's grandson treated his Hebrew in much the
same way as the translators of Job and Proverbs
treated their Hebrew sources. Their claims about
the translation technique of the grandson

notwithstanding, neither Smend, Peters, nor Box and
Oesterley is reticent about using the Greek as an
indicator of what Ben Sira's original Hebrew was.[8]

Since none of the authors cited above presented any systematic treatment of the grandson's
translation technique, it is not clear on what
grounds their evaluations of the translation have
been made. In some instances a few examples are
cited; in most, only the assertion is made.
Reiterer's previously mentioned study is the only
one of which I am aware that attempts to treat this
issue in a systematic fashion. In order to examine
the translation technique of the beginning of the
Praise of the Ancestors section, he has carefully
set out the extant Hebrew, Greek, Latin, and Syriac
texts and compared them with one another. He then
uses the data from these comparisons in his
discussion of each line of the text. In his
concluding remarks he argues that the Greek of Sir
is a valuable witness to an early form of the
Hebrew, but he offers little in the way of general
characterizations of the Greek except to say that
the Greek of Sir does not tend to rely on the Greek
Pentateuch for lexical equivalents.[9]

Despite the extensive use of the Greek as a
basis for reconstructing Ben Sira's Hebrew, the
crucial question remains open as to whether the
grandson actually translates in such a way that the
process of reconstruction is even possible. What
kind of a translation did Ben Sira's grandson
actually produce? Did he follow the Hebrew that was
in front of him literally or translate it freely?
What liberties did he take with his parent text?
What aspects of his translation provide data for

reconstructions of that parent text? What aspects
of his activity obscure the Hebrew? A more thorough
understanding of the grandson's approach to his
Hebrew parent text will provide the necessary data
for any attempt to answer these questions. The
pursuit of answers to some of these questions is
the focus of this chapter.

2.1.2 "LITERAL," "FREE," AND THE STUDY OF TRANSLATION TECHNIQUE

Emanuel Tov has thoroughly treated the issue
of reconstructing the Hebrew parent text of the OG,[10]
both in its theoretical and practical aspects. In
light of his treatment some subsequent issues need
to be raised, issues that become acute when
attempting to reconstruct the Hebrew parent text of
the Greek Sir. These issues can conveniently be set
out under three headings: (1) the scope of the
study of translation technique; (2) the categories
"literal" and "free" and their impact on reconstructing Hebrew parent texts; (3) terminological
clarity.

2.1.2.1 The Scope of the Study of Translation Technique

When one examines the issue of translation
technique, one of two basic approaches can be
taken. On the one hand, the focus could be on
specific, individual techniques of translation,
such as how a translator handles Hebrew infinitives
or Hebrew temporal constructions.[11] This approach
has the advantage of exhaustively treating a number
of individual techniques of translation on a more
narrow, or what might be called the micro level.
This approach, however, cannot practically cover

every technique that a translator used, and as a
result, it applies to reconstructions of the parent
text limited to the individual technique alone. On
the other hand, an approach on the broader or macro
level could provide basic indications of the way in
which translators generally approached their Hebrew
texts. Such an approach would give broader
indications that could be used in the process of
reconstruction. Additionally, a more general
approach may help to isolate the most important
techniques of translation on the micro level that
should occupy the scholar for any given translation. Ideally then, the use in combination of the
macro and micro approaches to the study of
translation technique should provide the most
complete and practical results.

This point can be illustrated quite well with
regard to Sir. If the primary goal is to reconstruct or even to investigate the possibility of
reconstructing the missing Hebrew sections of Sir,
as well as the places in the extant texts that are
corrupt, a study of the use of the definite article
or of the aorist tense in Greek would be of limited
value when faced with the prospect of reconstructing a complete Hebrew text. What would be
more instructive, at least at the beginning, is
information on how the translator viewed his Hebrew
text in general, the overall approach. Once this
broader picture is brought into focus, studies of
specific techniques could be undertaken and
utilized to examine individual aspects of the
Hebrew parent text.

Unfortunately, certain necessities must be
faced, and the problem is, in fact, a very

practical one where Sir is concerned. An understanding of the translation technique of a
particular Greek translation is important for three
basic and related enterprises: (1) the possible
reconstruction of the Hebrew parent text of the
Greek; (2) the textual criticism of the Hebrew text
of the book; (3) the textual criticism of the Greek
translation.[12] Therefore, when encountering a
significant difference between the Greek translation and the available Hebrew text, one will want
to know: (1) if the difference reflects the
original Greek translation; (2) if that difference
was one that resulted from the translator's
exegesis; (3) if the difference represents an
actual Hebrew textual reading found in the
translator's parent text.

If there has been no systematic study of the
problem at hand, as, for example, I. Soisalon-
Soininen has done for the infinitive in the
Pentateuch or Emanuel Tov has done for the
causative verbs,[13] the scholar must either do a
complete study of the specific issue or rely on
existing characterizations of the translation in
order to get an impression of how closely the
translator followed the Hebrew. Earlier characterizations, such as those by Thackeray, were not
made by systematic examination of data, but
according to subjective impressions and sometimes
changing criteria.[14] Characterizations based on
more complete data would give the scholar firmer
ground on which to proceed. Yet many of these kinds
of studies have still to be done.

The need for more general studies does not
mitigate the need for complete detailed studies of

translation technique, such as those by Soisalon-
Soininen and Tov. By using the traditional methods
of scholarship, it is unlikely that all of the
translation techniques of the biblical translations
can be investigated completely on an individually
detailed basis in the near future. Consequently,
there exists a very practical need for data to
which scholars can turn when faced with such
text-critical problems or difficulties in
reconstruction.[15]

2.1.2.2 "Literal" and "Free"

Since Reiterer's examination of translation
technique in Sir is limited to such a small section
of the book, any attempt to treat the entire
translation should begin with the goal of providing
a generally reliable description of the translation. Traditionally, such descriptions have taken
the form of describing an entire translation as
either "free" or "literal." Unfortunately, the
basis for these descriptions has not always been
clear. It seems that the individual scholar's
intuition about a particular translation usually
has been the primary criterion for descriptions of
this sort.[16]

Yet, the inadequacy of these grounds for
characterizing translations has been recognized by
scholars. Two recent studies by James Barr and
Emanuel Tov have argued that the general descriptions "free" and "literal" are not adequate at
all.[17] First, Barr argues that the biblical
translators are for the most part using a basically
literal approach, and that one should be concerned

with describing various degrees of that literalism.
He writes,

> A sophisticated study of the LXX, at least in
> many books, rather than dealing with a
> contrast between free and literal, has to
> concern itself much of the time with
> variations within a basically literal
> approach: different kinds of literality,
> diverse levels of literal connection, and
> various kinds of departure from the literal.
> For this reason the idea of literality, rather
> than the idea of free translation, can
> properly form the basis for our definition. It
> is the various kinds of literalism that we
> seek to analyze and define: for each of them
> "free" means the opposite to this particular
> literalism.[18]

Second, as Barr and Tov indicate, literalism, as a
general approach to translation, has different
aspects, and these aspects can and should be
investigated individually.

Of the several aspects of literalism described
by Barr and Tov, four may be seen as capable of
quantification. They are: (1) the representation of
the word order of the Hebrew; (2) the representation of the constituent parts of Hebrew words by
individual Greek elements (segmentation); (3) the
addition or subtraction in the Greek translation of
elements in the Hebrew (quantitative representation
of elements); (4) the consistency of lexical
rendering between the Greek and Hebrew (stereotyping). In addition, both Barr and Tov include a
category called the linguistic adequacy of lexical
choices, while Barr adds two other groups: (1)
coded "etymological" indication of formal/semantic
relationships in the vocabulary of the original
language, and (2) level of text and level of
analysis.[19]

The recognition of the fact that literalism
consists of a number of aspects leads to the
conclusion that most translations cannot be
effectively characterized as literal or free in a
generalizing and all-encompassing manner, but that
the issue is more properly focused on how closely a
translator represents the Hebrew parent text in any
of these particular aspects of literalness. In
other words, since each aspect of the Hebrew could
be rendered literally or freely by the translator,
the different aspects of literalism need to be
examined independently, because any given translator may take a literal approach to the Hebrew
parent text in some ways and a more free approach
in others. For example, a translator may adhere
closely to the word order of the source text while
at the same time trying to impart to the lexical
equivalents in Greek a sense of the nuance of the
words in the Hebrew. What results is a translation
that would be considered at the same time quite
literal regarding word order and quite free
regarding lexical equivalence. How one assesses the
literal or free nature of any translation, then,
probably depends on what aspect(s) of literalism is
(are) considered determinative. At the same time
that these categories are more specific in their
focus, they are still broad enough in their scope
to help to provide general information on the
overall approach of the translator to the Hebrew
text.

When one describes a translation or aspects of
that translation as literal or free, what exactly
is being measured? The description "literal" could

mean a number of things. First, it could refer to
the success with which a translator transfers the
overall meaning of the source text into the target
language. Thus, a satisfactory "literal" translation of a symbolic passage would not be expected
to reproduce in the translation an exact verbal
representation of the source text, but rather the
meaning and tone. Second, the term "literal" could
be taken as synonymous with the adequacy of the
translation in conveying the meaning of the
original. For instance, a translator may use a
number of ways to represent parataxis in the Hebrew
text, all of them equally possible ways of
conveying the meaning of the Hebrew construction,
and each of these ways might be regarded as a
literal representation. Finally, the term might be
applied to the degree to which the translator is
consistent in reproducing in a mechanical or wooden
manner as many of the formal aspects of the Hebrew
text as possible. That is, a translation could be
described as "literal" if the translator has
attempted to reproduce in a rigid way in Greek the
actual form of the various elements of the parent
text. Does the translation show a tendency to
translate all occurrences of a Hebrew word "A" with
a Greek word "A" regardless of the context or
nuance? Does it follow the word order of the Hebrew
parent text despite the artificiality such
adherence might produce in Greek? If literalism is
thought of in this last way, criteria could be
developed, most conveniently around the aspects of
literalism set out by Barr and Tov, that could be
used to characterize translations and give some
indication of their relative value for the purposes

of textual criticism and the reconstruction of the
Hebrew parent text.

In this chapter, the term "literal" is
employed in accord with this last description.[20] As
a result, for the purposes of trying to develop
some means of characterizing translations by using
something other than subjective criteria or
scholarly intuition, it is the degree of mechanicalness or woodenness of the translation that is
examined, not necessarily the symbolic or commu-
nicative adequacy of the translation. In fact, a
more mechanical approach to translation may result
in a less meaningful translation, but it may
provide ample evidence for what the parent text
looked like. Perhaps the best example of this kind
of approach would be Aquila's translation.

It should be emphasized at this point that
what I propose to examine for the Greek translation
of Sir is a combination of two elements: (1) the
mechanicalness that a translator uses to represent
certain formal elements of the Hebrew parent text,
and (2) the consistency of the appearance of these
mechanical representations. In a recent article
that in part examines issues raised by E. Tov and
me, I. Soisalon-Soininen has argued that a free
representation (that is, a non-mechanical representation) can be used consistently, and therefore,
consistency in and of itself cannot necessarily be
used as an indication of literalness.[21] As a
criticism of the methodological stance taken in our
article, Soisalon-Soininen is quite correct, since
the issue was set out by us in precisely those
terms. This argument, however, is correct only as
far as it goes. In the article, Tov and I stated,

"Strictly speaking, we measure <u>consistency</u> and not
<u>literalness</u>, but that consistency is taken as <u>one</u>
[emphasis added] of the main exponents of literalness."[22] At this stage, I would restate this idea
to include the issue of mechanicalness or woodenness
of representation combined with the consistency of
that mechanical approach as a major exponent of
literalness. For example, if a translator
reproduces the word order of the Hebrew, even at
the expense of good, or perhaps even decent Greek,
and the Hebrew word order is reproduced with a high
degree of consistency, that translator can be said
to translate the Hebrew word order literally.

2.1.2.3 Terminology

Given the various uses and perhaps even
confusion attached to the terms "literal" and
"free," they may be more of a hindrance than a help
in their use as general descriptions of translations. Since I propose to examine certain
particular aspects of the translation technique of
Sir and not to make sweeping, all-inclusive
judgments about the translation as a whole, the
terms should probably not be used in this way at
all. In the discussions in this chapter, I have
attempted to avoid the terms for the most part.
Where they have been used, they are intended as
comparative terms to distinguish one group of
translations from another regarding a specific
aspect of translation technique.

The use of the term "literal" to indicate a
word-for-word technique is not adequate either
since some of the aspects studied in this chapter

go beyond the word-for-word approach. Hence, in
keeping with the two elements described above, I
have used the terms "mechanical" or "wooden" in
place of "literal." These terms denote an approach
to the Hebrew text in which the translator attempts
to represent as closely as possible certain
elements of the Hebrew in Greek regardless of the
character of the resultant Greek. Sometimes this
simply produces rather plain, repetitive Greek;
sometimes it results in ungrammatical, even
unintelligible Greek. On the other end of the
scale, I have used the term "free" to indicate
Greek translation that is not a mechanical
representation of the Hebrew, but Greek that
produces certain types of deviations from the
strict representation of the Hebrew because the
translator shows more regard for Greek style or
introduces exegetical elements into the
translation. In other words, translations that are
not wooden or mechanical.[23]

2.1.3 THE APPROACH OF THIS CHAPTER

The Wisdom of Ben Sira is unique among the
corpus of Jewish-Greek translations. For all the
other translations, one of two conditions exists.
Either there is a complete Hebrew(-Aramaic) text
available with which to compare the translation,
such as the biblical translations, or there is no
Hebrew text available at all, such as with 1 Maccabees. For Sir, Hebrew texts are available for
only about two-thirds of the book. As a result, the
major aim of this chapter is to examine the general
approach of Ben Sira's grandson to the Hebrew text

in order to understand better the prospects for
recovering his Hebrew parent text in those places
where it is not available.

Every aspect of the grandson's translation
technique cannot conceivably be examined here, so I
have used Barr's and Tov's categories of literalism
to provide insight into the grandson's general
approach. Each of these four categories (word
order; segmentation; quantitative representation;
stereotyping) has been examined separately for Sir
and for several other translations. The complete
set of data is outlined in tables in each section,
and then some summary remarks are made concerning
the Greek translation of Sir for each category.
More general remarks concerning the prospects for
recovering the Hebrew parent text of the Greek Sir
and any possible relations to other translations
are reserved for Chapter 4 below.

A few remarks on the use of statistics are
also called for here. One must always be careful
when relying on statistical information not to make
it say too much. Indeed cautions to this effect
have been issued by scholars.[24] If one is to treat
various aspects of entire translations, however,
the use of statistics as a comparative tool can be
very helpful. In the following sections, each
passage that was initially contained in the raw
data was examined for its applicability to the
category under study. Also, the results given in
the categories chosen are meant to be used as broad
indicators; they are not intended to give the
impression that every difference between the Hebrew
and Greek for those aspects can be categorized with
certainty as either a Hebrew variant or a free

translation. It is of the utmost importance to
examine each individual difference on its own
merits. What the results of these analyses show are
general approaches of certain translators to
specific aspects of their parent texts. These
indications should certainly provide some help when
reconstructing these aspects of the Hebrew, but
should not be considered determinative in and of
themselves.

For Sir in particular, the unfortunate state
of the Hebrew text as it has been transmitted in
the extant manuscripts has undoubtedly created
problems in these analyses that simply cannot be
detected. The procedure of formal equivalence
described in section 1.4 is difficult to apply
consistently in passages in which the second Hebrew
recension is brought into consideration, since each
Hebrew word is treated formally as the parent text
of the Greek. Often this second recension,
especially when it consists of single words or
small phrases, cannot be effectively identified,
and thus, it probably has an effect on some of the
statistical analyses. Every attempt has been made,
however, to compensate for the problematic state of
the Hebrew text. If a consistent and complete
Hebrew text were available in a form such as is
available for the biblical books, the overall
evaluation of the grandson on the aspects of
translation technique examined here would perhaps
be higher than it sometimes turn out to be. Yet, I
believe that, despite this particular difficulty,
the results achieved for Sir in this chapter help
to produce a clearer picture of how the grandson
approached certain basic aspects of his Hebrew, and

they give useful indications of the possibilities
for recovering the Hebrew of his parent text
through reconstructions based on the Greek.

2.2 ADHERENCE TO THE HEBREW WORD ORDER

2.2.1 INTRODUCTION

Of all the criteria that could be examined
with regard to the issue of literal and free
translations, the way in which the translator
reproduces the word order of the source is one of
the most revealing. For someone with the same
perspective toward the sacred writings as Jerome,
that even the order of the words contains a
mystery, the reproduction of the word order of the[25]
Hebrew would almost certainly have been important.
A translator who, for whatever reasons, desired to
produce a mechanically faithful representation of
the Hebrew parent text could be expected to place
great importance on approximating as closely as
possible the source text's word order. Understandably, then, Sebastian Brock calls faithfulness
to word order "the most obvious mark of any literal
translation."[26]

For those who translated the Hebrew scriptures
into Greek, word-order correspondence was facili-
tated by the flexible nature of Greek word order in
contrast to the more inflexible Hebrew order. This
flexibility in Greek permitted the translators the
latitude to follow their Hebrew text without, in
most instances, creating Greek that was incoherent.
In those translations where the Greek word order
closely follows that of the Hebrew, one of the

products is the creation of so-called Hebraisms in
the translations.[27]

Nevertheless, not every translator was concerned to produce a wooden representation of the
Hebrew parent text and thus did not feel con-
strained to follow the word order of the Hebrew.
These translators were inclined to employ more
usual Greek style, which resulted in more frequent
variation from the source text's word order. Thus,
the extent to which the Jewish-Greek translations
vary from the sequence of the Hebrew would appear
to constitute an important criterion for assessing
the degree to which a translation woodenly reflects
its source. For Sir specifically, the degree to
which the grandson followed the word order of his
Hebrew exemplar is an important element in
understanding his translation and in determining
the prospects for recovering his Hebrew parent
text, especially in those places where no Hebrew is
available.

2.2.2 TYPES OF WORD-ORDER VARIATIONS

Simply to present the raw data on word-order
variation is not sufficient for present purposes
because not all word-order variations are of the
same sort. An initial and obvious distinction is
between those variations that are actual, those
that represent the decision of the translator to
depart from the Hebrew order, and those that are
only apparent, due to the preservation of a parent
text different from that used by the translator.
Variations that are only apparent are by no means
easily distinguished from actual variations, and

each alleged variation must be examined individually to determine if it, in fact, derived from the
translator's source text. This determination can
only be made, however, after the general approach
of the translator to the word order of the source
is examined. If one encounters an apparent word-
order variation in a translation that elsewhere
deviates from its parent text only rarely, the
probabilities increase that the variation is a
reflection of the source and not a stylistic
contribution by the translator. In contrast, little
confidence can be placed in attributing a variant
word order to the parent text of a translation that
is shown elsewhere frequently to deviate from the
order of its source text.

Actual word-order variations can be either
syntactic or displacement variations. The
designation "syntactic" refers to the fact that in
Hebrew a number of constructions have a fixed
order, whereas Greek allows a number of possible
ways of rendering those orders. These constructions
can be found both within the Hebrew morpheme, such
as the conjunctive ו plus verb or noun, and within
the larger Hebrew sentence unit. J. M. Rife gives a
list of these elements in his article "The
Mechanics of Translation Greek." In Hebrew, these
include the fact that: (1) no word can come between
the definite article and its noun; (2) adjectives
immediately follow their substantives; (3) conjunctions are not postpositive; (4) genitives
follow their constructs; (5) "direct, personal,
pronomial" objects follow the verbs that govern
them; (6) demonstrative pronouns follow their
substantives.[28] Variations in Greek from these

orders must be stylistic in nature, a product of
the activity of the translator (or later copyists),
and they cannot be the result of a different parent
text, since the Hebrew sequence for all of these
grammatical constructions is absolutely fixed.
Further, other orders exist in Hebrew that are not
fixed, but usual, such as the normal sentence order
of the direct object following the verb. Variations
on this level may also indicate stylistic changes
by the translator, although, since Hebrew word
order is not absolutely fixed for these relationships, one cannot be certain a priori that the
change was not already present in the translator's
parent text.

Some differences in word order between the
Hebrew and Greek may be solely the result of the
displacement of certain elements in the sentence to
another place. These displacements may be as short
as the simple reversal of two words as in Sir 7.11.
מרים ומשפיל (MS A) // ὁ ταπεινῶν καὶ ἀνυψῶν Or,
they might involve phrases, clauses, or even entire
sentences, as in the following examples.

Sir 47.24 (Heb = MS B)

להדיחם	---
[מ]אדמתם	---
וחגדל	καὶ ἐπληθύνθησαν
חטאתו	αἱ ἁμαρτίαι αὐτῶν
מאד	σφόδρα
---	ἀποστῆσαι αὐτοὺς
---	ἀπὸ τῆς γῆς αὐτῶν

Sir 49.13 (Heb = MS B)

---	καὶ στήσαντος
---	πύλας
---	καὶ μοχλοὺς
וירפא	καὶ ἀνεγείραντος

אֵת הרימסחינו	τὰ οἰκόπεδα ἡμῶν
וייצב	---
דלחים	---
וברִיח	---

Unlike word-order differences of a syntactic
type, there are no convenient means for determining
whether the examples given above are the result of
the translator's own style or sense of the source
text, or whether they represent a parent text
different from the extant Hebrew manuscripts,
although it does seem likely that the longer texts,
especially those comprising entire clauses or
sentences, will have a higher probability of being
variations that were already in the Hebrew.
Shemaryahu Talmon has given strong indication,
however, that even cases such as these longer texts
could stem from a translator's assessment of an
entire passage, and consequently, features such as
chiastic structure may be changed at the level of
translation rather than in the parent text.[29] In
this section, for the purpose of initial characterizations, all differences in word order are
treated as if they were the result of translational
activity. This procedure is consistent with the
approach of considering the MT as the parent text
of the OG in a formal way.[30] Nevertheless, it is
clear that some of these differences will have
derived from a parent text different from the
surviving Hebrew textual tradition. Once
assessments can be made about the relative
strictness with which a translator follows the
source text's word order, any individual instance
can be examined to determine the probabilities of
whether or not it is the result of a difference in
the parent text.[31]

The type of word-order difference may well
affect reconstructions of the Hebrew parent text.
Certainly syntactical differences are easier to
reconstruct, since the Hebrew must follow a certain
order. For example, if in Greek the possessive
pronoun precedes the noun, any reconstruction of
the possessive in Hebrew will require the noun to
have a pronominal suffix. A translation that has
numerous syntactical differences in word order
poses less of a problem than a translation that
contains numerous displacement differences. What
the syntactical differences indicate, however, is a
willingness on the part of the translator to ignore
word order as a controlling element in the
preparation of the translation.

Another problem arises when one attempts to
determine how to represent word-order variations in
a statistical enumeration of the data. In this
study, a word-order difference between the Hebrew
and the Greek is defined in terms of the entire
unit of variation, and each unit has the
statistical value of one. The clear majority of
instances concerns only one or at most two words,
and these pose little difficulty. The example of
Sir 7.11 given above would be counted as one unit
of word-order variation because it involves simply
the reversal of the order of two adjacent nouns.
This also appears to be the situation with units
longer than just a couple of words. If we look at
the other two examples given above, the translator
apparently considered the phrase להדיחם מאדמחם in
47.24 and the clause ויצב דלתים ובריח in 49.13 as
intact or discrete units (presuming that they were
not already in a different order in the parent

text). Therefore, each of these contexts should be
considered one unit of variation rather than two or
three in the statistical summaries below.

The importance of clarity on this issue is
highlighted in Galen Marquis's study of word-order
changes in the Greek of Ezekiel. Marquis nowhere
indicates what for him constitutes a change in word
order. His only comment in this regard comes at the
beginning of his statistical summary where he
speaks of instances when the word order "in the
translation deviated in one or more details from
the MT."[32] In most instances no problem really
exists. Yet, would Marquis treat syntactical word-
order differences, like the use of the postposition
conjunction δέ, within a larger displaced clause,
as one or two instances of word-order difference?
How would he treat a displacement within a larger
displacement? Marquis does not say. To judge from
the examples that he gives subsequently, one can
surmise that a word-order change is for him similar
to my own definition, although his lack of clarity
on this issue causes some potential confusion in
using his statistical summary.

Unfortunately, in treating all units (individual words; phrases; clauses) equally, certain
frequently occurring word-order differences,
especially of a syntactic type, receive a significance disproportionate to their actual importance
for characterizing a translation. The most
frequently occurring culprit is the postpositive
particle δέ. In some translations that have
traditionally been viewed as free or paraphrastic,
such as Job, Proverbs, and Isaiah, this particle is
used frequently. In translations such as these, the

preponderance of δέ can easily give misleading
results. That is not to say that the use of δέ is
not in any way indicative of a translator's
approach to the source text. Since even in the
least wooden translations the occurrences of καί
outnumber those of δέ,[33] the use of δέ, when it
translates a conjunction in Hebrew, represents a
choice by the translator to deviate from the Hebrew
word order, and it is significant for understanding
the approach to translating. If, on the other hand,
the use of δέ outweighs all the other word-order
differences, one might justifiably view the
significance of the statistical data differently.
In Genesis, for example, word-order differences
involving δέ constitute 70 percent of the total
number. This percentage is a much more significant
portion in Genesis than the 7 percent figure for
word-order differences involving δέ in the so-
called Theodotion text of Daniel. Therefore, when
the data are given below, two different ratios will
appear -- one including all occurrences of δέ, and
one excluding those occurrences.[34]

Since the data on word order are so numerous,
some concessions to completeness have of necessity
been made. In the discussion that follows, other
than the occurrences of δέ, word-order differences
are not separated into sub-groupings, such as the
reversal of nouns, the placing of a possessive
pronoun before its noun, or the displacement of a
prepositional phrase. The conclusions reached will,
as a result, be general rather than specific. More
detailed studies form a next stage in research
along these lines, a stage based on development and
criticism of the initial research. In subsequent

studies, a number of other areas, which will not be
treated here, could be pursued that relate to the
problem of word-order differences. For instance,
the data could be examined to see if specific
phrases or words in some translations routinely
vary from the Hebrew word order.[35] Issues such as
whether certain translators shift particular parts
of speech, such as prepositions, away from the
sequence of their parent text, or whether the
majority of differences is affected by syntax or is
intentional could easily be examined.

2.2.3 COMPARATIVE DATA

For the category of word order, all the books
of the Jewish-Greek biblical corpus were examined,
in contrast to other categories treated in this
chapter, which are only examined in selected books.
The reasons for this decision are entirely practical. It seemed advisable that, if possible, at
least one of the criteria of literalness discussed
in this chapter should be investigated for the
entire corpus, and since the data on word-order
differences are so easily garnered, this criterion
was selected.

The data are presented here in a way that is
fundamentally different from the way that Marquis
has presented his data in his aforementioned study
of Ezekiel, where he took a ratio of the word-order
changes to the number of verses in each section of
text treated. His resulting percentages are much
higher than those presented in the tables below.
This situation results from the fact that in my
study I have not dealt with verses as a unit of

comparison, but with computer records, or lines,
which contain, for the most part, one Hebrew word.
Thus, since Sir has 310 word-order changes marked
in a file of 9288 lines, its word-order deviation
is 3.33 percent or about 3 word-order deviations
per 100 Hebrew words.[36]

The higher percentage at which Marquis arrives
can leave an impression that is somewhat misleading. If one encounters, in a given verse, the
Greek possessive pronoun preceding its noun,
something impossible in Hebrew, a difference in
word order results. The other perhaps eight or nine
words in the verse still follow the Hebrew word
order. In a ratio based on number of variations per
number of verses, that one variation is equated to
the faithfulness to the parent text of all the
other words. In other words, the deviation of one
word is being equated with the faithfulness to the
word order of a whole verse. This approach results
in percentages of variation like 46.2 percent
deviation in Job, when, in fact, the word order in
Job does not actually vary 46.2 percent of the
time.[37] The point is not that the percentage is
incorrect, since it is in any event relative, but
that the reader may be led to think that word-order
variation is much more pervasive in Job than it
actually is.

This criticism is not intended to mitigate
Marquis's general conclusions concerning word
order. The major importance of the percentages is
not in the absolute numbers derived, but in their
comparative value, and Marquis says as much.[38] How
do the results that I reach in this section compare
to those achieved by Marquis? Do we reach the same

or different conclusions concerning the character
of the translations that we have studied? These are
the more overriding questions; numbers and
percentages are only the means of comparison.

The relevant data appear in the following
three tables. The first, Table 1A (p. 46), provides
the ratio of the total number of word-order
variations per number of computer file lines and
the ratio of the number of variations excluding δέ
per number of computer file lines.[39] The second,
Table 1B (p. 48), gives the same data for each of
the Minor Prophets individually. In both Table 1A
and 1B, column A gives the total number of word-
order variations followed by the number of
occurrences of δέ that involve word-order
differences, column B gives the adjusted number of
lines in the CATSS computer file for that book,
column C gives the percentage of word-order
deviation including δέ, and column D gives the
percentage of deviation excluding δέ. The third
table, Table 2 (p. 49), lists, for both ratios,
each of the books in descending order from the
translation that most consistently adheres to the
Hebrew word order to the translation that is least
consistent.

TABLE 1A - RATIO OF WORD-ORDER DIFFERENCES TO
          NUMBER OF LINES

BOOK	A	B	C	D
GEN[a]	1108 / 772	20526	5.39	1.63
EXOD[a]	628 / 333	16856	3.72	1.75
LEV[a]	219 / 108	11746	1.86	.92
NUM	206 / 67	16055	1.28	.86
DEUT	189 / 47	14297	1.32	.99
JOSH(B)	193 / 39	10062	1.91	1.53
JUDG(A)	67 / 14	9834	.68	.53
JUDG(B)[a]	43 / 6	9693	.44	.38
α	80 / 9	13476	.59	.49
ββ[a]	30 / 4	3800	.78	.68
βγ	46 / 10	8390	.54	.42
γγ[a]	108 / 6	12249	.88	.83
γδ[a]	59 / 7	13232	.44	.39
ISA[a]	710 / 99	17826	3.98	3.42
JER[a]	166 / 20	18461	.89	.79
EZEK(α')[a]	80 / 15[b]	9110	.87	.71
EZEK(β')	72 / 6	5470	1.31	1.20
EZEK(γ')	87 / 7	4076	2.13	1.96
MP[a]	114 / 49	14411	.79	.45

PS	197 / 78	19977	.98	.59
JOB	952 / 345	7938	11.99	7.64
PROV	687 / 338	7691	8.92	4.53
RUTH	31 / 20	1314	2.35	.83
CANT	0 / 0	1264	0.00	0.00
QOH	3 / 0	2938	.10	.10
LAM	8 / 0	1575	.50	.50
ESTH[a]	223 / 55	3158	7.06	5.31
DAN o' [a]	155 / 9	7160	2.16	2.03
DAN θ'	27 / 2	5766	.46	.43
EZRA	14 / 1	3570	.39	.36
NEH	24 / 1	5061	.47	.45
1 CHR	45 / 9	10239	.43	.35
2 CHR	80 / 1	13062	.61	.60
SIR[a]	309 / 15	9288	3.32	3.16

TABLE 1B - MINOR PROPHETS

HOS	32 / 15	2407	1.32	.70
JOEL	7 / 3	961	.72	.41
AMOS	10 / 4	2015	.49	.29
OBAD	5 / 3	288	1.73	.69
JONAH	12 / 4	684	1.75	1.16
MIC	9 / 4	1426	.63	.35
NAH	2 / 0	561	.35	.35
HAB	8 / 3	672	1.19	.74
ZEPH	2 / 0	778	.25	.25
HAG	3 / 2	631	.47	.15
ZECH	17 / 8	3108	.54	.28
MAL	7 / 3	880	.79	.45

[a]For each of the following books all the occurrences of word-order differences longer than four Hebrew words are listed. GEN - 31.26, 31.32, 31.33, 47.5; EXOD 36.9; LEV - 5.2, 26.6; JUDG(B) - 20.27; ββ - 2 SAM 5.5; γγ - 1 KGS 11.4; γδ - 2 KGS 14.13; ISA - 10.14; JER - 16.4, 40.12, 41.10, 51.34, 52.22; EZEK - 5.12; MP - ZECH 3.5; DAN ο' 4.28, 4.29, 5.6, 5.29, 9.26; ESTH - 2.7, 9.12; SIR - 20.4, 31.23, 33.39.

[b]For reasons that are not apparent, Marquis's total number of word-order differences in Ezek 1-39 is quite different from mine. He lists (p. 64) 100 cases of word-order differences out of 1013 verses. I have found 152 marked in the CATSS computer files. Since Marquis nowhere defines what a word-order difference is, or whether more than one variation in a given verse is counted as one or more variations per verse, I am at a loss to explain the discrepancy.

TABLE 2 - LISTING OF BOOKS IN ORDER OF CONSISTENCY
(IN %)

1. CANT	- 0.00	1. CANT	- 0.00
2. QOH	- .10	2. QOH	- .10
3. EZRA	- .39	3. 1 CHR	- .35
4. 1 CHR	- .43	4. EZRA	- .36
5. γδ	- .44	5. JUDG(B)	- .38
6. JUDG(B)	- .44	6. γδ	- .39
7. DAN θ'	- .46	7. βγ	- .42
8. NEH	- .47	8. DAN θ'	- .43
9. LAM	- .50	9. NEH	- .45
10. βγ	- .54	10. MP	- .45
11. α	- .59	11. α	- .49
12. 2 CHR	- .61	12. LAM	- .50
13. JUDG(A)	- .68	13. JUDG(A)	- .53
14. ββ	- .78	14. PS	- .59
15. MP	- .79	15. 2 CHR	- .60
16. EZEK(α')	- .87	16. ββ	- .68
17. γγ	- .88	17. EZEK(α')	- .71
18. JER	- .89	18. JER	- .79
19. PS	- .98	19. γγ	- .83
20. NUM	- 1.28	20. RUTH	- .83
21. EZEK(β')	- 1.31	21. NUM	- .86
22 DEUT	- 1.32	22. LEV	- .92
23. LEV	- 1.86	23. DEUT	- .99
24. JOSH(B)	- 1.91	24. EZEK(β')	- 1.20
25. EZEK(γ')	- 2.13	25. JOSH(B)	- 1.53
26. DAN o'	- 2.16	26. GEN	- 1.63
27. RUTH	- 2.35	27. EXOD	- 1.75
28. SIR	- 3.32	28. EZEK(γ')	- 1.96
29. EXOD	- 3.72	29. DAN o'	- 2.03
30. ISA	- 3.98	30. SIR	- 3.16
31. GEN	- 5.39	31. ISA	- 3.42
32. ESTH	- 7.06	32. PROV	- 4.52
33. PROV	- 8.91	33. ESTH	- 5.31
34. JOB	- 11.99	34. JOB	- 7.64

2.2.4 CONCLUSIONS CONCERNING WORD-ORDER VARIATION

The tables suggest a number of interesting conclusions. With respect to the OG materials in general, Barr's conclusion that in the Jewish-Greek translations one is faced with "variations within a basically literal approach," seems confirmed for word order.[40] Even the translation that most frequently varies from the Hebrew word order, Job, still retains the order of its source almost 90 percent of the time. When judged, however, against Song of Songs, which does not have any deviations noted, the translator of Job is seen to have taken a much more liberal attitude towards the Hebrew text. Most of the books can be characterized as to the nature of their adherence to the word order of their parent texts, although in some cases the percentages are so close as to make clear distinctions unwarranted.

The translations that follow the word order of the Hebrew most closely are Song of Songs and Qoheleth. After them come among others, Ezra, 1 Chronicles, the $\gamma\delta$ section of Samuel-Kings, Judges(B), and the Theodotion text of Daniel. Books such as Ezekiel(α'), Psalms, the Minor Prophets, and the $\beta\beta$ section of Samuel-Kings fall in the middle and could be regarded as trying to be faithful to the Hebrew while not totally disregarding Greek style. On the other end of the scale, Job, Proverbs, and Esther stand by themselves as most frequently deviating from their parent texts. When including the occurrences of $\delta\acute{\epsilon}$, Genesis stands with this trio of translations, but when $\delta\acute{\epsilon}$ is excluded, Genesis stands close to its companions in the Pentateuch.[41]

While Job, Proverbs, and Esther stand together
as taking the least rigorous approach to following
the Hebrew word order, some other books fall
together at a distance sufficiently removed from
these three and from the more slavish end of the
spectrum to justify grouping them together as
relatively free. Among these are Old Greek Daniel,
Isaiah, and Ezekiel(γ'). Also included in this
latter group is Sir. Among all the translations,
Sir most consistently stands close to Isaiah. While
certainly not taking the same "free" approach as
the translations of Proverbs, Job, or Esther, it is
clear that the grandson was not as concerned with
the exact word order of his parent text as most of
the other translations. A number of specific
observations about Sir help to fill out the
picture.[42]

Although δέ is not used very frequently in
Sir (only 15 times where the Hebrew texts are
extant), Sir often uses the postpositive γάρ for
'כ, which produces the same effect as δέ.[43] The
frequency of γάρ, combined with the use of δέ,
leaves the distinct impression that Ben Sira's
grandson did make some concessions to Greek style.
This conclusion is further confirmed by the more
than occasional position of the possessive pronoun
before the noun it governs (cf. for example, 7.21;
8.2; 16.17; 41.1)[44] and the position of the
pronominal direct object before the verb (cf. for
example, 7.1; 13.9; 33.22).

One of the most acute problems facing any
student of Sir is the nature of the extant Hebrew
texts. Because of the current state of the Hebrew

manuscripts of Sir, possible textual corruption may
account for the frequent occurrence of word-order
differences consisting of the interchange of words,
especially nouns, joined by καί.[45] When compared
to the other translations, Sir also seems to have a
large proportion of displacement differences. This
situation could be the result of textual corruption
in the Hebrew manuscripts or of the liberal
attitude of the grandson towards his grandfather's
Hebrew. Further, only Genesis has more transpositions of four words or more than Sir, and Sir has
a large number of three word transpositions,
transpositions that are not listed separately.
Since the data for Sir have been derived by
formally using the available Hebrew as the parent
text of the Greek, these observations suggest that
Sir, more than most other books examined in this
section, may owe its positions in the tables to
issues connected with a different parent text. This
conclusion might be expected since none of the
other translations from Hebrew examined has such a
diverse and problematic textual base.

Finally, the data given in the tables can be
compared with other studies of translation
technique. For word order, the data given here
generally support the conclusions reached by
Marquis in his study in which he examined Ezekiel
1-39, Job 1-30, Psalms 1-78, Isaiah, Jeremiah,
1 Samuel, and 2 Kings. He concluded that for the
criterion of word order, Ezekiel seemed to fit with
Jeremiah and 1 Samuel, and to a lesser degree with
Psalms and 2 Kings. The data here suggest that
Ezekiel, Jeremiah, and Psalms stand close together,
but that 1 Samuel and 2 Kings are more wooden in

reproducing Hebrew word order than Ezekiel. Job and
Isaiah are indeed at quite a distance from Ezekiel.
Yet, I would disagree with Marquis that Ezekiel is
"quite literal according to the criterion of word
order."[46] Of the books listed above that are close
to Ezekiel, according to the data compiled here,
Ezekiel would much more accurately be termed
"relatively literal" or "relatively wooden" with
some accommodations made for Greek style.

Two other studies provide characterizations of
translations that can be compared with the results
attained in this study, Raija Sollamo's study of
the so-called semiprepositions and the study of
Emanuel Tov and me, which focuses on the consistent
or inconsistent rendering of certain lexical
elements.[47] Sollamo divides the translations into
four groups, two of which are given labels. Group
1, called by her "most freely rendered," is Esther
o', Proverbs, Exodus, Isaiah, Job, and Daniel o'.
Group 2 is less freely rendered and contains
Leviticus, Genesis, Joshua, Numbers, and
Deuteronomy. Group 3 consists of translations that
are more slavish than the previous two. To this
group belong 1 Chronicles, 2 Chronicles, Daniel θ',
Minor Prophets, 1 Kings, 1 Samuel, and Psalms.
Group 4, her "slavish" group, has 2 Esdras,
Jeremiah, Ezekiel, Judges(A), 2 Kings, 2 Samuel,
and Judges(B).[48] The results of this study make it
difficult to separate the translations into such
groupings, but generally, those translations that
fall into Sollamo's groups 3 and 4 come at the top
of Table 2 above, and those that fall into her
groups 1 and 2 are at the bottom of that table.
When one looks at the second ranking in Table 2

(excluding δέ), Sollamo's group 1 falls all the
way to the bottom, and her group 2 comes together
just above. The major difference from Sollamo comes
in the last two sections of Ezekiel, which fall
near the bottom of the table. Sollamo treated
Ezekiel as one book, but the three-fold division
used here suggests that the faithfulness to the
Hebrew word order is different for each of the
three divisions.

Tov and Wright have five groups, four of which
correspond to Sollamo's groups. They are designated
free, relatively free, relatively literal, literal,
and inconsistent. The final group is made up of
translations whose consistency of rendering varied
between the various elements studied by Tov and
Wright.[49] For word order, those translations
labelled "literal" in Tov and Wright come at the
top of the rankings given in Table 2. These are
Song of Songs, Qoheleth, Ezra (studied separately
from Nehemiah), and 2 Kings. The "relatively
literal" and "relatively free" groups are difficult
to distinguish for word order. Even though Tov's
and Wright's "relatively literal" group (2 Samuel,
Judges[A], Jeremiah, and Ruth) comes together above
their "relatively free" translations (Numbers and
Deuteronomy) in Table 2, the percentages for
Jeremiah, Ruth, Numbers, and Deuteronomy come close
together and prevent any clear distinction. The
"free" translations, Job and Proverbs, are also
free regarding word-order deviation. In general,
then, the results of the word-order data seem to
confirm the characterizations of Sollamo and Tov
and Wright.

2.3 THE SEGMENTATION OF HEBREW WORDS

2.3.1 INTRODUCTION

In this section and the next, I will be examining two related aspects of the way in which translators attempt to imitate the exact form of their Hebrew texts in their translations. As was argued above, for the purposes of attempting to reconstruct the Hebrew parent text of a Greek translation, the evaluation of literalism in translations must take into account the extent to which translators endeavored mechanically to preserve the form of the original Hebrew as much as the content. The results of these next two sections thus become important as evaluative criteria for assessing the extent to which reconstructions can be made of certain features of the Hebrew that served as the parent text for these translations. Whereas word-order adherence involves the translator's representation of the sequence of the Hebrew source text, segmentation and quantitative representation (section 2.4 below) are two ways of examining the rendering in translation of the quantitative form of the Hebrew.

Both Barr and Tov emphasize segmentation as an important element of the broader phenomenon of literalism. In fact, Barr remarks that segmentation is often regarded "as the essential differentiating characteristic which divides between literal and free translations," although he himself does not hold so strongly to such a characterization.[50] In this section, the term segmentation refers to the translators' technique of dividing Hebrew <u>words</u>

into their constituent parts in order to represent
each part in the Greek translation. Quantitative
representation differs from segmentation in that it
concerns the one-to-one representation (or lack of
it) of multi-word Hebrew phrases, clauses and
sentences. In other words, segmentation and
quantitative representation are related issues, one
treating the micro aspects of form (segmentation)
and the other, the macro aspects (quantitative
representation). For each of these two aspects of
literalism, the more mechanical or wooden translations attempt to achieve a complete one-to-one
correspondence in the Greek translation of each
element in the Hebrew source text.

By defining segmentation in this way, I have
deviated somewhat from the way in which Barr uses
the term. In his study of literalism, Barr actually
uses the term in a number of different senses. In
the way that corresponds most closely to the way in
which I use the term, Barr defines segmentation as
the dividing of Hebrew words into constituent
elements and the translation of each element into
Greek.[51] I certainly have no basic disagreement
with this definition. Barr in practice, however,
seems to confuse this idea with the problems of
lexical consistency and lexical adequacy. As an
example of a "less literal approach" (by "less
literal" I assume non-segmented) he offers Deut
32.8.[52]

בהנחל עליון גוים
ὅτε διεμέριζεν ὁ ὕψιστος ἔθνη

Barr regards the Greek as something other than a
literal (segmented) translation because the
preposition ב is rendered by a conjunction. This

translation results in a normal Greek temporal
phrase rather than what would be a more stilted
phrase using ἐν as a translation of ב. In my
opinion, Barr's argument is not strictly based on
issues of segmentation, but on lexical consistency
and adequacy. That is, the translator has chosen
not to give a rigorously wooden translation of the
Hebrew part of speech, even though each element of
the Hebrew word has been rendered into Greek. By
the definition for segmentation that I gave above,
this sentence would be segmented equally, precisely
because each element in the word בהנחל has a Greek
equivalent with ב represented by ὅτε and הנחל by
διεμέριζεν. Nothing is missing in Greek that is in
the Hebrew.[53] The translator has recognized the
function of the Hebrew preposition, has given it a
more idiomatic Greek translation, and at the same
time, has represented in Greek all of the segments
in the Hebrew word.

A second way that Barr has used the term is
with regard to Hebrew idioms. He cites the example
of the phrase כרת ברית rendered into Greek almost
everywhere as διατιθέναι διαθήκην. In contrast to
this not so literal translation, he cites Aquila's
translation of κόψω . . . συνθήκην in Jer
31(38).31 as an overly zealous and "barbarous"[54]
adherence to the principle of segmentation. This
instance seems to be purely and simply a problem of
lexical adequacy or lexical choice, not segmentation. Rather than a problem of the representation
of the same Hebrew part of speech, as was the case
with Deut 32.8, the translators did not match the
exact meanings of the words in the Hebrew idiom,
and thus, according to Barr, they have not

segmented their Hebrew. According to my use of the
term segmentation, however, this phrase could not
even qualify initially for consideration, since
neither Hebrew word has more than one segment.

Finally, Barr has also used the concept of
segmentation to refer to division below the level
of the Hebrew word, especially as practiced by
Aquila. With this technique, a translator may
attempt to segment on the level of apparent word
formation. For example, Barr notes that, Aquila,
perhaps not understanding the meaning of צלצל in
Isa 18.1, rendered it as σκιὰ σκιά. Thus, he
treated the word as if it were actually two
occurrences of the Hebrew word צל, "shadow."[55]

I have not used the term segmentation in
either of Barr's last two ways, and I have tried
not to import the issues of lexical adequacy into
the discussion of segmentation. What I have
attempted to examine in the translations studied in
this section is the extent to which Greek
translators divided segmentable Hebrew words into
their constituent parts and then rendered each part
into Greek in some way. The issues of lexical
consistency and adequacy require a separate
treatment.

Additionally, a little more precision is
needed to differentiate segmentation from its
relative, quantitative representation. Since
segmentation has been defined here as the one-to-
one representation of each element in a Hebrew
word, it follows that a Hebrew word must have more
than one segment to be considered in this section.
For example, each of the constituent parts of the
word ובטובח (MS A) are present in the Greek of Sir

14.4, καὶ ἐν τοῖς ἀγαθοῖς αὐτοῦ. Here there are
four elements to be put into Greek: the conjunction;
preposition; noun; possessive pronoun. In Barr's
example of Deut 32.8, only one word is capable of
segmentation, בהנחל. If the Hebrew word cannot be
segmented, anything added to it in Greek, such as a
possessive pronoun, constitutes a problem of quantitative representation. Similarly, if a non-seg-
mentable word in Hebrew is missing in the Greek, it
is also a problem of quantitative representation.
In fact, according to my definition of segmentation,
there can be no such entity as a _longer_ non-
segmented text. If some element is added in Greek
and is not likely to represent a different Hebrew
parent text, it is always a problem of quantitative
addition, not segmentation. Thus, in Num 29.27
where במשפט in MT corresponds to κατὰ τὴν
σύγκρισιν αὐτῶν, the additional Greek pronoun is
treated under quantitative representation, not
segmentation, because there is no segment to which
αὐτῶν can correspond. Of course, one could
suggest a different Hebrew parent text here that
had the possessive. As I argued above, however,
that possibility can only be more clearly evaluated
when all the data have been studied based on the
procedure of formal equivalence.

2.3.2 PROBLEMS OF METHOD IN EVALUATING SEGMENTATION

Unfortunately, the entire issue of segmentation is not so cut and dried as it may seem, and
a number of problems attend any examination of it.
Theoretically, it seems possible that any Hebrew
word that can be segmented can have a corresponding

Greek word for each Hebrew element, but in the
actual practice of translation from Hebrew to
Greek, the translators encountered a number of
words whose segments could only be represented in
Greek with great difficulty. Most of these words
were treated as though they were only one word. For
the most part, I have treated these words as the
translators treated them. Some of these words are
handled consistently throughout the translations
and pose no difficulty. The majority of cases
involve the use of the definite article with certain parts of speech in Hebrew, such as pronouns.
In these instances, the article is almost always
incorporated into the Greek word. For example, ההוא
is almost always ἐκεῖνος, or הזה is almost always
some form of οὗτος. The definite article functions
this way with a number of nouns as well. Words such
as הבקר or היום are almost invariably one word in
Greek. All cases such as these are treated in this
section as incapable of being segmented.

Nouns and pronouns with the definite article
make up only a small number of the words that are
usually treated as if they were not capable of
segmentation. A much larger number of other words
presents greater difficulty because sometimes they
are broken into segments by the translators and
sometimes they are not, even within the same
translation. The words in this group are mostly
conjunctions, adverbs, and, most frequently, the
so-called semiprepositions.

The issue can be seen most clearly with the
semiprepositions. In her study of semiprepositions,
Sollamo defines these words as "combinations of a
preposition and a noun . . . whose function is

prepositional."[56] This category includes such prepositions as לפני, בעיני, and בתוך. Translators will at times render these words as one preposition in Greek and at others give what Sollamo calls "slavish" translations, which render both the preposition and the noun.[57] Of the translations studied by her, only Esther shows no "slavish" renderings of the semiprepositions that occur in the Hebrew, while every other translation has a mixture of "slavish" and "free" renderings.[58] Although some books show a predominance of free renderings, they may also show a tendency to be consistent in the renderings that are used for the various Hebrew semiprepositions. Due to these circumstances, in an attempt to keep the problems of lexical consistency and lexical choice at bay in this section, I have treated the semiprepositions as segmentable words that may occasionally be treated as one word by the translator. Thus, because of the ambiguous nature of these words, if a translator renders לפני as ἐνώπιον in some places and as ἐν προσώπῳ in others, both have been considered as examples of equal segmentation. I have also extended this principle to certain conjunctions and adverbs, such as למען, בטרם, and כמו, which translators most often tend to render by one Greek word. In most cases, other than with the semiprepositions, these words are rarely segmented by the translators. The question of the specific rendering or renderings used by a translator is best answered when speaking of lexical consistency in translations. Sollamo, to her credit, has succeeded in maintaining a clear separation between these two issues.[59]

Perhaps the single most difficult case to treat is the preposition ל. Whereas most of the prepositions in Hebrew are usually given some representation in the Greek translation, the many different uses of ל and their subsequent treatments by the translators make it virtually impossible to treat adequately as an issue of segmentation. In many cases, the preposition simply cannot be made to fit into Greek translation, even by the most rigorous of translators. Two uses of ל comprise the majority of such cases: (1) the use of ל with the infinitive, and (2) the use of ל to designate the indirect object. In neither case is the preposition usually rendered in Greek. To try to separate out each instance of these uses would require the detailed examination of every single occurrence of ל not rendered in Greek, a proposal that is not practical in the present study because ל only forms a small part of a much broader study. The close analysis required to treat ל adequately cannot be undertaken in this context. As a provisional solution to this problem, I have not included the occurrences of ל in the data presented in the tables in this section, but have included them in a separate table attached at the end (p. 67), which gives the number of occurrences of ל excerpted from the text files for each book studied here along with the number of those occurrences where the translator has used a Greek preposition to render the Hebrew preposition. Clearly, this material is extensive enough to warrant a separate study that would be able to take into account the different uses of ל and the various renderings given them by the translators.

One other word that is handled in a special
way is the <u>nota accusativi</u>, את. This word is
discounted altogether, since, with the notable
exception of Aquila, it is not translated into
Greek. The Hebrew phrases in which it occurs are
treated as if את were not present. So the phrase את
העם in Isa 29.14 is considered exactly as if it
were העם, the phrase ואת רעיך in Job 35.4, as if it
were ורעיך. The result is that some phrases with את
will be considered capable of segmentation and
others will not.

Finally, there will be some occasions when a
Hebrew word or words and the corresponding Greek
translation may contain elements appropriate for
both segmentation and quantitative representation.
In these cases the occurrence will be included in
the data for both sections. For example, in Sir
44.2, MS B has the phrase מימות עולם, while the
Greek has ἀπ᾽ αἰῶνος.[60] The representation of
the preposition מן by ἀπό in Greek is considered
a legitimate example of segmentation by the translator, and at the same time, the representation of
ימות עולם by αἰῶνος is relevant to quantitative
representation.

2.3.3 COMPARATIVE DATA

The biblical books selected for study in this
section were chosen to represent a wide range of
literal or free renderings based on their[61]
characterizations in other studies. They are,
besides Sir: Numbers; 2 Kings; Isaiah; Amos; Job;[62]
Proverbs; Ruth; Song of Songs; and Qoheleth.

Table 3 below (p. 65) lists each of these
translations in order from the translations that
most consistently represent all the segments of
Hebrew words to those that do this least
consistently. The table reads across from left to
right. The first column, headed by the "equals"
sign ("="), gives the number of Hebrew words for
which the Greek translator has represented all the
constituent elements. The second column, headed by
the "greater than" sign (">"), gives the number of
Hebrew words for which one or more elements are not
formally represented in the translation. The third
column, simply the first two added together, gives
the total number of words that could possibly be
segmented. Finally, the fourth column gives the
ratio (expressed in a percentage) of the number of
equally segmented words represented in column one
to the total number of words that could possibly be
segmented equally (the third column). The table at
the end of the chapter (p. 67) gives the total
number of occurrences of the preposition ל for each
book, the number of occurrences where the
preposition has been rendered into Greek (the
column is marked with "="), and the number of
occurrences where the preposition has not been
rendered by a preposition in the Greek translation
(the column is marked with ">").[63]

TABLE 3 - CONSISTENCY OF SEGMENTATION OF HEBREW
          WORDS

BOOK	=	>	TOTAL	%
QOH	997	38	1035	96.32
2 KGS	4609	250	4859	94.85
CANT	522	45	567	92.06
RUTH	468	42	510	91.76
AMOS	643	68	711	90.43
NUM	4908	758	5666	86.62
ISA	4084	1289	5373	76.00
SIR	1643	661	2304	71.31
JOB	1459	720	2179	66.95
PROV	1101	584	1685	65.34

The relative order of the books listed in
Table 3 shows some differences from the order of
consistency obtained above for word-order
differences. As with word order, Qoheleth, Song of
Songs, and 2 Kings are very consistent in their
representation of the constituent elements of
Hebrew words. Ruth and Amos are also quite
consistent in this regard. Numbers falls close to
these top five at 86.62 percent of equally segmented translations. After Numbers, there is a
significant drop off to Isaiah, Sirach, Job, and
Proverbs. These latter four translations fall
closely together for this aspect of translation as
did Isaiah, Sirach, and Proverbs for word-order
differences, whereas Job stood alone in that
category.

These results also compare favorably to the
characterizations made by Sollamo and Tov and
Wright. Of the translations studied by Sollamo, the
only major difference is Numbers, which Sollamo
places in a group of relatively free translations.
For segmentation, Numbers comes together with Amos,
a translation included in Sollamo's group 3
(relatively literal).[64] In comparison with Tov's
and Wright's results, Ruth, called relatively
literal, is allied more closely with the literal
translations of Qoheleth, Song of Songs, and 2
Kings. Amos, called inconsistent, is also among
this group. Sir, also in the inconsistent group,
falls at the bottom of the table with the free
translations, Isaiah, Proverbs, and Job.[65]

Among all the translations studied, there do
not seem to be any consistent ways in which they
deviate from equal representation of the constituent elements of the Hebrew words. Since there is
really a limited number of possibilities for this
category, certain types occur frequently. The lack
of the definite article, the lack of prepositions,
the lack of possessive or object pronouns, the lack
of representation for conjunctive ו all are quite
numerous. In this regard, Sir is no different from
the other translations in this section, but the
same caveat must be reiterated here that was noted
above for word order. It seems probable a priori
that some of these very elements, especially
elements such as the definite article, would
probably be affected by the poor state of the
Hebrew text. So again with Sir, even more caution
must be exercised when making pronouncements in
this regard.

TABLE 4 - THE OCCURRENCES OF THE PREPOSITION ל

BK	TOTAL	=	>
QOH	323	29	294
2 KGS	532	83	449
CANT	70	8	62
RUTH	111	12	99
AMOS	81	35	46
NUM	1249	302	947
ISA	782	206	576
SIR	383	93	290
JOB	260	55	260
PROV	320	50	270

2.4 QUANTITATIVE REPRESENTATION OF THE HEBREW PARENT TEXT

2.4.1 INTRODUCTION

As Barr and Tov both point out, the translator who strives to make a close representation of the Hebrew parent text works toward a one-to-one correspondence between the Hebrew and the resulting Greek translation.[66] Thus, in an absolutely mechanical translation every Hebrew element would be represented by a corresponding element in Greek. The use of this technique, called quantitatively equal representation, is quite widespread in the Jewish-Greek translations, especially as compared to other translations, such as the Aramaic Targums, which tend toward a more paraphrastic rendering of

their source texts. Barr notes that on the whole
the Greek translators of the Hebrew scriptures seem
to have added or subtracted few elements in their
works.[67] Nevertheless, even though in a general
sense the Jewish-Greek translations are clearly
more concerned to give a close representation of
the Hebrew than are the Targums, the degree to
which a translator adds to or subtracts words from
the Hebrew parent text gives a good indication of
the translator's approach to rendering the Hebrew
text and helps in understanding the confidence with
which such additions or subtractions should be
accepted in reconstructions based on the Greek
translations.

   Quantitative representation is related to, but
different from, the technique of segmentation.
Whereas segmentation takes place on the level of
the Hebrew word, quantitative representation
operates at the multi-word level. As I have defined
it elsewhere, quantitatively equal representation
is "the division by the translator of multi-word
Hebrew units into their constituent parts producing
a one-to-one representation in Greek."[68] That is,
quantitative representation concerns the word-by-
word (but not necessarily in sequence) representation in translation of the form of the source
text. Thus, the addition of a pronoun in the Greek
translation or the elimination of a subject that is
explicit in Hebrew constitute quantitative
differences between the parent text and the
translation. For example, the following passage
from Sir 12.12 illustrates quantitatively equal
representation.

Sir 12.12 אל חושיבהו לימינך (MS A)
    μὴ καθίσῃς αὐτὸν ἐκ δεξιῶν σου

In this case, each element of the Hebrew (negative
particle, verb with attendent object, prepositional
phrase) is present in the Greek translation with no
elements added or subtracted. The following two
examples show translations that are quantitatively
longer and shorter.

(Longer)

Sir 6.29 וחבלחה בגדי כתם (MS A, 2Q18)
    καὶ οἱ κλοιοὶ αὐτῆς εἰς στολὴν δόξης

(Shorter)

Sir 5.14 אל תקרא בעל שתים (MS A)
    μὴ κληθῇς ψίθυρος

In the Greek of Sir 6.29, all the elements of the
Hebrew are represented, but the formal representation of this clause shows the addition of the
preposition εἰς before στολήν. In the context of
the whole verse, this addition probably represents
a compensation for the fact that the clause lacks
an explicit verb, which is understood from the
preceding clause in the Hebrew (assuming that the
translator did not read the Hebrew as בבגדי). On
the other hand, in the second example, the Hebrew
idiom בעל שתים, which means "double tongued"
(literally "master of two"), has been rendered by a
single Greek word ψίθυρος, "slanderer" or
"whisperer."
    There are, however, no translations in the
Jewish-Greek corpus that show 100 percent
quantitative representation throughout. Every one
of these translations contains some deviations from
perfectly equal quantitative representation. The

translators' motivations for these deviations
probably vary. In most cases of quantitatively
longer translation, it seems that the translators
are concerned to clarify or explain certain
conceptual or grammatical elements in the Hebrew.
In cases of quantitatively shorter translations,
translators seem to be concerned to eliminate
repetitive elements or elements that are deemed
unnecessary. Thus, where segmentation shows the
translator's sensitivity to each unit within a
Hebrew word, the degree of quantitatively equal
representation can give a good indication of the
translator's awareness of the larger context of the
material that is being translated. Every quantitative deviation, however, is probably not the
result of exegetical motivations. Quantitative
deviation could also result from the translator's
desire for variety in the translation or from well-
known and conventional ways of rendering certain
Hebrew constructions and idioms. But no matter what
the motivation, the more a translator attempts to
give a one-to-one representation of the
quantitative form of the Hebrew text, the more
literal the resulting translation can be
considered.

In the discussion that follows, both longer
and shorter quantitative deviations are considered.
Here, as in the preceding section on segmentation,
in addition to Sir, a number of translations have
been selected based on their characterizations by
previous scholars. For this section I have examined
Numbers, Amos, Proverbs, Ruth, Song of Songs, and
Qoheleth.

2.4.2 QUANTITATIVELY LONGER TRANSLATIONS[69]

This section is concerned with those deviations from quantitatively equal representation that introduce elements into the translation that are not represented in the formal Hebrew parent text. At the outset of this investigation a number of types of occurrences have been excluded from consideration. In general, additional elements that could easily represent an actual Hebrew textual variant are excluded. That is, since certain elements might well have been in the parent text, they are excluded in order to avoid counting as longer quantitative translations places where the translator was simply following the Hebrew text. Occurrences of this type to be excluded are: the Greek definite article; the addition of καί or δέ; forms of the relative pronoun that do not render participles; duals; pronouns used as the indirect object. These kinds of elements are very difficult, if not impossible, to reconstruct with any certainty.[70] The following passages provide examples of some of the kinds of elements to be excluded.

καί or δέ

    Cant 4.16 יזלו
        καὶ ῥευσάτωσαν

Relative Pronoun

    Sir 44.8 יש מהם הניחו שם
        εἰσὶν αὐτῶν οἳ κατέλιπον ὄνομα

Indirect Object

    Num 20.10 שמעו
        ἀκούσατέ μου

In other instances, certain types of words or
Hebrew idioms are excluded because they are almost
never rendered into Greek with quantitatively equal
translations. These exclusions include proper
names, numbers, and words for which Greek does not
have an adequate means of representing equally. Two
examples of the latter type are אין, which is
almost always translated οὐκ ἔστιν, and בין,
which almost always appears in Greek as ἀνὰ μέσον
or ἐν μέσῳ.

Since I take a minimalist stand on issues
related to possible differences in the parent text,
the elements just discussed are not counted,
because they could reduce the significance of the
results. Obviously, however, some of the excluded
elements could be, and probably are, genuine
additions introduced by the translator. In order to
compensate somewhat for this problem, I have
provided two tables of data below. In Table 5
(p. 75), the data are presented following my stated
procedure of excluding certain elements; Table 6
(p. 75) gives all of the data, including those
occurrences excluded from the first table.

2.4.2.1 TYPES OF LONGER QUANTITATIVE TRANSLATIONS

In the books chosen for this section, I was
able to isolate eleven different ways in which
translators include additional elements in their
translations. For all of the different types, the
common thread that links them is that in Greek
there are ways of avoiding the use of additional
elements. Here I will list each type of expansion
and give an example from Sir. For more detailed

explanation and examples see my paper "The
Quantitative Representation of Elements: Evaluating
'Literalism' in the LXX."

1. Making the Subject of a Verb Explicit

Sir 46.9 ויתן לכלב עצמה (MS B)
καὶ ἔδωκεν ὁ κύριος τῷ χαλεβ ἰσχύν

2. Prepositions

Sir 42.18 מב[ו] אחיות עולם‎ (MS M)
καὶ ἐνέβλεψεν εἰς σημεῖον αἰῶνος [71]

3. Particles or Conjunctions

Sir 12.10 כי כנחשת רועו יחליא (MS A)
ὡς γὰρ ὁ χαλκὸς ἰοῦται οὕτως ἡ
πονηρία αὐτοῦ

4. Forms of εἰμι and γίγνομαι

Sir 37.18 מושלת (MS B)
καὶ ἡ κυριεύουσα. . .ἐστιν

5. Negative and Affirmative Particles

Sir 45.19 וירא יהוה ויתאנף (MS B)
εἶδεν κύριος καὶ οὐκ εὐδόκησεν

6. Differences Produced by Changes of Voice

Sir 6.27 בקש ומצא (MS A)
καὶ ζήτησον καὶ γνωσθήσεταί σοι

7. Personal Pronouns

Sir 7.36 אחרית (MS A)
τὰ ἔσχατά σου

8. Relative Pronouns

Sir 39.18 ואין מעצור לחשועתו מעשה (MS B)
καὶ οὐκ ἔστιν ὃς ἐλαττώσει τὸ
σωτήριον αὐτοῦ ἔργα

9. Idiomatic Expressions

Sir 37.26 עולם (MSS C, D)
εἰς τὸν αἰῶνα

10. Composite Renderings

Sir 33.20 חמשׁיל (MS E)
        δῷς ἐξουσίαν

11. Exegetical Renderings

Sir 6.37 יחבמך (MS A)
        τῆς σοφίας δοθήσεταί σοι

2.4.2.2 COMPARATIVE DATA

These different types of deviations from
quantitatively equal representation can be used as
indicators of how closely a translator has followed
the form of the Hebrew parent text. In the tables
below, a ratio is given for each book, which is a
percentage of the number of quantitatively unequal
units to the total number of records in the
computer file for that book.[72] The percentages can
then be used to compare the different translations
for this characteristic of literalness.

The data presented here have not been broken
down into the types of deviations outlined above.
In any further investigation of this issue, each
deviation could be marked as to which of the types
it represents, and data could be gathered for those
narrower categories. Studies such as this could
provide significant insight into the particular
ways in which a translator introduces elements into
the translation. Such insight would greatly assist
in the task of reconstructing particular elements
in the Hebrew parent text of the translations.

In each table presented below, line 1 shows
the total number of deviations from one-to-one
correspondence between the Greek translation and

the Hebrew collected from the CATSS computer files.
Line 2 gives the number of lines in the CATSS
parallel file for each book, and line 3 lists the
percentage of deviation from equal quantitative
representation.

TABLE 5 - DEVIATIONS PRODUCING LONGER TRANSLATIONS
          (LESS EXCLUSIONS)

	QOH	CANT	NUM	RUTH	SIR	AMOS	PROV
DEVS.	33	20	418	44	312	97	549
LINES	2938	1264	16055	1314	9288	2015	7691
%	1.1%	1.5%	2.6%	3.3%	3.4%	4.8%	7.1%

TABLE 6 - DEVIATIONS PRODUCING LONGER TRANSLATIONS
          (PLUS EXCLUSIONS)

	QOH	NUM	CANT	RUTH	SIR	AMOS	PROV
DEVS.	66	428	35	54	423	110	713
LINES	2938	16055	1264	1314	9288	2015	7691
%	2.2%	2.7%	2.8%	4.1%	4.6%	5.5%	9.3%

The tables above show clearly that the
translators of Qoheleth and Song of Songs take the
most rigorous approach to quantitative representation. Numbers is fairly close behind, and when
all the deviations are considered in Table 6,
Numbers, because it uses few of the particular
translations that were excluded, stands even closer
to Qoheleth and Song of Songs. At the other end of
the scale, Proverbs stands out as the least
rigorous regarding quantitative representation.

The conclusions to be derived from these data
underscore the importance of evaluating aspects of
literalism rather than simply giving blanket
descriptions of translations based on somewhat
vague criteria. If the results here are compared
with those of Sollamo and Tov and Wright, some
differing characterizations of translations can be
reached. In Tov and Wright, Qoheleth and Song of
Songs were characterized as literal, Ruth and Amos
were relatively literal. Numbers was called
relatively free; Proverbs, free; and Sirach,
inconsistent.[73] Sollamo described Proverbs as
"freely rendered." Numbers is included in her
second group (relatively free), while Amos,
included with the Minor Prophets, is in the third
group (relatively literal).[74] Thus, the evaluations
of the translations of Qoheleth, Song of Songs,
Ruth, and Proverbs agree well with these previous
descriptions. Sir falls in the middle, but
certainly closer to Numbers and Ruth than to
Proverbs, or even Amos. Amos and Numbers are the
two anomalies. They have, in effect, switched their
previous roles. For this category, Numbers is
relatively consistent in its correspondence between
the Greek and Hebrew, and it differs from previous
descriptions as relatively free. Amos, as a part of
the Minor Prophets, has usually been regarded as
relatively literal, a description that is not
applicable on the basis of the present criterion.
The fact that these two books can be regarded in
different ways using different criteria argues for
the position taken at the beginning of this chapter
that general descriptions of translations are not
adequate, but that more detailed criteria need to

be developed, and that translations need to be characterized on the basis of these specific criteria.

This is also true with reference to Sir. In contrast to its position in the previous two categories, where the Greek Sir was not very wooden in its renderings, for this criterion, Sir demonstrates a relatively consistent pattern of resisting the addition of elements in translation that are not in the Hebrew. In this respect, Sir is very close to Ruth in both tables of data. The large jump in Sir in the total number of deviations from Table 5 to Table 6 is largely due to the frequent presence in Greek of καί where there is no corresponding conjunction in the extant Hebrew manuscripts. As a result, in this instance, Greek Sir parts company with Proverbs, a translation with which it had a certain closeness in the previous two sections. This may indicate less of a tendency in Sir to paraphrase, a tendency often claimed for Proverbs and supported by the analysis in this section.

2.4.3 QUANTITATIVELY SHORTER TRANSLATIONS

The situation with quantitatively shorter translations is much simpler than with the longer texts. This is the case because the shorter quantitative differences are more closely related to problems of segmentation than the longer quantitative texts are. I argued above that on a formal level there can be no such thing as a longer segmented translation. If the Greek is longer than the Hebrew when the procedure of formal equivalence

is applied, the issue automatically becomes one of
quantitative representation. This categorization,
however, is made simply for matters of convenience,
even though there is a relation between some
quantitative problems and segmentation. In cases
such as Num 29.27 (MT = כבשמפט; LXX = κατὰ τὴν
σύγκρισιν αὐτῶν) cited above in section 2.3.1, a
different parent text, one that had the possessive
pronoun, would constitute an example of segmentation, but it is included under quantitative
representation because there is no possessive in
the MT. Only when the data for segmentation and
quantitative representation are fully analyzed can
one effectively determine whether or not quantitatively longer elements are likely to represent
elements in the translator's parent text, and thus,
constitute an equally segmented Hebrew. One
possibility for further research along these lines
would be to separate the quantitative problems into
two categories: (1) those that could potentially be
segmentation issues, and (2) those that could not.
Such a division could provide even further insight
into possible differences between the available
Hebrew texts and the translators' source texts.

Similarly, quantitatively shorter translations
reflect the absence of one or more elements from
multi-word Hebrew phrases, clauses, or sentences.
For example, in Sir 3.13 κἂν represents אם גם of
MS A. This is not a problem of shorter quantitative
representation, because καί renders גם and ἔαν
renders אם. The only problem is one of segmentation
between גם and καί. Some other cases might appear
to be problems of segmentation when they are really
quantitative problems. A good example is found in

Qoh 2.25 where חוץ ממנ' is translated by πάρεξ
αὐτοῦ. Although one might argue that the issue is
one of segmentation between ממנ' and αὐτοῦ, a
more satisfactory explanation is that πάρεξ
combines both חוץ and מן, and thereby the problem
becomes one of quantitative representation.

A second problem concerns the treatment of
words in Hebrew that have no counterpart in the
Greek translation. How should these be evaluated?
The lack of a translation for a word such as כל in
the phrase את כל מלאכח'ך in Sir 3.17 (MS C; the
Greek has τὰ ἔργα σου) is certainly different
from the lack in Greek of a Hebrew phrase like כל
'מ' in Sir 3.12 (MS A). Further, what is to be done
about shorter texts like that in Sir 3.25 where
eight words in Hebrew MS A find no Greek
representation? To operate in the same way as with
the longer quantitative texts and to exclude
anything that could likely represent an alternative
parent text would mean excluding all such cases.

The problem could be solved in one of two
ways. First, one could arbitrarily decide on a
length of text to include, such as two Hebrew words
not represented in Greek. All others would be
excluded. This solution ignores the problem of
whether a Hebrew word or words genuinely have no
corresponding word in the Greek translation (such
as the example of Sir 3.17 above), or whether the
word has been considered together with another word
as with חוץ and מן in Qoh 2.25. The second
solution, which I have adopted here, is to give
different presentations of the data. In this
section I will present the data in the following
manner. In Table 7 (p. 88), all of the Hebrew texts

that have quantitatively shorter Greek translations
will be combined with those for passages where the
Greek translation is quantitatively shorter due to
the fact that one Hebrew word is not represented in
the Greek. This is done primarily for two reasons,
one methodological and the other practical.
Methodologically, to exclude all shorter texts
where one word of the Hebrew is lacking a Greek
correspondent would be to work contrary to a basic
principle of the formal equivalence of the
surviving Hebrew textual traditions to the Greek.
There is no way <u>a priori</u> to tell whether or not כל
in Sir 3.17 was in the translator's Hebrew. Only an
analysis based on principles of formal equivalence
will give an indication of the probability that כל
was or was not in the grandson's Hebrew text.
Practically, the texts used for this study are set
up in such a way that these cases cannot be
effectively distinguished from some other cases,
such as the lack of an equivalent in Greek for a
Hebrew preposition. If a Hebrew preposition could
be represented implicitly by a Greek case ending,
the Hebrew preposition will often be listed
together with the inflected noun rather than
separately with some indication that it is missing
in the Greek. Thus, in Sir 9.3, for the Hebrew of
MS A, אל תקרב אל אשה זרה, the Greek has μή
corresponding to אל, ὑπάντα to תקרב, ἑταιριζομένη
to זרה, but only γυναικί, a dative case noun, to
the phrase אל אשה. This is a genuine shorter
quantitative translation, but nothing explicitly
indicates that the Greek is lacking the Hebrew אל.
Consequently, I have adopted a policy of grouping
all such cases together with all cases of

quantitatively shorter texts where the Greek lacks
a correspondent for one Hebrew word.

A second set of data will be given showing the
number of quantitatively shorter texts comprised of
multi-word phrases and clauses. For these
occurrences Table 8 (p. 88) will give, on separate
lines, the number of phrases and clauses missing in
the Greek translation. The number of missing
phrases will be combined in Table 9 (p. 88) with
the results of Table 7 described above. The number
of clauses will not be combined in this table.

This approach assumes that Hebrew clauses
lacking in Greek translation will most likely be
predominantly problems of a different parent text,
and not problems that result from the translator
eliminating them or from omissions originating in
the process of the transmission of the Greek. This
is especially likely in Sir, where the Hebrew
manuscripts clearly contain elements of an expanded
second Hebrew recension. If all of these clauses
were included in a single presentation of the data,
the second Hebrew recensional readings would be
counted against the translator even though they
were almost certainly not in his parent text.
Multi-word Hebrew phrases, elements like
prepositional phrases or noun phrases, are more
ambiguous and will be treated separately. They are
not of the same sort as readings involving one
word, but also are different from longer clauses.
In the case of Hebrew phrases, the principle of
formal equivalence must be modified in order to
deal with the ambiguity they present.

One kind of shorter reading has been excluded
from this group. These are instances where one

Greek word translates two Hebrew words, and both
Hebrew words have been incorporated intact into the
Greek term. For example, in Sir 5.4, the Hebrew
words ארך אפים (MSS A, C) have been rendered as
μακρόθυμος by Ben Sira's grandson. The one Greek
word has incorporated each of the Hebrew terms into
the translation, ארך represented by μακρο- and אפים
by -θυμος. In cases such as these, even though the
Greek is formally shorter, it does accurately and
separately represent each element of the Hebrew.
This situation is of a completely different type
from the example of בעל שׁחים translated as ψίθυρος
in Sir 5.14, a type that is considered a genuine
shorter quantitative translation because the Greek
paraphrases the Hebrew words.

2.4.3.1 TYPES OF SHORTER QUANTITATIVE TRANSLATIONS

Although they are not as numerous as the
different types of longer quantitative
translations, shorter quantitative translations
seem to fall into various types, the most prominent
of which are described below.

1. The Representation of a Hebrew Preposition

This is perhaps the most frequent way in which
shorter quantitative translations are produced. In
many instances, where a preposition is required in
Hebrew, a Greek case ending will suffice. The
translator who is more concerned with Greek content
and style than with representing the form of the
source text will often use the simple Greek case
ending rather than include the superfluous

preposition. This situation often results from an
interpretation of the source text by the
translator, as the example from Prov 19.3 below
illustrates.

Sir 9.3 ‎אל תקרב אל אשה זרה‎ (MS A)
     μὴ ὑπάντα γυναικὶ ἑταιριζομένῃ

Prov 19.3 ‎ועל יהוה יזעף לבו‎
     τὸν δὲ θεὸν αἰτιᾶται τῇ καρδίᾳ αὐτοῦ

2. An Explicit Subject in Hebrew Condensed in Greek

In some instances, where the Hebrew subject is
explicit, especially if it is an independent
pronoun, the Greek translator will not provide a
separate rendering in Greek, but will allow the
ending of the verb to suffice.

Sir 33.17 ‎ב]ברכ]ת אל גם אני קדמחי‎   (MS E)
     ἐν εὐλογίᾳ κυρίου ἔφθασα

Qoh 8.2 ‎אני פי מלך שמור‎
     στόμα βασιλέως φύλαξον

3. Condensation of Hebrew Periphrastic Tenses

Whereas the Greek translators will sometimes
use εἰμί or γίγνομαι in periphrastic tenses, and
as a result, produce a longer quantitative
translation, so will they occasionally condense
Hebrew periphrastic tenses into one Greek main
verb, which produces a shorter quantitative
translation. In some instances, the translators may
also choose not to render the independent personal
pronoun when it functions as the copula, or when it
is simply deemed superfluous.

Sir 5.9 אל תהיה זורה לכל רוח (MS A)
μὴ λίκμα ἐν παντὶ ἀνέμῳ

Sir 41.7 כי [ב]גללו היו בוז (MS M)
ὅτι δι' αὐτὸν ὀνειδισθήσονται

Sir 11.11 וכדי כן הוא מתאחר (MS A)
καὶ τόσῳ μᾶλλον ὑστερεῖται

4. The Omission of Individual Words

For a variety of reasons, individual words in
Hebrew may not be represented in Greek. Certain
words, such as לא and אשר, are often eliminated, as
are certain types of words, especially conjunctions
and particles. In other cases however, nouns,
verbs, or other "content" words may be eliminated
in translation. In most instances, it is impossible
to tell the reason for the shorter translation, but
stylistic or exegetical concerns seem most likely.
In some translations certain words or types of
words may be routinely eliminated in translation,
especially in those cases where Greek grammatical
considerations demand it. For example, a number of
instances of כל and of גם found in MT do not appear
in the Greek translation of Proverbs.[75]

Prov 1.25 ותפרעו כל עצתי
ἀλλὰ ἀκύρους ἐποιεῖτε ἐμὰς βουλάς

Num 14.17 ועתה יגדל נא כח אדני
καὶ νῦν ὑψωθήτω ἡ ἰσχύς σου κύριε

Sir 13.8 השמר אל תרהב מאד (MS A)
πρόσεχε μὴ ἀποπλανηθῇς

Sir 45.23 ויכפר על בני ישראל (MS B)
καὶ ἐξιλάσατο τοῦ ισραηλ

5. The Combination of Two Words into One in Translation

Often a translator will use one Greek word to
render two Hebrew words, which results in a
translation quantitatively shorter than the source
text. Sometimes the resulting translation will be a
clear reflection of both Hebrew words. At other
times, the result may emphasize one of the two
Hebrew terms, and thereby, it may look as if one of
the words has been disregarded. In cases such as
this, it is often difficult to determine whether
one word has simply been eliminated in translation,
or whether both have been considered together. A
good example of this latter type involves איש with
an adjective rendered in Greek by the adjective
alone. In the examples that follow, each results in
a quantitatively unequal translation, even though
the way in which the Hebrew words are combined is a
little different.

Sir 10.30 איש עשיר (MS B)
           πλούσιος

Sir 44.14 לדור ודור (MS M)
           εἰς γενεάς

Sir 9.16 בעלי לחמך (MS A)
          σύνδειπνοί σου

Prov 17.18 חסר לב
           ἄφρονι

6. Paraphrasing

Although strict paraphrasing seems to be
relatively infrequent in most of the translations
in the Jewish Greek corpus, its use in translation
often produces shorter quantitative translations.
Some paraphrasing is probably conventional. A

translator may have a way to render a particular
Hebrew phrase into Greek in a quantitatively equal
way, but the translation would be awkward or
uncomfortable, so the translator paraphrases in
order to avoid the difficulty. In some instances, a
more paraphrastic rendering may be more natural for
the translator. The best example involves the
translation of יש with ל to indicate possession.
Greek could render this construction in a quantitatively equal manner using εἰμί with a dative
case. In fact, this more wooden translation is
sometimes used.[76] Yet, in the overwhelming majority
of cases, some Greek verb of possession, like
ἔχω, is used. Sir 14.11, given below, provides a
good example. The two examples from Proverbs
demonstrate paraphrasing of entire cola. In Prov
10.4 the translator has rendered "The one who works
with hands of deceit is poor" as "Poverty brings a
man low." In Prov 17.8, "A precious gem is a bribe
in the eyes of its owner" is rendered into Greek as
"A gracious reward is instruction to those who use
(it)." In both cases, the entire colon has been
paraphrased, and despite the fact that there is
some connection between the lexical elements of the
Hebrew and Greek texts, in each case, the Greek
rendering has resulted in a quantitatively shorter
translation.

Sir 14.11 יש לך (MS A)
ἔχῃς

Prov 10.4 ראש עשה כף רמיה
πενία ἄνδρα ταπεινοῖ

Prov 17.8 אבן חן השחד בעיני בעליו
μισθὸς χαρίτων ἡ παιδεία τοῖς χρωνένοις

2.4.3.2 COMPARATIVE DATA

In Table 7 (p. 88) a ratio (expressed in percentage) of the number of deviations that produce shorter quantitative translations to the number of lines in the CATSS computer files is given for each translation studied. The number of shorter deviations is smaller than the number for longer quantitative translations for each book. This situation results because many shorter deviations are actually subsumed under the rubric of segmentation since, rather than having a separate Hebrew word that is not in the Greek translation, the shorter translation results from a missing <u>segment</u> of a Hebrew word. For example, in Sir 45.19, ויכלם is rendered καὶ συνετελέσθησαν. The difference in voice and meaning between the two verbs renders the Hebrew direct object unnecessary in the translation. If that direct object had been a separate noun, its omission would have been a matter of a quantitatively unequal translation. As it stands, however, the shorter translation falls under segmentation.

The same general policy has been followed here as above for longer quantitative translations. The data have not been broken down into the various types of deviations outlined above -- that remains a possibility for future study. Table 8 below provides the number of multiple word phrases and clauses for each translation that were not included in the data given in Table 7. Table 9 below gives the same information as Table 8, but with the number of phrases included in the totals.

SIRACH AND ITS PARENT TEXT

TABLE 7 - DEVIATIONS PRODUCING SHORTER TRANSLATIONS

	CANT	QOH	RUTH	AMOS	NUM	PROV	SIR
DEVS.	6	17	15	29	315	202	291
LINES	1264	2938	1314	2015	16055	7691	9288
%	.47	.57	1.14	1.43	1.96	2.62	3.13

TABLE 8 - PHRASES AND CLAUSES

	NUM	AMOS	PROV	RUTH	CANT	QOH	SIR
PHRASE	32	0	10	1	2	0	23
CLAUSE	11	2	31	1	0	0	83

TABLE 9 - DEVIATIONS FROM TABLE 7 PLUS PHRASES

	QOH	CANT	RUTH	AMOS	NUM	PROV	SIR
DEVS.	17	8	16	29	347	212	314
LINES	2938	1264	1314	2015	16055	7691	9288
%	.57	.63	1.21	1.43	2.16	2.75	3.38

For shorter quantitative translations, as for
longer, Qoheleth and Song of Songs stand alone in
an extremely close quantitative representation of
the MT. Ruth and Amos fall together in the middle,
but still retain a close representation of the
Hebrew. Numbers, Proverbs, and Sirach, however,
give different results from those for quantitatively longer translations. Numbers has moved
toward the more free translations here. One
possible reason for Numbers being more free for

shorter quantitative translations than for longer
ones may be that a large number of cases of shorter
translations in Numbers concerns the translation of
peoples' ages, and although the renderings of
numbers were excluded, the frequent use of כן or בה
with no Greek equivalent has inflated the data for
Numbers. Conversely, Proverbs is somewhat less free
in this case than might have been expected. Of
course, this is a relative judgment, since the
percentage of deviation is almost six times higher
for Proverbs than for Song of Songs. Proverbs,
however, is a difficult translation to evaluate on
criteria such as this, since many verses in Hebrew
have been interpreted by the translator, and yet
the individual elements still have formal
equivalents, as we saw above in the examples of
paraphrasing. Further, many more examples are
likely to fall under the category of segmentation.

Sir is a completely different situation. As it
appears in the tables, Sir is the most free of all
the translations, including Proverbs. Although
many, perhaps most, of these occurrences are
probably due to a free approach by the translator
on these matters, some, perhaps many, instances are
certainly the result of the complex text-critical
situation in the book. This is most readily seen in
those places where more than one manuscript is
extant for the same passage, especially where MSS A
and B overlap. In some instances, one manuscript
will have a Hebrew word in the text where the Greek
has no corresponding translation. The other
manuscript will agree with the Greek and have no
Hebrew word. In these cases, I presume that the
Hebrew that agrees with the Greek was most likely

its parent text. The additional word in the one
manuscript may well reflect a reading of the second
Hebrew recension, and thus, it could not have been
part of the translator's parent text. Consequently,
these instances are not counted in the data given
above because the parent text of the Greek probably
lacked the words. Unfortunately, in most places
where Hebrew is extant for Sir, only one manuscript
is extant, and such clear text-critical judgments
cannot be made.[77] Undoubtedly, there are numerous
other instances where the Hebrew would present
similar situations were other Hebrew manuscripts
extant. With the difficulty of identifying all of
the second Hebrew recension readings in the extant
Hebrew manuscripts, one can only guess as to where
these problems might occur elsewhere, and thus, the
numbers for Sir are probably higher than if the
second Hebrew recension could be entirely
eliminated. The present state of the Hebrew texts
also most likely accounts for what seems to be an
inordinate number of longer clauses in Sir for
which there is no corresponding Hebrew.

2.4.4 CONCLUSIONS

As a conclusion to this section I have taken
the number of longer quantitative translations
given in Table 5 and combined them with the number
of shorter quantitative translations given in Table
7. The results are found in Table 10 below. This
combined tally gives a different perspective on the
extent to which the translators of these books
woodenly represented the quantitative form of their
Hebrew text. When the data for longer and shorter
quantitative translations are combined, Qoheleth

and Song of Songs remain the most wooden of the
group, and Proverbs, the least wooden. Ruth and
Numbers fall close together, as do Amos and Sirach.
On the basis of these data, one might call Ruth and
Numbers relatively wooden for this characteristic
of literalness, and Amos and Sir could be termed
relatively free. It must be noted, however, that
even the least wooden of these translations,
Proverbs, retains the quantitative form of its
Hebrew about 90 percent of the time. This picture,
then, together with the conclusions for word order,
seems further to bear out the aforementioned
impressions of Barr that the translators of the
Jewish-Greek materials added or subtracted few
elements from their Hebrew source texts.

TABLE 10 - COMBINED DATA FROM TABLES 5 AND 7

	QOH	CANT	RUTH	NUM	AMOS	SIR	PROV
DEVS.	50	26	59	733	126	603	751
LINES	2938	1264	1314	16055	2015	9288	7691
%	1.70	2.05	4.49	4.56	6.25	6.49	9.76

2.5 CONSISTENCY OF LEXICAL REPRESENTATION

2.5.1 INTRODUCTION

The fourth aspect of translation to be
examined in this chapter is the degree to which
translators consistently use one Greek word as a
representation of one Hebrew word. The extent to
which this approach, which has been variously
termed stereotyping, verbal linkage, concordant
relationship, and regular lexical concordance,[78] is

used by a translator gives an additional indication
of the degree to which the translation demonstrates
adherence to the source text. The higher the
stereotyping tendency on the part of the translator, the more confidence one has in reconstructing
the lexical elements of the Hebrew parent text of
the translation. In this section, however, a
different approach will be taken to this issue from
that taken by most scholars who have treated it.

Almost universally, when discussing
stereotyping, the starting point is the Hebrew text
from which the translation is made.[79] The idea of
stereotyping has been seen as the extent to which
translators represent a particular word in Hebrew
by a particular word in Greek. That is, in the
perfectly stereotyped translation, the same Greek
word would translate a specific Hebrew word in all
of its occurrences, and that Hebrew word would be
the only word translated by that Greek. Thus,
stereotyping is considered from the perspective of
the variety or consistency of renderings given to
any Hebrew word.

This ideal situation could be likened to the
use by the translator of an inflexible word list
for each Hebrew to Greek correspondence; any
deviation from that list would be impossible.[80]
Naturally, no student of the Hebrew-Greek translations actually imagines that this kind of procedure
was at work, but it is the picture that is built up
of perfect lexical correspondence. As a result, the
usual approach has been to start by taking a Hebrew
term and then finding the Greek word or words that
translate it. If one Greek word predominates
(although no criteria seem to exist for what

constitutes predominance), it is called a stereotyped rendering. Since frequently the same Greek
word translates more than one particular Hebrew
word, one Greek word may be called a stereotyped
rendering for more than one Hebrew word.

The present study will move in the opposite
direction, from the Greek translation to the
Hebrew. Stereotyping in this case refers to the
variety or consistency of words in the source
language that any Greek word represents, rather
than the variety of renderings in Greek for any
Hebrew word. The reasons for this approach are
relatively straightforward, and they address the
particular difficulties of working in Sir. As I
argued in the introduction to this chapter, a major
difficulty with Sir, or any translation for that
matter, is the problem of whether or in what
aspects the Hebrew parent text can be reconstructed
with any certainty. The studies of translation
technique undertaken here have the expressed
purpose of trying to reach conclusions concerning
the prognosis for that enterprise. If the scholar
who wishes to reconstruct the Hebrew parent text
cares primarily about the degree to which the
translator represented the _form_ of the Hebrew text,
then an important element is what Hebrew word or
words each Greek word represents, and how
consistently they are represented, as well as _vice
versa_. In order to be able to attempt reconstructions of lexical elements in the source
language, the ideal picture of one Greek word for
one Hebrew word represents only part of the
problem. It is necessary to examine the other side,
that is, what Hebrew word or words any Greek word
translates, and how consistently this is done.

This concern is especially acute when one
studies the Greek Sir. This one translation is
different from all the others in the Jewish-Greek
corpus in that no Hebrew text is extant for the
entire book. Whereas in Proverbs or Genesis, or any
other book, there is a Hebrew from which to
proceed, that is not the case for approximately
one-third of Sir. This reality changes the focus.
For example, in a translation which has Hebrew for
the entire book, if a strange looking lexical
equivalent were encountered, one would look at how
that Hebrew word is rendered in its other
occurrences. Then, based on the consistency of
representation or some pattern of usage, one could
make a decision regarding the parent text of the
Greek, and if it were warranted, attempt some
reconstruction. In Sir, this is not always
possible. The attempt to reconstruct often involves
passages where there is no Hebrew available, and so
a different approach is necessary, an approach that
targets the Greek first. For instance, in order to
reconstruct the Hebrew parent text of Sir 17.6,
where no Hebrew is yet available, one would
encounter γλῶσσα. It would be necessary to look
elsewhere in Sir and to find out which Hebrew terms
the grandson translates as γλῶσσα. Based on the
consistency or lack of consistency in the
translation, or perhaps the context, a reconstruction of this term might be attempted. In fact, in
Sir, where γλῶσσα does occur with a Hebrew
equivalent, it translates both לשׁון and שׂפה (in the
plural). Since the Greek noun is in the singular,
לשׁון seems to be the more likely Hebrew reading

based on the available data. What causes additional
difficulty, however, is that of the 26 occurrences
of γλῶσσα in the Greek Sir, 13 occur in places
where no Hebrew is extant. Thus, a significant
amount of important data cannot be used.

Not only other studies of stereotyping, but
also the other sections of this chapter have taken
the Hebrew as a starting point and then proceeded
to the Greek. Word order, segmentation, and
quantitative representation, however, differ
significantly from stereotyping. In each of the
first three sections, one limited aspect of the
Hebrew text was being considered, and, for the most
part, each involved a relatively simple comparison
of the Greek and Hebrew texts on these issues.
Consequently, for each issue a relatively clear
picture could be derived as to what was happening
in each translation. The representation of Hebrew
lexical elements in Greek is necessarily more
complicated in that one is dealing with many
different words, each capable of being treated in a
variety of ways by the translator. In order to get
an idea of the degree to which each translator
consistently represented the lexical elements of
the Hebrew text, it seemed that the Greek to Hebrew
approach would work the best.

A simple example that illustrates this
approach involves the two synonymous Greek nouns
meaning "sword," μάχαιρα and ῥομφαία. In
Numbers, μάχαιρα occurs four times, each time as a
translation of חרב. In my opinion, this concordance
represents a stereotyped rendering, whether or not
ῥομφαία translates חרב or some other word for a
weapon. What matters is that when μάχαιρα occurs,

it renders the same Hebrew word. The translator of
Numbers evidently decided that μάχαιρα would
translate only חרב, regardless of what other
possible translations חרב might have. In fact, the
synonym ῥομφαία occurs twice in Numbers, and both
times it renders חרב. Thus, both ῥομφαία and
μάχαιρα could be called stereotyped renderings.

2.5.2 OTHER STUDIES OF LEXICAL CONSISTENCY

Several studies either have focused on the
issue of lexical consistency or have included it as
an important aspect of the analysis. The study of
Tov and me works from the Hebrew to Greek approach.
Three of the five categories that we selected
involved the rendering of a Hebrew word or suffix
by a Greek term: ב translated by ἐν, כי by ὅτι
or διότι, and the representation in Greek of the
Hebrew third person singular masculine suffix. In
each case, we were able to see the degree to which
the Hebrew was represented by a single Greek
equivalent as expressed in a percentage of the
total Hebrew occurrences, as well as the number of
times they were translated by the same Greek word.
Although we did reach some conclusions regarding
literalness, we did not really arrive at any
conclusions concerning stereotyping as I have used
the term here, because ἐν was used for other
Hebrew prepositions, and ὅτι and διότι were used
for other Hebrew conjunctions.

A second attempt to describe stereotyping is
made by G. Marquis in his article "Consistency of
Lexical Equivalents as a Criterion for the
Evaluation of Translation Technique as Exemplified

in the LXX of Ezekiel."[81] In this study, Marquis
develops a mathematical formula that, he argues,
reflects the degree of literalness of a translation
based on what he defines as the consistency of the
translator in reflecting the source text. This
formula is based on a rather idiosyncratic definition of consistency. For Marquis, consistency "is
measured by the translator's method of translating
as ascertained by an in-depth examination of the
textual data: when he translated one Hebrew word
more than once by the same Greek word, the
translation is consistent."[82] He contrasts
consistent translations with singular translations,
which can be faithful to the source text, can
reflect an actual Hebrew variant, or can be "free"
translations. The degree of literalness, then, is
the percentage of consistent translations plus the
percentage of the singular translations that
faithfully reflect the source text. The percentage
of singular translations that reflect the source
text is taken to be the same ratio as that of
consistent to singular translations for the entire
corpus.[83] According to Marquis, once the
translation equivalents have been determined for
any book, the data can then be plugged into this
formula to derive a degree of literalness, which
can then be used in comparing different
translations.

Two major difficulties attend this approach.
First, I am not sure what help comes from defining
consistency in the way Marquis has defined it. With
this approach, a given Hebrew word can have more
than one "consistent" translation, and it is the
degree of consistency of these translations that is

the major constituent of the degree of literalness.
Yet, by this measure, a high degree of consistency
(and a subsequent high degree of literalness) does
not seem to lend any additional certainty to the
process of reconstruction. For example, a translation may be characterized by a situation such as
with שׂיח in Sir. In the six places where there is a
Greek translation, three are λαλιά (13.11; 32.6;
35.17), two are λόγος (13.11; 44.4) and one is
παραβολή (13.26). Thus there are two "consistent"
translations and one singular translation, which
may or may not reflect the source text. Such a
situation throughout a translation could produce a
high or relatively high degree of literalness via
Marquis's formula, and yet confidence in any
reconstructions to be made would not seem to be
enhanced.

Second, it is not clear why the percentage of
singular translations that faithfully reflect the
source text can be taken "to be approximately the
same as the percentage of consistent translations."
Marquis does not show how this is the case. He only
comments,

> We were able to check on the basis of concrete
> data what is the amount of consistent trans-
> lations, and from this datum we deduce a
> similar percentage among singular transla-
> tions, whose subservience to the source cannot
> be ascertained directly . . . and which reveal
> to the same extent translations that from the
> aspect of the translator's literalness do not
> reflect a free approach.[84]

Yet, this percentage constitutes an important value
in the final mathematical formula intended to
determine a degree of literalness. On what basis
does he make this claim? One is ultimately left

with the impression that Marquis's mathematical
formula is a somewhat artificial construction that
does not, at least for purposes of reconstruction,
provide a great deal of assistance.

The work of Sollamo on the so-called semiprepositions relies heavily on stereotyping as a
means of analysis. In addition to speaking of
certain translations as the "stereotype" of any
particular Hebrew term, she has also examined what
she calls the "stereotyping tendency," the degree
to which translators consistently use the
"stereotype" for a Hebrew word. The examination of
this tendency is kept quite distinct from the
problem of "slavish" renderings, Sollamo's term for
literal, and "free" renderings of individual Hebrew
terms. For example, both ἐναντίον and πρὸ προσώπου
are used to translate the semipreposition לפני.
πρὸ προσώπου is considered "slavish" because it
reflects both the preposition and the noun.
ἐναντίον, on the other hand, is free because it
does not represent both elements. Either of the two
words could be stereotypes for the Hebrew word in
any given translation. Thus, for Sollamo, the
stereotyping tendency concerns the consistent use
of the term not its more narrow reflection of the
individual elements of the Hebrew semipreposition.
By measuring the stereotyping tendency, Sollamo
only treats the issue of consistency of use.

Two concerns arise when considering Sollamo's
approach to the issue of stereotyping. The first is
a problem that this study faces. What constitutes a
stereotype? Sollamo arbitrarily decides that the
term "stereotype" will refer to any translation
that "covers at least 50 per cent of all the

translated cases."[85] Although, as I will argue
below, I do not think that this is a sufficiently
high percentage, it really has little impact on her
statistics for stereotyping tendency, which is the
most important point for this study.

The way that she derives a stereotyping
tendency is somewhat unclear, however. Sollamo
calculates this tendency in the following way:

> The intensity of the stereotyping tendency can
> be measured by calculating the number of all
> translated cases that are covered by the most
> usual equivalents. This means that the
> occurrences of the most common equivalent of
> each semipreposition are added to [sic] in
> each book. Then the final sum is compared with
> the total number of renderings of the
> semiprepositions in the book in question.[86]

Although this explanation does not make the issue
completely clear, what Sollamo seems to be doing is
to take the most common rendering for each
semipreposition (she does not say the stereotype),
to add the number of their occurrences together,
and to compare that number to the total number of
renderings in order to derive a percentage that she
calls the "intensity" of the stereotyping tendency.
By including all the semiprepositions together,
however, she runs the risk of distorting the
conclusions to be reached by her statistical
summaries. If, for instance, the "most common
equivalent" of one or two semiprepositions comprised less than 50 percent of the occurrences and
one or two others comprised 90 to 95 percent,
depending on the total number of renderings, the
intensity of the stereotyping tendency could be
quite high for the whole book, when in fact, it
might be high for only some, maybe even a minority,

of the total number of semiprepositions. A somewhat
different approach, the examination of each
semipreposition separately and the derivation of a
percentage for each, would have shown more clearly
which semiprepositions were rendered consistently
and which ones were not.

2.5.3 METHODOLOGICAL CONSIDERATIONS

The studies of Marquis and Sollamo bring into
relief the question of the relationship between
literalness and consistency. Marquis tackles this
question directly and, based on his definitions of
consistency and literalness, concludes that they
are different. For him, literalness is "absolute
faithfulness to the source."[87] By this definition,
and this is reflected in his mathematical formula,
a singular translation that is faithful to the
source is literal, whereas consistency only
contributes to an understanding of literalness.
Although Sollamo does not address this issue
directly, her separation of free and "slavish"
translations from the problem of stereotyping
demonstrates that it is a concern. She really is
dealing with two aspects of lexical representation,
one concerning the possible ways that a semipreposition can be represented in Greek and the other
concerning the consistency of the use of any
particular rendering.

These different approaches underscore the
argument made in the introduction to this chapter
that the term literal is simply inadequate to the
descriptive task. In the examination of stereotyping undertaken below, I am actually looking at

the degree of consistency of any given translation,
and therefore, I am closer to the general approach
of Sollamo to the issue.

The degree of consistency of representation is
probably, then, best expressed in the term "stereotyping tendency." This term as used by Sollamo in
her analysis of the semiprepositions makes a great
deal of sense. Ideally, a translation in which
every Greek word is stereotyped would mean that the
same Hebrew word is represented by every occurrence
of a particular Greek word, even in a situation
such as was noted above with μάχαιρα and ρομφαία
in Numbers. There, each Greek word translates only
one particular Hebrew word; it just so happens that
they both render the same Hebrew word. None of the
Greek scriptural translations would be expected to
demonstrate this consistency for every word, and
thus, what is at stake is the degree to which any
translation approaches the ideal.

The following discussion is based on the idea
that not only entire translations can show a
stereotyping tendency, but that the concept applies
to individual words as well. By viewing the
tendency to stereotype on the level of the
individual word, the problem of what constitutes a
stereotype can be addressed. There do not seem to
be any concrete, objective criteria for determining
what percentage of occurrences constitutes a
stereotyped rendering, and I will not argue for any
absolute criteria because they would be as
arbitrary as any already in use. What I have
attempted to do is to rank translations from most
to least consistent over a certain range and to see
the relative positions of these translations over
that range.

Finally, because of the way that different
types of words are used, it is important to
separate parts of speech for analysis. Since
Sollamo is studying only the semiprepositions, a
sub-group of prepositions, this does not have to be
a concern for her. Marquis selects nouns and verbs
for his study. The advisability of this procedure
is clear, since translators may be more sensitive
to the nuances of certain parts of speech, or they
may treat others more automatically or routinely.
Certain types of words may provide a greater
richness or paucity of expression, which further
dictates the possibilities presented to the
translator. A translator may be more inclined to
nuance the various types of action indicated by
verbs, but may regard nouns more as labels and
treat them more consistently. Ultimately, by
analyzing different parts of speech separately, a
better picture may be obtained regarding the
lexical decisions made by translators.

In the data analyzed below, I have selected
the nouns and verbs. These two parts of speech, at
least a priori, seem to be the easiest to handle,
although as will become evident they are treated
differently by different translators. As a result,
conclusions can only be drawn concerning the
consistency in the representation of nouns and
verbs. Subsequent studies would necessarily take
into account other parts of speech, and they would
use a larger number of translations for comparison.
I have also chosen to treat only the lexical
rendering and not the tense, person, and number of
verbs nor have I considered the case or number of

nouns. Certainly in some contexts these elements
are important, and they should be studied. That
analysis, however, is beyond the present
undertaking.[88]

Since I am using the Greek translation as the
starting point for my analysis, my approach is
necessarily different from the studies discussed
above. Basically, I decided to determine a stereotyping tendency for each Greek noun and verb used
in the translations selected for this section.[89]
That figure is a percentage derived from the ratio
of the most common equivalent for the word under
consideration to the total number of occurrences of
that word for which a Hebrew equivalent is listed
in the text files. For example, out of the four
occurrences in Sir of the noun ἀγαλλίαμα, two
render the Hebrew noun שמחה (15.6; 31.36), one
renders תפארה (6.31), and one, גיל (30.23). Since
שמחה is the most common equivalent the ratio is 2
out of 4 for a sterotyping tendency of 50 percent.
Because such percentages have varying significance
depending on the number of occurrences, the nouns
and verbs were divided into two groups, those
occurring from 5 to 9 times and those occurring 10
or more times. Nouns and verbs occurring 4 or fewer
times were not counted.

After a stereotyping tendency was determined
for each word, the entire translation was
considered. To derive a figure for the entire
translation, a percentage was derived by taking all
the words in each category (10 times or above and 5
to 9 times) whose stereotyping tendency was above a
certain percentage and then comparing them to the
total number of words in that category. Since there

are no objective criteria for determining a
specific percentage that constitutes a sterotype, I
took three separate ratios: one for words whose
stereotyping tendency was 75 percent or above, one
for words with a stereotyping tendency of 66
percent and above, and one for words with a
stereotyping tendency of 60 percent or above. The
upper limit of 75 percent is a somewhat arbitrary
limit, except to say that I felt that if a translator consistently used a Greek word to render the
same Hebrew word over 75 percent of the time, it
probably reflected a self-conscious attempt on the
translator's part to be lexically consistent.[90] The
translations were then ranked from the highest
stereotyping tendency to the lowest for each ratio.

2.5.4 COMPARATIVE DATA

For this section, ten translations were used:
Sirach; Numbers; 2 Kings; Isaiah; Amos; Job;
Proverbs; Ruth; Song of Songs; Qoheleth. The
results of the investigations are contained in the
following six tables (pp. 106-108). The first four
tables give the results for each of the two groups
of nouns and verbs. The three ratios described in
the previous section are labeled "75% & UP," "66% &
UP," and "60% & UP." The percentage listed next to
the name of each book represents the percentage of
the total number of words in that category whose
stereotyping tendency exceeded the limits given at
the top of the column. Thus, in Table 11 column 1,
Sir is ranked tenth out of ten with a stereotyping
tendency of 30.64 percent. This means that out of
the nouns used 10 times or more in Sir, 30.64

percent have individual stereotyping tendencies of
75 to 100 percent. In Table 11 column 2, Sir is
again tenth out of ten with a stereotyping tendency
of 46.77 percent. This percentage indicates that
46.77 percent of the nouns in Sir have individual
stereotyping tendencies of 66 percent or above. The
difference in stereotyping tendency from column 1
to column 2 indicates that Sir has some nouns that
have stereotyping tendencies between 66 and 74
percent, which results in a higher percentage in
column 2 than in column 1. Some translations show
the same percentage across all three columns, such
as Amos in Table 12. In this case, all of the nouns
that occur between 5 and 9 times in Amos have
individual stereotyping tendencies that are either
above 75 percent or below 60 percent. Thus, the
percentage in the three columns does not change.
The last two tables, 15 and 16, operate in the same
way, except that they show the stereotyping
tendency for each book by using all the nouns and
all the verbs that occur 5 times or more.

TABLE 11 - NOUNS USED 10 OR MORE TIMES

75% & UP		66% & UP		60% & UP	
1.	Ruth 100%	Ruth	100%	Ruth	100%
2.	Qoh 100%	Qoh	100%	Qoh	100%
3.	2Kgs 96.55%	Amos	100%	Amos	100%
4.	Num 84.34%	2Kgs	96.55%	Cant	100%
5.	Cant 80%[a]	Num	88.69%	2Kgs	96.55%
6.	Amos 80%[b]	Cant	80%	Num	95.65%
7.	Job 54%	Isa	61.53%	Isa	69.23%
8.	Prov 50%	Prov	58.62%	Job	66%
9.	Isa 48.71%	Job	56%	Prov	65.61%
10.	Sir 30.64%	Sir	46.77%	Sir	62.90%

TABLE 12 - NOUNS USED BETWEEN 5 AND 9 TIMES

75% & UP		66% & UP		60% & UP	
1.	Ruth 100%	Ruth 100%		Ruth 100%	
2.	Cant 100%	Cant 100%		Cant 100%	
3.	2Kgs 89.39%	Qoh 92.85%		2Kgs 96.96%	
4.	Qoh 89.28%	2Kgs 92.42%		Qoh 92.85%	
5.	Amos 88.23%	Amos 88.23%		Amos 88.23%	
6.	Num 76.11%	Num 80.59%		Num 86.56%	
7.	Prov 45.45%	Prov 57.57%		Prov 65.15%	
8.	Job 44.26%	Job 54.09%		Job 63.93%	
9.	Isa 41.07%	Isa 47.32%		Isa 62.50%	
10.	Sir 33.33%	Sir 41.97%		Sir 56.79%	

TABLE 13 - VERBS USED 10 OR MORE TIMES

75% & UP		66% & UP		60% & UP	
1.	Cant --[c]	Cant --		Cant --	
2.	Ruth 100%	Ruth 100%		Ruth 100%	
3.	Qoh 100%	Qoh 100%		Qoh 100%	
4.	2Kgs 92.85%	Amos 100%		Amos 100%	
5.	Num 80.30%[d]	2Kgs 92.85%		2Kgs 96.42%	
6.	Amos 66.66%	Num 86.36%		Num 89.39%	
7	Prov 48.38%	Prov 61.29%		Prov 64.51%	
8.	Isa 35.34%	Isa 43.10%		Isa 54.31%	
9.	Job 35.29%	Job 41.17%		Sir 50%	
10.	Sir 27.27%	Sir 36.36%		Job 47.05%	

TABLE 14 - VERBS USED BETWEEN 5 AND 9 TIMES

75% & UP		66% & UP		60% & UP	
1.	Qoh 100%	Qoh 100%		Qoh 100%	
2.	Ruth 93.75%	Ruth 93.75%		Cant 100%	
3.	Cant 88.88%[e]	Cant 88.88%		Ruth 93.75%	
4.	2Kgs 81.13%	2Kgs 83.01%		2Kgs 90.56%	
5.	Amos 70.58%	Amos 70.58%		Amos 82.35%	
6.	Num 62.50%	Num 70.31%		Num 78.12%	
7.	Isa 35.92%	Isa 44.66%		Isa 55.33%	
8.	Prov 30%	Job 41.33%		Job 48%	
9.	Job 28%	Prov 38.57%		Prov 45.71%	
10.	Sir 25.64%	Sir 32.05%		Sir 44.87%	

TABLE 15 - TOTALS OF TABLES 11 AND 12 (COMBINED)

75% & UP	66% & UP	60% & UP
1. Ruth 100%	Ruth 100%	Ruth 100%
2. Cant 96.55%	Cant 96.55%	Cant 100%
3. Qoh 94%	Qoh 96%	2Kgs 96.77
4. 2Kgs 92.74%	2Kgs 94.35%	Qoh 96%
5. Amos 85.18%	Amos 92.59%	Amos 92.59
6. Num 81.31%	Num 85.71%	Num 92.30
7. Job 48.64%	Prov 58.06%	Isa 65.93
8. Prov 47.58%	Job 54.95%	Prov 65.32
9. Isa 44.97%	Isa 54.58%	Job 64.86
10. Sir 32.16%	Sir 44.05%	Sir 59.44

TABLE 16 - TOTALS OF TABLES 13 AND 14 (COMBINED)

75% & UP	66% & UP	60% & UP
1. Qoh 100%	Qoh 100%	Qoh 100%
2. Ruth 95.45% f	Ruth 95.45%	Cant 100%
3. Cant 88.88%	Cant 88.88%	Ruth 95.45
4. 2Kgs 87.15%	2Kgs 88.07%	2Kgs 93.57
5. Num 71.53%	Num 78.46%	Amos 85%
6. Amos 70%	Amos 75%	Num 83.84
7. Prov 35.64%	Prov 45.54%	Isa 54.79
8. Isa 35.61%	Isa 43.83%	Prov 51.48
9. Job 30.27%	Job 41.28%	Job 47.70
10. Sir 26%	Sir 33%	Sir 46%

[a]This percentage represents 4 out of 5 occurrences of nouns used 10 times or more.

[b]This percentage represents 8 out of 10 occurrences.

[c]Song of Songs has no occurrences of verbs used more than 10 times.

[d]This percentage represents 2 out of 3 occurrences.

[e]This percentage represents 8 out of 9 occurrences.

[f]This percentage represents 8 out of 9 occurrences.

The results of the data are interesting.
Almost without exception, throughout all the
tables, the order of the translations stays the
same, and the translations break into three groups.
The first is comprised of Qoheleth, Song of Songs,
Ruth, and 2 Kings. The second contains Numbers and
Amos, while the third group includes Job, Proverbs,
Isaiah, and Sirach. In almost every case there is a
radical break between the stereotyping tendencies
of the first two groups and the third. Clearly the
most consistent group is the group of Ruth, Song of
Songs, Qoheleth, and 2 Kings. These translations in
almost every case have stereotyping tendencies of
90 percent or better and oftentimes have 100
percent of their nouns and verbs with individual
stereotyping tendencies above 75 percent.[91] On the
other end of the scale, Sir is ranked at the bottom
most often, and in most cases, it has fewer than 50
percent of its words at or above the particular
limit for individual stereotyping tendencies.
Numbers and Amos frequently come together in the
same area although both fluctuate somewhat.

If these three groups are compared to
Sollamo's and Tov's and Wright's groupings, the
results are similar. For lexical representation,
Ruth is close to the more literal translations,
whereas Tov and Wright characterize Ruth as
relatively literal. The third group corresponds
well to Sollamo's and Tov's and Wright's free
translations. For this criterion, Amos comes toward
the top of the tables, and thus, it agrees with the
way that Sollamo has characterized it in her third
group. Numbers, again, is somewhat of an anomaly in
that both Sollamo and Tov and Wright include it

with relatively free translations, but in this case
it is close to Amos, as well as the more lexically
consistent translations.

When looking specifically at Sir, no pattern
of use is immediately apparent. There does not seem
to be any distinction made, for example, between
concrete and abstract nouns. Terms as varied as
ἀδικία, ἀλήθεια, δέησις, θυμός, ἰσχύς, and χάρις
all have stereotyping tendencies of less than 50
percent, and similar kinds of words have stereotyping tendencies of over 75 percent. Even words
that receive very consistent treatment in the OG,
such as διαθήκη, do not receive consistent
treatment in Sir.[92] Nor is any pattern apparent for
the verbs -- no difference between more concrete
and abstract, no difference in the handling of
simplex and compound.

The one very noticeable feature of the
grandson's treatment of nouns and verbs is that the
percentages given in the tables do not vary nearly
as much between them as in the three other
translations that fall at the bottom with Sir. The
statistics suggest that Proverbs, Job, and Isaiah
demonstrate much greater differences in the
handling of nouns and verbs. In each case the
percentages are lower for the verbs, indicating
less of a tendency to stereotype them. Sir,
however, falls much more consistently in the same
general areas for both nouns and verbs.

At this point, the question must be raised
concerning the extent to which the occurrence of
certain words that present a limited number of
possibilities for translation may have affected the
results given above. This does not present as much

of a problem as it might first appear. In translations that are consistent in their approach to
lexical choices, all Hebrew words are treated
equally, hence a high degree of consistency with
regard to lexical choice. In the translations given
above, it would be difficult to argue that in
Qoheleth, Song of Songs, Ruth, and 2 Kings, all of
which had very high stereotyping tendencies, the
majority of words were words for which only very
limited translation possibilities existed. In 2
Kings, for example, nouns such as ἁμαρτία,
δικαίωμα, δυναστεία, and λόγος all have very high
stereotyping tendencies along with nouns like
ἀγρός, ἔτος, or θυγάτηρ. Terms like the latter
group may have raised the percentage somewhat, but
it hardly seems reasonable to account for a 100
percent stereotyping tendency in this manner. On
the other side, in translations that have very low
stereotyping tendencies, these types of words may
make the results a little higher, but at times even
these words may evidence some variety. In Job, for
example, only 50 percent (12 out of 24) of the
occurrences of δίδωμι render ןתנ.

Even though the tables suggest that certain
translations show a higher degree of consistency
regarding the lexical equivalence of nouns and
verbs, when one reconstructs lexical elements each
case needs to be considered on an individual basis.
Very often even the cases that do not use the
stereotype may show some inner consistency, and
this possibility must be considered. It may be that
a word in a certain context is translated with a
term other than the usual one, but it may be
entirely predictable. In Amos, for example, λέγω

is used 50 times totally, and it translates אמר 31
times for a stereotyping tendency of 62 percent.
The other 19 instances all translate the same word,
נאם, in the phrase נאם אדני. The consistent nature
of the minority 19 cases cannot be denied even
though the individual stereotyping tendency for
λέγω is rather low. Data such as these, however,
can frequently be isolated. One interesting
possibility along similar lines would be to look at
words used less than 5 times. In some cases in
different translations where, for instance, a Greek
word occurs 2 times and translates two different
Hebrew words, the two occurrences are separated by
a large amount of intervening text, which suggests
that perhaps the translator simply forgot what the
earlier equivalent was. The extent to which
different translations tend to exhibit this feature
or others like it, and what the impact is for
understanding these translations, could be easily
examined using the raw data that were utilized for
this section.

2.6 GENERAL CONCLUSIONS

For each of the analyses of the four aspects
of translation technique conducted in this chapter,
a set of statistical data was given, and the
translations were ranked according to those data.
How should this information be considered? In each
of the aspects of translation studied, the statistical information gave a relative relationship of
one translation to another. For example, even
though Sir ranked 30 out of 34 translations
regarding word order (when δέ was discounted), the

percentage of deviation was rather small. Sir's position needs to be viewed relative to translations like Song of Songs or Qoheleth where there was practically no deviation from the word order of the MT. Although there may not appear to be firm controls on this material, the relative position of translations to each other is significant. This is especially true when the results are compared with other studies of translation technique, such as those of Sollamo or Tov and Wright, which may use different statistical measurements, but still compare translations to each other. These statistics must be understood as a means of comparison, not an absolute standard.

In concluding this chapter, it must be reiterated that the investigations conducted above concern only those aspects of translation technique that Barr and Tov argued were elemental for understanding the "literal" nature of translations. The evaluation of such broad aspects of translation technique allows the scholar to form impressions of the overall approach of the translator to the source text that are based on data rather than some intuition or subjective criterion about a particular translation and that do not necessitate a complete study of all aspects of the translation technique. In this regard, the results are only to be broadly applied, and they should not be substituted for a case by case examination of the evidence. The knowledge, however, that the translator of Job was not very consistent in the lexical representation of nouns and verbs should assist the scholar who studies this text by giving an indication of how much confidence to place in

reconstructions based on those aspects of the
translation. This kind of analysis performed on
several broad aspects of translation also alle-
viates the need to describe an entire translation
by means of sweeping generalizations. By studying
certain of these aspects of translation, the
scholar may also find indications for further study
that would provide more specific clues as to how
the translator of a particular book worked.
Finally, the study of these areas reinforces the
inadequacy of simply describing a translation as
"literal" or "free." Translations can vary in the
ways that different aspects of the source text are
treated, and thus, they could possibly be called
"literal" and "free" at the same time.

2.6.1 ASPECTS OF TRANSLATION TECHNIQUE IN SIRACH

This conclusion can be seen when looking
specifically at the Greek Sir. This translation
demonstrates some variation in its approach to the
four elements of translation studied here. For word
order, we saw that Sir fell toward the bottom of
the rankings of the 34 translations studied (28
when δέ was included, 30 when it was not). In
these rankings, it was close to Isaiah in both
cases. For segmentation, Sir ranked with Isaiah,
Job, and Proverbs as the four least consistent
translations of the 10 studied. When longer
quantitative translations were considered, Sir fell
close to Numbers and Ruth in the middle rather than
at the "free" end of the scale with Proverbs, but
it was the most likely of all the translations
studied to produce shorter quantitative transla-

tions, although some special problems were noted
for Sir in this case. In the last category, lexical
representation, Sir was the least consistent of all
the translations in its representation of nouns and
verbs, again falling close to Isaiah.

In what ways, then, can the Greek Sir be used
as a basis for the reconstruction of the elements
studied. In four out of the five separate analyses
(longer and shorter quantitative translations are
considered separately), the grandson's translation
could be characterized as not representing the
Hebrew closely. As a result, for the categories of
segmentation, shorter quantitative translations,
lexical representation, and to a lesser extent word
order, the Greek Sir would not seem to provide a
firm basis for reconstructions. The grandson's
approach to the Hebrew seems to reflect more of a
concern for the message than the medium. This is
especially true of lexical representation in that
the grandson seems primarily concerned with what is
communicated rather than consistency of representation. With respect to longer quantitative
translations, the grandson appears generally to
have avoided the addition of elements that were not
in his Hebrew, although his practice in this area
is clearly not that of the translators of Qoheleth
or Song of Songs.

The qualifications given in Chapter 1 need
also to be recalled, however. Undoubtedly, the poor
state of the Hebrew texts of Sir together with the
presence of some elements of the second Hebrew
recension has affected the statistical picture. Any
conclusions drawn from these data for Sir need to
be made tentatively. This situation sets up an

intractable difficulty. An understanding of
translation technique is necessary in order to know
how confidently reconstructions can be made, but
the textual situation in Sir leads one to think
that a variant parent text probably plays a greater
role in evaluations of Sir than in other books,
even though this this assumption is not fully
substantiated by the data. In my opinion, even if
evaluations of Sir are affected to a greater degree
by a different Hebrew parent text, I do not think
that the conclusions drawn above for Sir are too
far off the mark. The general conclusion that the
grandson was not concerned to give a close formal
representation of Ben Sira's Hebrew still seems to
be accurate.

In addition, the results of these comparative
analyses point to what could be an important area
for further investigation of the grandson's
translation, the apparent close similarity for
particular aspects of translation between Sirach
and Isaiah rather than between Sirach and Proverbs
and Job, two translations to which Sir might have
been expected to be most similar.[93] More detailed
studies of some of the sub-divisions of the aspects
studied in this chapter and of some narrower
aspects of translation technique may show whether
the two translators take a genuinely similar
approach to their source texts or whether the
similarity suggested by these analyses is merely
coincidental.

2.6.2 ASPECTS OF TRANSLATION TECHNIQUE IN THE OTHER BOOKS

Although this is a study of the Greek translation of Sir, enough data has been marshaled to warrant a few remarks about the other translations included. I will confine my remarks to those translations studied for all four areas of translation technique. Most of the translations remain relatively constant for all four aspects of translation technique. Qoheleth, Song of Songs, and 2 Kings maintain a consistently close representation of the Hebrew. In contrast, Job, Proverbs, and Isaiah rank as the least consistent throughout. The other three translations demonstrate the need for studying aspects of translation, because all three could be called literal or free at different times. Although Ruth falls close to the three most consistent translations, it is near the bottom in its representation of word order. Numbers and Amos are the least constant translations of the nine because their positions fluctuate in the different categories.

The results derived here for these translations also demonstrate the value of comparing them with other studies that attempt to provide characterizations of the translations. The comparisons between the results in this chapter and those of Sollamo and Tov and Wright again show a general constancy with some fluctuation in different translations, especially Numbers and Amos. As these kinds of data continue to be studied for the Greek scriptural translations, the evaluations of them

will become clearer and more precise. Such
increasing precision will provide a firmer base
from which to reconstruct the Hebrew parent texts
of these translations.

CHAPTER 3

THE INFLUENCE OF JEWISH-GREEK BIBLICAL
TRANSLATIONS ON THE GREEK TRANSLATION OF BEN SIRA

3.1 INTRODUCTION

In the prologue to his translation, Ben Sira's
grandson shows his awareness of Greek translations
of "the Law," "the Prophets," and "the rest of the
books." He refers to these works in an apology for
any shortcomings perceived in his translation, and
he notes that there "is no small difference" (οὐ
μικρὰν ἔχει τὴν διαφοράν) between the Hebrew and
Greek forms of these works. In addition, he informs
us that his grandfather knew the Hebrew of these
books well. These two pieces of information raise
some interesting questions regarding, first, the
nature of the relationship between the translation
of the grandson and the Greek traditions of the
Jewish Scriptures, second, the relationship between
the Hebrew of Ben Sira and the Hebrew scriptural
traditions and their impact on the Greek translator,
and third, the effect of these relationships on
understanding the nature of the Hebrew text that
lay before the grandson in any given passage.

These issues are by no means unrelated, and
the answers to these questions determine how
extensively and with how much confidence the OG
translations can be used in reconstructions of the
Hebrew Sir. On the one hand, if the grandson can be
shown to have relied on these Greek translations,
or if he used them as models for his own work, the
frequent scholarly practice of reconstructing the
Hebrew parent text of the grandson by appropriating
Hebrew words or phrases from the MT, which correspond to words and phrases used both in the OG and

Greek Sir, receives support. On the other hand, if
the grandson did not utilize these translations in
his own work, these Hebrew-Greek equivalences can
provide little assistance in trying to recover Ben
Sira's Hebrew.

Unfortunately, simply because the grandson
knew of Greek translations of the scriptures, it is
often assumed on that basis that he must have been
dependent on them in some way. Rudolph Smend in his
classic commentary on Sir expresses what seems to
be the working assumption of many scholars when he
says, "Without doubt he [the grandson] was capable
of comparing the LXX with the Hebrew text, for the
Pentateuch and for the historical books, working
very carefully throughout; it often served him as a
dictionary."[1] Yet, to date, only Reiterer's
previously mentioned study specifically targets the
Greek, but even in the beginning of the Praise of
the Ancestors, where one would expect a priori the
greatest influence of the OG, Reiterer concludes
that the grandson did not depend much on the Greek
Pentateuch.[2] To rely primarily on the results of a
study of such a limited portion of the translation
as a basis for describing the grandson's procedure
in the rest of the book would simply be inadequate,
because, (1) Reiterer only looks at the grandson's
dependence on the Pentateuch, not other scriptural
materials, and (2) the nature of the material in
the Praise of the Ancestors section is different
from elsewhere in the book. Outside of this work,
there has been no systematic examination of this
issue. So, in contrast to the analyses of broad
aspects of translation technique that were
presented in Chapter 2, this chapter focuses on

what is one, specific "translation technique" of
the grandson, his use (or non-use) of the OG
translations in his own work and the degree to
which his use of those translations reflects the
same Hebrew-Greek equivalences between the MT and
OG. The primary result of such an investigation
will be to ascertain what value these equivalences
have in reconstructions of the grandson's Hebrew
parent text.

When one considers the possibility that the
grandson depended on earlier Greek translations for
his work, one must ask in what ways he may have
used them. One of the most obvious is pointed to in
Smend's assertion that the grandson had access to
both the Hebrew and Greek scriptures and could
compare them. When Ben Sira uses a passage or
phrase from the Hebrew scriptures does the grandson
betray his recognition of that usage by using the
corresponding Greek scriptural passage for its
translation? Are Ben Sira's uses of the Hebrew
scriptures transparent enough to create such a
scenario? Or, does the grandson use the Greek
translations independently of any awareness of his
grandfather's dependence on the Hebrew scriptures?
Would the authoritative status (or conversely, non-
authoritative status) of these books affect how Ben
Sira or his grandson may have used them? These
questions point to the importance of the connection
between Ben Sira's use of the Hebrew scriptures and
the grandson's use of Greek translations of them.
Thus, an analysis of the uses by Ben Sira and his
grandson of their respective scriptural traditions
and the relationships between the Hebrew and Greek
of Sir where scriptural passages are used would

seem to have direct bearing on solving some of
questions posed here.

3.1.1 THE HEBREW OF BEN SIRA AND THE HEBREW BIBLE

Following the discovery of the Cairo Geniza
manuscripts of Sir[3] a great deal of scholarly
effort was spent analyzing the Hebrew of these
texts. The use of Aramaic, Mishnaic vocabulary, and
so-called "biblical Hebrew" were primary focuses of
early scholarship on these materials. One of the
early judgments on Ben Sira was that he was a
meticulous imitator of the Hebrew Bible and that he
borrowed from it frequently.[4] In fact, to read some
of the commentaries, with their myriads of references to the Hebrew Bible, it would be easy to get
the impression that Ben Sira's work was nothing but
a _pastiche_ of "biblical" words, phrases, and
quotations. In this vein, Schechter and Taylor
write, "Ben Sira, though not entirely devoid of
original ideas, was, as is well known, a conscious
imitator both as to form and as to matter." They go
on to suggest that he had partially failed in his
work because of his occasional use of non-biblical
phraseology.[5]

A number of studies have attempted to provide
lists of those passages in Sir presumed to derive
from the Hebrew Bible (i.e., in the form preserved
in the MT). These lists are often quite extensive.
For example, Schechter and Taylor in their initial
publication of the Cairo Geniza manuscripts give a
list of passages prefaced by the statement, "The
following list containing the phrases, idioms,
typical expressions and even whole verses about

which there can be <u>no reasonable doubt</u> [emphasis
added] that they were suggested to him by or
directly copied from the Scriptures will best show
how well he was acquainted with the Bible and how
much use he made of it."[6] This list numbers almost
365 passages (including references to the Book of
Daniel which probably reached its preserved form
after Ben Sira wrote his book).

The major issue, as it is reflected in the
statement from Schechter and Taylor cited above,
seems to be that the appearance of these phrases in
Ben Sira's book indicates a conscious and deliberate
use by him of the biblical text. Yet, included in
Schechter's and Taylor's list are phrases that seem
likely to have been fairly common, like כל בשׂר (Sir
9.19). How does the occurrence of a phrase such as
this, without any wider contextual parallel,
constitute evidence of a deliberate and conscious
dependence on the Hebrew scriptures by Ben Sira?
Frequently, Hebrew expressions are included in
these lists that occur throughout the Hebrew
scriptures and could well represent common usage.
Why should these be cited as illustrating beyond a
"reasonable doubt" dependence on the Hebrew scriptures?[7] Finally, many phrases in these lists are
taken from Psalms, Proverbs, Job, and Qoheleth.
Could there not be, due to the subject matter of
these works, a proverbial language, which is shared
among these works, especially Job, Proverbs, and
Sirach?[8] The evidence provided by these lists for
Ben Sira's presumed dependence on the Hebrew
scriptures seems ambiguous, and the question
remains open as to the extent of Ben Sira's
conscious dependence on the text of the Hebrew
scriptures.

That Ben Sira knew and borrowed from the
Hebrew scriptures in his work is clear. This is
corroborated by his grandson when he says in his
prologue, "My grandfather Jesus, having given
himself much to the reading of the Law, the
Prophets, and the other books of the ancestors, and
having acquired considerable familiarity therein,
was induced also himself to take part in writing
somewhat pertaining to instruction and wisdom. . ."
(Prol. 7-12). Thus, one should not be surprised to
find many allusions to the Hebrew scriptures in the
Hebrew of Sir. The crucial issue is the extent to
which Ben Sira was dependent on the text of the
Bible. Some recent studies, especially those by J.
G. Snaith, Reiterer, and Middendorp, suggest that
the incidence of textual borrowing from the Hebrew
scriptures by Ben Sira may be less than scholars
such as Schechter and Taylor previously thought.[9]

Evaluations of the Hebrew Sir like that of
Schechter and Taylor seem to be based primarily
upon two suppositions. The first is the assumption
that every phrase that looks like the Hebrew
scriptures actually derives from them. If one were
to accept this assumption, Schechter and Taylor's
conclusion would be hard to avoid. This assumption,
however, is not a necessary one, and it ignores
other possible ways of construing this evidence.
Such phrases could just as readily be explained as
deriving from contexts of everyday speech, school
traditions, or liturgy and worship, that is, from
contexts other than direct dependence on the
biblical text. As other studies, such as that of
Snaith (discussed below), have pointed out, this

initial assumption seems unwarranted, and many of
those places, which, according to Schechter and
Taylor, were "suggested to him [Ben Sira] by or
were directly copied from the Scriptures," can be
explained in alternative ways.

The second factor affecting such estimations
of Ben Sira's work is the introduction of changes
made to the Hebrew at the hands of copyists over
the course of the centuries, especially revisions
toward the more familiar biblical wording of texts
that are reminiscent of the Bible. To be sure, many
corruptions in the Hebrew have been recognized, but
the comment of Box and Oesterley that "Ben Sira's
language constantly echoes that of the Old
Testament, and it is remarkable how clearly and
frequently these reminiscences display themselves
in the text of H [the Geniza Hebrew]," reflects a
prevalent attitude toward the Hebrew Sir.[10] If the
Hebrew text made sense, had poetic balance, and
looked like the Hebrew scriptures, it was usually
depicted as representing the Hebrew of Ben Sira. A
good example would be the acceptance by Box and
Oesterley of the text of MS A for Sir 15.14, which
differs from the Greek (and from MS B, which they
did not know for this verse). MS A bears a close
resemblance to Gen 1.1 through its use of אלהים and
בראשית, but the Greek probably represents the
earlier and better form of the text, the Hebrew of
which subsequently came to light in MS B. As we
shall see, a large number of harmonizations to the
Hebrew Bible have crept into the text of Ben Sira,
and the presence of this harmonizing activity must
be kept in mind when attempting to speak about Ben
Sira's imitation of the Hebrew Bible.[11]

Snaith, in his excellent article "Biblical Quotations in the Hebrew Ecclesiasticus,"[12] points out some of the methodological difficulties with this approach. In addition, he lists some helpful criteria for determining which Hebrew words or phrases may have been taken from scriptural materials.

With respect to method, he first points out the possibility that any given passage in the Hebrew Sir may have been harmonized toward biblical passages by editors or copyists. Particularly suspicious are those places where no corresponding Greek phrase exists, such as Sir 49.5. Here ἔθνει ἀλλοτρίῳ ("foreign nation") corresponds to גוי נבל נכרי in MS B. Snaith argues that נבל is a gloss based on Deut 32.21, and that the Hebrew parent text of the Greek most likely read גוי נכרי.[13] I would add here that the occurrence of variant Hebrew readings in which one corresponds to a scriptural passage, even though both could be legitimate equivalents of the Greek, also indicates revision toward the Hebrew Bible. An example is found in Sir. 5.7. Here MS A reads וביום נקם ("in the day of tribulation"), and MS C reads ובעת נקם ("in the time of tribulation"). The Greek for this phrase is καὶ ἐν καιρῷ ἐκδικήσεως, which agrees more closely with ובעת in MS C and probably represents its parent text, while וביום is a gloss, which harmonizes towards a number of places in Isaiah where the phrase יום נקם occurs.

Middendorp in <u>Die Stellung Jesu ben Siras zwischen Judentums und Hellenismus</u>[14] also argues that glosses or revisions that harmonize a passage toward MT are the source of many similarities to

scriptural texts. This process is the result of
what he calls "recollection errors" ("Memorier-
fehlen"). That is, although Ben Sira himself may
not have used a specific passage from the Hebrew
scriptures in his work, his Hebrew was close enough
to a scriptural text that in the process of the
transmission of the text a scribe wrote the scriptural form instead of the authentic text of Ben
Sira. Though I consider Middendorp's thesis to be
plausible, even probable, he unfortunately bases
his argument on an unsubstantiated presupposition
about the Greek translation technique of Sir. In a
discussion of the phrase אֶת הַטּוֹב (Gk = τὸ
ἀριστὸν κυρίῳ) he says, "Since I hold the Greek
to be a true representation of its parent text, I
accept that the parent text contained הישׁר לײ." He
goes on to argue that אֶת הַטּוֹב is an error caused by
remembering 2 Kgs 18.3.[15]

Middendorp has not established, however, that
the Greek of Sir is, in fact, "a faithful representation of its parent text," which seems to mean a
word-for-word translation that reflects the same
translation equivalents as those found in the OG
translations of the Bible. Although the idea of
"recollection errors" seems a likely possibility in
many cases, the results of the analysis of
translation technique above in Chapter 2 challenge
the assumption that the Greek translation is a
"faithful representation," if that means literal or
word-for-word. At best, one might argue that enough
is not known about the translation technique of the
grandson to establish Middendorp's assumption; at
worst the conclusions reached above throw
considerable doubt on his argument.

A second difficulty raised by Snaith is that
of "distinguishing deliberate reference and
quotation from common literary or popular usage."[16]
This would seem to be an obvious methodological
caveat for anyone working with such texts,
especially considering the paucity of knowledge
concerning the Hebrew language in this period. One
needs to use caution in ascribing phrases that
occur frequently and widely in the Hebrew
scriptures to some biblical influence, unless other
compelling reasons, such as similarity of context
can be cited. A good example is the Hebrew phrase
. . .בעיני חן ומצא in Sir 42.1, which A. Eberharter
lists as dependent on Gen 6.8, where Noah is said
to have found favor in the eyes of the Lord.[17] Even
a cursory glance at a Hebrew concordance will show
that the phrase is extremely common and widespread.[18] The use of this phrase in Sir 42.1 does
not show Ben Sira to be deliberately using a
specific passage from Genesis, but conversely,
shows him to be using a common Hebrew idiom. This
conclusion is especially reinforced when the
different contexts of the phrase in Gen 6.8 and Sir
42.1 are taken into account.

For Snaith, the relationship between Ben
Sira's canon and his dependence on the Hebrew
scriptures is also important, especially because of
the importance for canon history attached to any
close biblical parallels in Sir. To what extent was
there a canon of Jewish scripture at the time of
Ben Sira? Did he utilize literature which has not
survived? Was the very idea of a canon meaningful
to someone writing at the beginning of the second
century BCE? The usual method of answering these

questions has been to argue that if Ben Sira uses
language parallel to that found in a book of the
Jewish canon, then that book must have had
canonical status (or at least quasi-canonical
status) for him. The use of material from a book
says little or nothing about its authoritative
status, however, for as Snaith rightly notes, "the
fact that the quotation was from the past literature of his national heritage may have been
sufficient to command respect from Ben Sira!"[19]
Conversely, the argument that if Ben Sira did not
quote a book, it did not have canonical status is
just as problematic. The absence of language
parallel to any particular book may mean nothing
more than Ben Sira did not use the book.

The question of Ben Sira's canonical con-
sciousness aside, the grandson, in his prologue,
does list three groups of works with which his
grandfather was familiar: "the Law," "the
Prophets," and "the other books." The Pentateuch
almost certainly constituted the group referred to
as "the Law" (ὁ νόμος).[20] That a prophetic corpus
existed seems clear from the use of the word
"Prophets" in a series with "Law," but which works
made up that group? Ben Sira's reference in 49.10
to שנים עשר הנביאים ("twelve prophets") may be
evidence for a corpus of the so-called Minor
Prophets. The explicit mention of Ezekiel's vision
of God's chariot (מרכבה),[21] of Isaiah and Jeremiah
(48.22; 49.6) may also indicate Ben Sira's knowledge of prophetic books under their names.[22] Did
the books of Joshua, Judges, Samuel, and Kings
belong to this group as they do in the modern
Hebrew Bible? Without attempting to provide compre-

hensive answers to such questions, what can be said
is that the Praise of the Ancestors section shows
familiarity with traditions that are also found in
these works.[23]

The third group, "the other books," is the
most difficult to delineate. Clearly, Ben Sira
wrote in a style reminiscent of those wisdom books,
which were later included in the Jewish canon, but
whether he extensively utilized and intentionally
modeled his book after the Book of Proverbs as
Schechter and Taylor state,[24] or simply used
popular and well known wisdom language, proverbs,
and ideas is sometimes hard to know. Ben Sira might
be expected to express himself in these ways and
some of the similarities in such words or phrases
may show the indirect influence of biblical
language rather than deliberate imitation.[25]

Snaith further suggests some specific criteria
for ascertaining whether or not the Hebrew of Sir
has been influenced by the Hebrew scriptures. I
have adhered to these criteria when dealing with
Ben Sira's Hebrew. First, and of foremost importance, is the context of the passage. There are
many places in the Hebrew Sir where phrases appear
that also occur in the Hebrew scriptures. If these
occur in contexts which are quite different from
the scriptural accounts and are not rare or unusual
occurrences of the word or phrase, the probability
of Ben Sira having excerpted these phrases directly
from the Hebrew scriptures decreases accordingly,
and they cannot be used with any certainty as
evidence of any textual dependence. They might be
nothing more than commonly available phrases in the
language, which happen to occur both in Sir and in

the Hebrew scriptures.[26] Some phrases may have
originated in scriptural contexts, and subsequently
they may have found their way into liturgy or
worship. These types of materials would have been
communicated as part of the environment in which
Ben Sira was raised and trained, and they would
likely be familiar to him.[27] A good analogy might
be the modern evangelical minister who, upon
entering the pulpit, speaks in King James English
phraseology without deliberately using any
particular scriptural passage. This language is
part of the environment.

Snaith lists a number of possible areas in
which direct borrowing from the Hebrew scriptures
by Ben Sira might be sought. These are: (1) pairs
of nouns linked with ו or pairs of nouns related
through a construct; (2) entire cola that closely
resemble biblical passages; (3) similarity of words
or phrases in similar context; (4) words used in
odd ways or ways different from their usual use.[28]
The evidence must be weighed carefully in each
instance to determine the possibility that direct
textual dependence by Ben Sira on the Hebrew
scriptures best explains the situation. Snaith
succinctly states, "We must guard against
recognizing references to the canon in every
possible case, and never allowing the author to
express himself naturally in his own way."[29]

3.1.2 THE GREEK OF BEN SIRA'S GRANDSON

Despite the lack of systematic work on the
influence of Greek scriptural translations on the
grandson's translation, one can find many passages

where the Greek Sir has been used to "correct"
extant Hebrew passages or to reconstruct the
missing Hebrew sections on the basis of Hebrew-
Greek translation equivalents drawn from OG
passages. In other words, even though the issue has
never been thoroughly studied, the Greek Sir has
often been treated as if the grandson had indeed
compared the Hebrew and Greek texts of the
scriptures with each other.

The reasons that scholarship has handled the
Greek Sir in this manner seem to be two-fold.
First, the extensive use of the Greek to "correct"
the Hebrew primarily stems from the implicit and
largely unsubstantiated assumption that the
grandson is using a word-for-word translation
technique, an assumption that, at least for those
aspects covered in Chapter 2, is not substantiated
by the data. That many corruptions exist in the
extant Hebrew texts of Sir is undeniable, but to
operate as if the Hebrew of Sir were corrupt in
those places where the extant Greek does not appear
to be a close translation of the extant Hebrew is
to ignore important aspects of the grandson's
approach to his translation. Some scholars, such as
Middendorp, use this confident assessment of the
Greek translation as their explicit working basis
without attempting to substantiate the claim.[30]
Other scholars state that the grandson did not
intend a word-for-word rendering of his grandfather's Hebrew, but then operate as if he were
doing just that.[31] In the following analysis, as
elsewhere in this study, the operating principle is
that the extant Hebrew should only be considered at
variance with the parent text of the Greek when a

clear exegetical path cannot be constructed between
the Hebrew and the Greek (as long as the Greek
itself cannot be considered corrupt due to the
process of the transmission of the text), or when
the presence of Hebrew variants makes the Hebrew
textual situation clear.

Second, the use of translation equivalents
found in OG passages as a basis for reconstructing
the Hebrew of Sir assumes that the grandson of Ben
Sira stood firmly enough in the traditions of
translation represented by the OG that, if he did
use a word-for-word technique of representation,
his translation equivalents would be recognizable
in relation to those represented in Hatch's and
Redpath's Concordance to the Septuagint. This
position largely ignores the fact that in many
instances Greek words in the OG materials represent
a variety of different Hebrew terms and vice versa,
and without a parallel context, which is often not
present in Sir, there is no way to choose one of a
number of possibilities. To what extent the grandson's translation may reflect lexical equivalents
found in OG translations simply has never been
treated.[32] As a result, an understanding of the
degree to which the grandson may have depended on
OG materials has direct bearing on the ability of
scholars to use the OG as a basis for reconstructing the parent text of the grandson where
that parent text is missing, or where the extant
Hebrew appears problematic.

It is also helpful to distinguish, on a
theoretical basis, the sorts of dependence that one
might expect to find if a text such as Sir did rely
consciously on OG terminology. Three types of

dependence seem to me to be most probable: informal
citations, intended allusions, and lexical equivalences. The first category, informal citations, is
called "informal" because Sir contains no formal
quotations -- that is, quotations preceded by an
introductory formula.[33] An informal citation may be
defined as an extended phrase, colon, or verse that
uses wording identical or nearly identical to the
source text, usually in a similar or identical
context to that of the source text. The appearance
in the Greek Sir of this type of parallel would
provide the clearest evidence for conscious
dependence on OG translations.

   After informal citations, intended allusions
to passages in the OG materials might provide some
indication that the grandson depended on OG
passages in his translation. The identification of
an allusion is a bit more subjective; "allusion" is
defined here as the use of key words or phrases,
which appear intended to bring the source text to
the mind of the reader, often in a context quite
different from that of the passage to which
allusion is being made. Here I am speaking of more
than mere parallels in language. I mean the
conscious use of a passage on the part of the
translator. Of course, the determination that an
allusion is conscious may be difficult to make, but
instances like that found in Sir 8.3 (see below)
where the grandson uses a very rare Greek verb may
indicate a conscious use of a text, even though the
context in the Greek Sir may be quite different
from that of the OG. Like informal citations,
allusions demonstrate the influence of specific
passages in OG translations, and only by their

relative frequency or infrequency do they indicate
any general textual dependence by the grandson on
OG materials.

The use of the term textual relationship or
dependence, however, does not necessarily mean that
the grandson was sitting with copies of Greek
translations and looking up every passage that he
found in his Hebrew. A number of possibilities
exist which may be difficult, if not impossible, to
sort out for any given passage. They might be
schematized as follows:

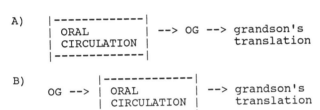

A) |-------------|
    | ORAL | --> OG --> grandson's
    | CIRCULATION | translation
    |-------------|

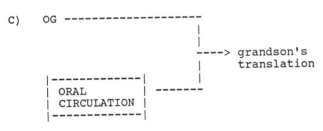

B) |-------------|
    OG --> | ORAL | --> grandson's
            | CIRCULATION | translation
            |-------------|

C) OG --------------------
                          |
                          |
                          ----> grandson's
                          | translation
    |-------------| |
    | ORAL | -------
CIRCULATION

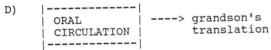

D) |-------------|
    | ORAL | ----> grandson's
    | CIRCULATION | translation
    |-------------|

In Model A, the oral transmission of material
within the Greek-speaking Jewish communities is one
of the streams that possibly influenced the
vocabulary and form of the OG translations.
Subsequently, Ben Sira's grandson used the written
translations as sources for his translation. In

Model B, presuming some length of time between the
OG translations and the grandson, the OG has come
into use in Jewish communities, and the written
form of the text influenced the language used in
transmitting the biblical materials in such
contexts as worship, liturgy, school, or home. The
grandson's knowledge of the scriptural materials
may have derived, for the most part, from these
contexts, and in this case, his translation is
influenced by the OG only indirectly and sporadically. Model C, which seems the most likely situation, presents a scenario in which both the written
OG text and the oral transmission of the material
have influenced the grandson. Model D, where any
similarity to OG passages is coincidental, may be
possible, but does not seem likely given the close
parallel in textual form found between the grandson's translation and the OG for some passages.

In some cases, however, it is impossible to
tell whether Model A, Model B, or Model C is the
most applicable in any given situation. That is,
the grandson may have been familiar with Greek
traditions about biblical persons or events, which
themselves were derived from the OG, and he shares
certain important vocabulary with the OG in the
same context, even though he may not be using the
OG per se. This may also explain the somewhat
haphazard fashion of usage that seems to
characterize his dependence on the OG. In this
study no attempt has been made to distinguish
between these three possibilities, and all three
could be understood by the term textual
relationship, if not textual dependence.[34]

Model B has an additional nuance that must
always be considered a possibility for the grandson
(and Ben Sira himself for that matter). Once the OG
translations were made, certain important terms
used in them may well have become embedded in the
subsequent oral transmission of the material. This
seems to be a likely possibility with material such
as that found in the Praise of the Ancestors.
Consequently, the translation of the grandson may
reflect words in some materials (for example, see
below under Sir 45.18-19) that are also in the OG
accounts, although the larger section in Sir does
not display textual dependence on the OG. Words of
this kind may well have come to the grandson in a
"fixed" oral tradition derived from the OG. To
distinguish between those passages in which there
is direct textual dependence and those in which the
dependence is more indirect is usually difficult
and may ultimately rely on the scholar's intuition
about the passage. As a consequence of this
problem, some of the examples discussed below may
be ambiguous enough to fit into more than one
category, and they have been placed where they are
on the basis of my intuitional assessment of the
various possibilities.

Lexical equivalence,[35] that is, the use in Sir
of the same Greek term as found in characteristic
OG renderings for the same Hebrew term, demonstrates
less of the influence of specific passages of the
OG than the more general relationship of the
grandson to the traditions of translation represented by the OG. The extent to which the grandson
uses the same or different translation equivalents
from the OG, especially for rare or unusual words,
or even neologisms in the OG, shows how much he

stands with the traditions of the OG translations
or apart from them.

The question of canon needs to be raised with
the Greek of Sir as well as with the Hebrew,
although posed in a slightly different way. If the
translator had no Greek translation of a particular
book, then he could not very well be dependent on
it. The issue then is not canon per se, but what
books the grandson might have had available to him
to influence his translation. As noted above, in
the prologue to his translation, the grandson
refers to the categories, "the Law," "the
Prophets," and the "rest of the books." He
indicates that he knows Greek translations of these
divisions when he says,

> You are entreated, therefore, to make your
> reading sympathetically and attentively and to
> have patience, if in anything of what we have
> labored to translate we seem to fail in some
> of the phrases. For things originally spoken
> in Hebrew do not have the same force in them
> when they are translated into another
> language. And not only these things, but also
> the Law itself and the Prophets and the rest
> of the books have no small difference when
> they are spoken in their original form.
> (Prologue 15-26)

What books comprise these three groups? When
were they available in Greek translation? It is
generally agreed that the Pentateuch would have
been translated long before Ben Sira and his
grandson worked, and we can have confidence
concerning the contents of "the Law." Just how much
of the remaining OG translations were available to
the grandson is problematic, and no scholarly
consensus exists on the issue.[36]

In an article entitled "Ben Sira and the
Dating of the Septuagint,"[37] G. B. Caird discusses
the problems associated with this issue. Caird
states that for ascertaining the existence of Greek
translations of books, scholarship has "three
rather blunt tools" at its disposal: citation,
style, and borrowing. When one looks for knowledge
of OG translations (other than the Pentateuch) in
literature prior to the Greek Sir very little can
be found. Eupolemus may show a familiarity with 2
Chr 2.12, Aristeas apparently knows some material
from Job, and the Wisdom of Solomon (though itself
of uncertain date) shows some familiarity with the
Greek of Isaiah.[38] On stylistic grounds, Thackeray
has examined and grouped the OG translations in a
chronological sequence, which Caird finds
unsatisfactory.[39]

Caird, for his discussion of the Greek Sir,
confines himself to the third "tool," borrowing. He
begins his study by saying, "For our purpose the
important point is this, that, whenever the
grandson recognizes such a scriptural borrowing in
his grandfather's Hebrew, he himself borrows from
the appropriate Greek translation, if one happens
to be available to him."[40] From this statement, he
argues that where parallel texts exist between the
Greek Sir and a book of the OG, that book must have
been available in Greek by the time of the
grandson. Conversely, if there is no parallel where
one might be expected (Caird primarily uses the
example of Joshua), then the Greek either was not
in existence or was not available to the grandson.

Here Caird's argument is almost completely
circular. He does not seem to have given sufficient
consideration to a number of other options, such

as: (1) the grandson chose not to use an OG
parallel of which he was aware; (2) he used other,
non-biblical traditions about certain figures
instead of OG material with which he was familiar;
(3) he used Greek translations of biblical books
that have not survived; (4) he simply failed to
recognize "scriptural borrowing" by his grandfather
in certain instances as such, and thus, his failure
to use OG language tells us nothing. The first
aspect of Caird's argument is probable, that is, if
the Hebrew Sir has parallel language to a Hebrew
biblical text, and the grandson's Greek also
coincides with an OG text, borrowing is a possible,
perhaps probable, explanation, although in some
instances so is coincidence of language. The
converse, that if there is no parallel language
where it might be expected, then a Greek
translation of that book was not known to the
grandson, is simply not a necessary conclusion.
Caird reaches this conclusion largely as a result
of the way he has set up the problem.

Given the paucity of information about OG
translations prior to the Greek Sir, Sir constitutes a primary source of data for answering this
question, as Caird has recognized, and a close
examination of the Greek Sir would undoubtedly
yield large dividends. Yet, if one were primarily
interested in the question of the availability of
the scriptural materials in Greek, the most that
one could say would be that certain books were
available to the grandson because he borrows from
them. A judgment about the non-availability of
translations is not possible. In this study I am
not primarily interested in answering the question

of the availability of books in Greek, although the
answer to that question will have a bearing on how
the results of this study are viewed, and vice
versa. I am concerned with the extent to which the
grandson shows dependence on OG translations of the
scriptural materials.

The preceding discussions presume that in both
the Hebrew and the Greek Sir the author and
translator have used written sources that are
identifiable. Snaith's criteria are pointed toward
elucidating a textual dependence of Ben Sira's
Hebrew on the Hebrew scriptures. The unexpressed
assumption that Ben Sira and his grandson used
textual sources exclusively seems to be made by
some scholars concerned with Ben Sira.[41] The
alternative that the biblical traditions were
learned through means other than the written text
of the scriptures does not seem to be seriously
considered despite the connection made in 51.23
between Ben Sira and a מדרש בית and the apparent
reference by the grandson in his prologue (4-6) to
both oral and written instruction.[42] The
possibility that sources other than written ones
are being used must always be kept in mind. The
assumption that Ben Sira and his grandson used only
written sources does not do justice to the social
and educational situations that most likely
obtained in their worlds. Certain texts, such as
the Shema (Deut 6.4-5), must have been very
familiar to both Ben Sira and his grandson, and one
might not expect to find an unambiguous textual
relationship between the Hebrew and Greek Sir and
the biblical source texts for such passages. The
researcher must always be aware that if a passage

does not appear to have a close textual
relationship to a specific biblical text, but shows
knowledge of the tradition, it may well be the
author's own version of familiar material.

Even if Ben Sira and his grandson used written
sources, a clear textual dependence may not be
evident. The text of the biblical books was fluid
in this period as the writings from Qumran have
demonstrated. The Greek tradition was most likely
no less fluid. Problems engendered by this textual
fluidity will be encountered below. Jack Sanders,
speaking about Ben Sira's use of Hellenistic
literature, makes an important distinction that
needs to be kept in mind when one looks at the use
of scriptural materials in Sir. He writes that one
must distinguish "between use of the work of
another author and the use of a phrase which may
have become so current that it was simply part of
the stock of 'expressions and allusions' available
to everyone."[43]

In the following investigations, the material
has been divided according to the translator's
stated categories of "Law," "Prophets," and "the
rest of the books." For the Law and Prophets, the
grandson's use of (1) informal citations and
allusions, and (2) lexical equivalences will be
examined. The third category, "the rest of the
books," has special problems of its own and will be
discussed separately. For each group, I have made
no attempt to be exhaustive, but have worked
primarily from previous studies, which have dealt
in some way with some of these issues. For each
section summary statistics will be given for all
the material, and the most important examples will
be discussed in detail.

3.2 PENTATEUCH

3.2.1 INFORMAL CITATIONS AND ALLUSIONS

Due to the way in which I have defined
informal citations and allusions above, the line
distinguishing them is often not a clear one.
Because both really provide evidence for the same
issue, the use of specific OG passages, they will
be treated together in one section.

When one examines the Greek of Sir for
allusions to Greek scriptural translations, the
relationship between the Hebrew and Greek of Sir
and their scriptural traditions helps to clarify
the way the translator has used the OG in his work.
Three basic relationships are suggested: (1) passages where the Hebrew of Sir can be shown to be
influenced by biblical passages and the translator
shows his recognition of this by using the
corresponding Greek scriptural passage; (2) those
passages where the Hebrew has been influenced by
the Hebrew scriptures, and the grandson translated
independently of the OG providing no evidence that
he was cognizant of the relationship; (3) passages
where the Greek shows influence of the OG while the
Hebrew shows no corresponding influence of the
Hebrew scriptures.

In this section, I have relied primarily on
the lists of presumed dependence of Ben Sira on the
Hebrew scriptures given in the studies of Schechter
and Taylor, Eberharter, Middendorp, and J.
Gasser.[44]   These lists have been supplemented by

individual passages given in other studies.[45] I
have analyzed the Hebrew of each passage according
to Snaith's suggested criteria to see if it can be
regarded as demonstrating a textual dependence on
the Hebrew scriptures. I have also examined the
corresponding Greek Sir to see if the translator
was influenced by the OG, even if the Hebrew shows
no influence of the Hebrew scriptures. Those
passages that demonstrate dependence on either the
OG or Hebrew scriptures have been included in the
overall tallies. If neither the Hebrew nor the
Greek of Sir shows a relationship to the respective
scriptural traditions, they have not been
considered. Finally, I have looked at the notes in
C. J. Ball's The Ecclesiastical or Deutero-
Canonical Books of the Old Testament Commonly
Called the Apocrypha and some of the commentaries
written before the publication of the Cairo Geniza
manuscripts in order to try to locate other
passages where the Greek of Sir may have affinities
to OG passages.[46] This procedure helps one to build
a picture of whether the translator recognized
allusions in his parent text, and if he felt com-
pelled to render them by means of a Greek scriptural text, or if he simply translated ad hoc. It
also helps to identify those places where he may
have been dependent on OG materials, even though
his Hebrew parent text showed no corresponding
dependence on the Hebrew scriptures.

The following chart summarizes the use made of
the passages listed in the studies above. Column A
gives the number of places listed in each study
that the respective authors concluded were
dependent on the Hebrew Pentateuch. Column B shows

the number of passages over which I felt enough
control, according to Snaith's criteria, to warrant
characterization as informal citations or allusions
to the Hebrew Bible. Finally, column C gives the
number of passages out of those in column B that I
judged to show a probable influence of the OG
translation on the Greek of Sir. The bottom of the
chart shows the number of different passages
identified in the studies used and the number of
those that seem to me to show probable influence of
the OG.

TABLE 1 - THE USE OF THE PENTATEUCH BY BEN SIRA AND
          HIS GRANDSON

Author[47]	A	B	C
Schechter/Taylor	88	27	9
Eberharter	211	42	12
Middendorp	47	21	7
Gasser	94	29	9
Total Number of Specific Texts		43	16

For the Hebrew Sir, these data support the
general conclusions of Snaith, Reiterer, and
Middendorp that Ben Sira was not as mechanically
dependent on the Hebrew scriptures as some scholars
thought. When the distinction between a parallel in
language and a textual relationship is applied to
the lists of passages given in the studies given
above, the number of places where the Hebrew can be
controlled and viewed as being dependent on the
Hebrew Pentateuch is drastically reduced.

On the other hand, the numbers given above do
not indicate the extent to which Ben Sira used
pentateuchal traditions. These traditions are found
most often, but not exclusively, in the Praise of
the Ancestors section, and they consist of summations of the traditions that also appear in the
Hebrew scriptures. A close enough relationship to
demand a textual dependence does not exist, but the
same events or persons are being described. P. C.
Beentjes refers to these places as the "structural
use of scripture," whereas Snaith uses the term
"anthological."[48] The basic framework of the event
or tradition is used, but no clear textual relationship can be established. Although Beentjes and
others implicitly assume that even in these places
Ben Sira and his grandson used written sources,
presumably scriptural accounts, the loose
connection of these materials to the scriptural
accounts show them to be the kind of material that
would have been communicated orally in school or
home traditions, or in worship and liturgy. This
explanation accounts for the presence of the
constituent elements of the traditions, while clear
textual dependence on the preserved textual forms
of those traditions is impossible to demonstrate.

The passages from column B produced 43
specific texts that show probable influence of the
Pentateuch on Ben Sira's Hebrew. Of these 43, 16
show a probable influence of OG materials on the
grandson's translation. 11 out of these 16 are
found in the Praise of the Ancestors section. Of
the remaining 5, one (7.30), has clear connections
with the "Shema," a "liturgical" passage likely to
be very familiar to the translator. Three passages

were simply too difficult to sort out. 24 passages,
then, remain where the Hebrew shows a dependence on
the Hebrew scriptures, but the Greek of Sir does
not reflect the OG. In addition to the 16 passages
where Ben Sira and his grandson show a dependence
on their respective scriptural accounts, three
additional passages show an influence of the OG on
the grandson where there is no apparent connection
between the Hebrew scriptures and the Hebrew of Ben
Sira. When one considers that 68 percent of the
passages that do show a dependence on the OG are in
the Praise of the Ancestors section, the prelimi-
nary conclusion can be drawn that where the context
of his parent text concerned some scriptural text,
event, or person that he recognized, the grandson
was more likely to borrow from the Pentateuch for
his Greek rendering. In the clear majority of
instances, however, he translated his Hebrew parent
text without resorting to the OG for help. The
translator's independence from the OG is
underscored by these results. These data do not
indicate that the grandson of Ben Sira was a
slavish imitator or replicator of the Greek Bible,
but rather they show that he demonstrates a
remarkable independence from it.

The examples discussed below are divided into
a number of types. These are: (1) those passages
where the Hebrew Sir contains an allusion to the
Hebrew biblical text, but the Greek Sir does not
reflect the OG; (2) those passages where both the
Hebrew and Greek Sir reflect their respective
scriptural traditions; (3) those places where the
Greek Sir has been influenced by the OG, but the
Hebrew Sir shows no clear relationship to the

Hebrew biblical text; (4) harmonizations in the
Hebrew Sir to the Hebrew scriptures, which occurred
during the transmission of the Hebrew Sir; (5)
summary, "anthological," or "structural"
reflections of scriptural traditions.

3.2.1.1 HEBREW DEPENDENCE / GREEK INDEPENDENCE

Of the 24 passages in this category, 14 fall
outside the Praise of the Ancestors section (3.8;
6.27?; 11.30?; 12.6; 15.15; 30.19; 35.14; 36.7;
36.14; 36.27; 39.23; 39.30; 40.9; 43.6).[49] The
remaining 10 are found in that section (45.3;
45.5?; 45.7; 45.10?; 45.14; 45.15; 45.21; 46.1;
48.15; 50.26). An interesting aspect of these
passages is that the independence of the translator
extends to various types of material. Examples from
ethical materials outside the Praise of the
Ancestors, from cultic and sacrificial contexts,
and from narrative materials can be marshaled to
show the extent of the translator's independence
from the Greek Pentateuch.

a. Sir 36.27 — ובאין אשה נע ונד (MS B)
καὶ οὗ οὐκ ἔστιν γυνή,
στενάξει πλανώμενος.

In this verse, Ben Sira makes a deliberate
comparison between a man with no wife and Cain,
whom God punished with wandering and homelessness.
He accomplishes this by using the identical phrase
to Gen 4.12, 14, נע ונד.[50] The wifeless man is like
Cain who is doomed to wander eternally and be
without permanent lodging. For this phrase, the
grandson shows no dependence on the OG. Where the

OG in both places has στένων καὶ τρέμων, the
grandson translates στενάξει πλανώμενος.

b. Sir 39.23 - ויהפך למלח משקה (MS B)
                        ὡς μετέστρεψεν ὕδατα εἰς
                        ἄλμην

The use of משקה ("well watered") in this
passage makes a connection to the story of the
destruction of the cities of the plain recounted in
Genesis. In Gen 13.10, the Jordan Valley is
described as well watered (משקה) "before God
destroyed Sodom and Gomorrah." In Sir, God dispos-
sesses the nations (23a)[51] and "turns a well
watered land into salt." The use of משקה here is
unusual, since it normally refers to drinking or to
a drinking vessel.[52] Snaith argues that the use of
this word "is probably intended to link the picture
of Yahweh's wrath against the nations, or Gentiles,
with the destruction of the cities of the plain in
the Genesis account."[53] The Greek Sir has ὕδατα
corresponding to משקה, whereas the OG uses
ποτιζόμενη. If the translator of Sir has recognized this rather veiled reference to Sodom and
Gomorrah, he does not resort to the biblical
account for his rendering.[54]

c. Sir 39.30 - [..] וחרב נקמות להחרים (MS B)
                        καὶ ρομφαία ἐκδικοῦσα εἰς
                        ὄλεθρον ἀσεβεῖς

Among the forces of God's punishment of the
wicked listed in 39.30 is a "sword of vengeance."
This phrase is only used one time in the Hebrew
scriptures. In Lev 26.25, it refers to Israel's
breaking of the covenant with God. The phrase in
Hebrew Sir may well have been taken from that

text.[55] In fact, the Hebrew Sir uses the language
of punishment in common with the Hebrew scriptures
in a number of passages, often transferring the
punishment from Israel to the nations or to evil
people.[56]

The Greek Sir has ῥομφαία ἐκδικοῦσα here;
Lev 26.25 has μάχαιραν ἐκδικοῦσαν. The similarity
of the two Greek texts raises the question of
whether the translator had a Greek text before him
which had ῥομφαία, even though this word does not
appear in the manuscript tradition for Lev 26.25.[57]
Could the Greek of Sir reflect a translation of
Leviticus that is no longer extant? On the other
hand, of the two synonyms for sword,[58] ῥομφαία is
preferred by the translator of Sir. For its part,
ἐκδικέω is the favorite translation of forms of
נקם throughout the OG, but it could have been used
by the translator here independently of the OG.
This text provides a good example of the ambiguity
that these kinds of passages often generate.

d. Sir 40.9 - ודם חרחר וחרב [דב]ר (MS B)
            θάνατος καὶ αἷμα καὶ ἔρις καὶ
            ῥομφαία

A similar situation to Sir 39.30 is found in
40.9. The phrase חרחר וחרב ("scorching heat and
drought") is used only one time in the Hebrew
scriptures (Deut 28.22). Like Sir 39.30, the phrase
is part of a list of calamities that befall the
ungodly, although in Deuteronomy it is part of a
list of punishments that would befall a disobedient
Israel. The grandson's translation, ἔρις καὶ
ῥομφαία, seems to represent a vocalization of the
text as חֲרְחֵר וְחֶרֶב ("strife and a sword"). The

translator of Deuteronomy also read חרחר as strife,
but used ἐρεθισμός, and apparently left חרב
untranslated.[59] That the two nouns in the Hebrew
Sir are intended to be natural disasters can be
seen from the parallel in v 9, "famine and
plague."[60] The grandson, however, has neither read
the Hebrew Sir correctly nor has he used the OG.

e. Sir 45.5 – ויגישהו לערפל (MS B)
       καὶ εἰσήγαγεν αὐτὸν εἰς τὸν γνόφον

In this verse, which describes Moses' approach
to God in the dark cloud, the Hebrew Sir uses the
same vocabulary as the MT of Exod 20.21. The Exodus
text reads ומשה נגש אל ערפל. Ben Sira probably
intended to allude to the Exodus tradition,
although the rest of the section about Moses has
very much the nature of a summary composition (see
below). This raises some doubt concerning a direct
textual dependence on the Hebrew scriptures by Ben
Sira.
   The Greek is also problematic. For יגישהו the
translator has used εἰσήγαγεν αὐτόν; the MT of
Exodus has the niphal and thus the Greek translator
used the intransitive εἰσῆλθεν.[61] The grandson's
translation closely follows Ben Sira's Hebrew in
which God leads Moses into the cloud. In Exodus, on
the other hand, Moses "enters" into the cloud. Both
translations use γνόφος to render ערפל. In the OG,
γνόφος can translate a variety of Hebrew words.
The Hebrew and Greek words only appear here in Sir.
It seems likely that the translator has learned
this tradition about Moses from some source other
than the OG, which would explain the ערפל/γνόφος
equivalence. On the other hand, he also translates

his Hebrew independently, giving a close rendering
of יגישהו, which differs from the OG. A textual
dependence seems unlikely here unless one argues
that the grandson is dependent on a Greek translation that no longer survives. One explanation might
be that this passage was learned by him in school
or worship contexts.

f. 45.14 - מנ[חחו בליל חקטר (MS B)
              θυσίαι αὐτοῦ ὀλοκαρπωθήσονται

The phrase בליל חקטר occurs one time in the
Hebrew scriptures, in Lev 6.15. The contexts of the
passage in the Hebrew of Leviticus and Sir are the
same, the presentation of the cereal offering twice
a day. A textual dependence on the Hebrew side
seems clear here. The Greek Sir in the treatment of
the phrase, however, shows a great difference from
the OG of Leviticus. The OG for Lev 6.15 has ἅπαν
ἐπιτελεσθήσεται. The grandson has apparently
included בליל within the verb and rendered the
phrase with ὀλοκαρπωθήσονται, thus showing no
dependence on the OG for his translation.[62]

g. 45.21 - יאכלון ייי אשי[63] (MS B)
              καὶ γὰρ θυσίας κυρίου φάγονται

The Hebrew phrase is probably taken directly
from Deut 18.1 where it is said that Aaron and his
sons have no inheritance within Israel, but that
they are to live on the offerings from the
sacrifices. Beentjes emphasizes that this passage
is an informal citation by pointing to the fact
that the whole discussion in Sir has been in the
third person singular, that is, concerning Aaron.
Only here does the narrative move to the third

person plural, including Aaron's sons as well.[64]
After this colon the text returns to the third
singular. In Greek, the key word is the rendering
of אשי by θυσίας. The Greek of Deuteronomy uses
καρπώματα.[65] ἐσθίω/φάγομαι is a common equivalent
for אכל in Sir and the OG, and the Greek Sir is
only coincidentally the same as Deuteronomy.[66] Any
textual dependence of the Greek Sir on the OG is to
be ruled out.[67]

h. 46.1 - משה בנבואה משרת משה בנבואה (MS B)
            καὶ διάδοχος Μωυσῆ ἐν προφητείαις

     The Hebrew phrase משרת משה ("servant of
Moses") is used in Exod 24.13, 33.11, Num 11.28,
Josh 1.1, and Sir 46.1 to describe Joshua. In no
instance in the Pentateuch or Joshua is the word
rendered by διάδοχος. Exod 24.13 and Num 11.28 use
παρεστηκώς; Exod 33.11 has θεράπων; Josh 1.1 uses
ὑπουργός. The use of διάδοχος by the grandson
seems to reflect an idea about the continuance of
the prophetic line. In this verse, Joshua succeeds
Moses. Later in 47.1, Nathan follows Samuel, and in
48.12, Elisha follows Elijah. The presence of this
scheme in the Greek Sir precludes the notion of a
different parent text for the grandson in this
verse.[68]

     The preceding examples show some of the
relatively clear cases where the grandson did not
follow his grandfather's dependence on the scriptural materials, as well as some of the problematic
examples. Thus, the possibilities are varied,
ranging from clear dependence in the Hebrew and
clear independence in the Greek to those instances
where the Hebrew may have an ambiguous relationship

to the Hebrew scriptures, or where the Greek may
show similar ambiguity in relation to the OG. It is
also important to note that these texts are found
inside the Praise of the Ancestors section as well
as outside of it. The grandson translates independently of the OG, even in places for which he could
presumably have located scriptural parallels. This
suggests that he is generally more concerned with
the Hebrew before him than he is with finding a
Greek scriptural parallel to use, although the next
set of examples shows clearly that when a context
was very clear to the translator he was more likely
to borrow from the OG.

3.2.1.2 HEBREW DEPENDENCE / GREEK DEPENDENCE

Of the 16 passages in this category 11 occur
in the Praise of the Ancestors section (44.16;
44.17; 44.18a; 44.18b; 44.19; 44.21; 45.9; 45.22;
47.20; 49.15; 50.16) and only five elsewhere (6.30;
7.30; 10.9; 10.17; 43.1). The examples fall into
two basic categories, those that reflect the text
of the OG and those that do not reflect the text,
but the content. A text that agrees with the text
of the OG, as for example, Sir 44.21, is stronger
evidence for borrowing than one which essentially
agrees in content and could have possibly had a
different Hebrew parent text from the preserved
Hebrew (as, for example, Sir 44.18). The following
examples are divided accordingly. As we saw in the
previous section, the examples come from a diverse
group of ethical, cultic and sacrificial, and
narrative contexts. The impression is reinforced

that the translator has no identifiable pattern for
borrowing from the OG or for maintaining
independence from it.

A. Examples That Reflect the OG Text

a. Sir 43.1 - חאר מרום ורקיע לטהר (MS M) /
                 עצם שמים מרביט הדרו (MSS M, B)
                 γαυρίαμα ὕψους στερέωμα
                 καθαρειότητος /
                 εἶδος οὐρανοῦ ἐν ὁράματι δόξης

The Hebrew of this verse is very close to Exod
24.10 and is probably an informal citation of it.
In Exodus, when Moses and the seventy elders go up
to the mountain, they see a pavement "as clear as
the sky itself" (כעצם השמים לטהר). The phrase is
translated in the OG as ὥσπερ εἶδος στερεώματος
τοῦ οὐρανοῦ τῇ καθαριότητι. This translation is
reflected in the Greek of Sir 43.1. Here the Masada
text preserves the best form of the Hebrew, and
where it has עצם שמים, the Greek has εἶδος
οὐρανοῦ, as well as στερέωμα καθαριότητος for
רקיע לטהר. In the OG, εἶδος ("appearance") only
renders עצם ("itself") in Exod 24.10. It seems
unlikely that the translators of Exodus and Sir
would arrive at this unusual rendering
independently. More likely, the Greek of Exod 24.10
influenced the translation of Sir 43.1.[69]

b. Sir 44.16 - והתהלך עם ייי ונלקח /
                 חנוך נמצא חמים (MS B)
                 Ἐνωχ εὐηρέστησεν κυρίῳ
                 καὶ μετετέθη

Although it is missing in the Masada text and
the Syriac, MS B has the statement about Enoch
here, and some statement about Enoch seems

presupposed by the Greek of Sir in this place.[70]
The text preserved in MS B is partially corrupt,
but can be reconciled with the Greek. As has been
widely observed, the phrase חמים נמצא, which has no
Greek equivalent, is most likely an intrusion from
v 17 where the phrase is used of Noah in accordance
with the Genesis description of him.[71] The key word
in this text is the verb התהלך. In Gen 5.22, 24,
Enoch is said to have "walked with God" (את התהלך
אלהים). This is translated into Greek as
εὐηρέστησεν τῷ θεῷ. In the Hebrew of Sir the phrase
is התהלך עם ''. The Greek has εὐηρέστησεν κυρίῳ.
The use of εὐαρεστέω for התהלך is not infrequent
in the OG, although it is confined to Genesis and
Psalms. The context of this equivalence, however,
combined with the use of the dative case and the
lack of a preposition (cf. Gen 17.1; 24.24; 48.15;
and Psalms where ἐναντίον or ἐνώπιον render the
Hebrew preposition) makes it more likely that the
translator was influenced by the Genesis account of
Enoch.[72]

c. Sir 44.19 - אברהם אב המון גוים (MS B)
          Ἀβρααμ μέγας πατὴρ πλήθους ἐθνῶν

Ben Sira begins his section on Abraham with a
description straight from the Hebrew scriptural
traditions, אב המון גוים (Gen 17.4). Its Greek
translation is an exact parallel to the OG language
except for one additional word. The OG of Gen 17.4
reads πατὴρ πλήθους ἐθνῶν; the Greek Sir adds μέγας
as an adjective modifying πατήρ. A comparison of
המון in other places in Sir points to the dependence of Sir on the biblical traditions in the
passage under consideration. In 45.9, המון is

rendered πλεῖστος, in 50.3, περίμετρον, and in
50.18, πλείστῳ. Only here in 44.19 is πλῆθος used.
This leaves the question of the addition of μέγας.
Peters argues that the addition comes as a parallel
to the adjectives for Noah in v 17 (חמים, צדיק).[73]
A more likely reason for this addition is that the
grandson is transmitting a Greek etymological
tradition for the Hebrew name אברם, Abraham's
previous name according to Genesis. He has divided
the name into the two words אב and רם, and rendered
רם as μέγας; or perhaps the translation reflects a
Greek reading based on רב. A similar attempt at a
Greek etymology of the name is found in Philo,
<u>Allegorical Laws</u>. 83, where he says that the name
᾿Αβραμ means πατὴρ μετέωρος ("uplifted father").[74]

d. Sir 44.21 - על כן בש[ב]ועה הקים לו (MS B) /
                  לברך בזרעו גוים (MS B)
                  διὰ τοῦτο ἐν ὅρκῳ ἔστησεν αὐτῷ /
                  ἐνευλογηθῆναι ἔθνη ἐν σπέρματι αὐτοῦ

These two cola have all the key vocabulary
words of Gen 22.16-18. The use of the oath (שבועה)
and the blessing of all the nations by Abraham's
seed (לברך בזרעם גוים) indicate that Hebrew Sir was
dependent on the Hebrew scriptural traditions about
Abraham for this narrative, although no extended
citations appear, just the key terms and ideas.[75]
The Greek of this verse is a faithful rendering of
the Hebrew, but is probably dependent on the OG
traditions about Abraham. This is made most clear
by the use of ἐνευλογηθῆναι. This verse constitutes
the only use of this verb in Sir; the other
instances of ברך are rendered by εὐλογέω.[76] It is
precisely this compound verb in the passive voice

that is used in Genesis in the context of the
blessing of the nations. In Gen 12.3 and 18.18, ברך
is used in the niphal, and in 22.18, it is
hithpael. All are rendered by ἐνευλογέω.

The only difference between the Hebrew and
Greek of Sir in this verse is that the Hebrew has
בזרעו גוים, and the Greek reverses the two nouns.
The most likely explanations of this situation are:
(1) the Hebrew of Sir is a later revision toward
the Hebrew biblical tradition, which has the nouns
in this order, or (2) the translator wanted to
bring the subject of the infinitive into closer
proximity to it, which necessitated a departure
from the Hebrew word order.

B. Examples That Reflect the Content of the OG

a. Sir 7.27-30 (MS A)

Deut 6.5, the second half of the Shema, forms
the basis for Sir 7.27-30. The Hebrew of 7.27-28 is
not extant due to a parablepsis; 7.27 began with
בכל, as does 7.29. Only two of the three elements
of Deut 6.5 are thus extant in Hebrew, בכל לבך and
בכל מאודך. The object of these two phrases is God
just as in the Deuteronomy passage, but according
to the Greek Sir, 7.27 applies to parents. By using
the three elements of the Shema, Ben Sira intended
to bring this familiar passage to the reader's
mind. The Greek translator recognized this connection, and he translated the phrases consistently
with the OG of Deuteronomy, especially by his use
of ὅλος for כל. In fact, the three uses of ὅλος
in Sir 7.27-30 are the only three times that the

word renders כל in all of Sir. An example of a
similar phrase in Hebrew where כל is rendered by
πᾶς is 47.8. In this verse, David is described as
loving God בכל לבו. The Greek has ἐν πάσῃ
καρδίᾳ.

The use of this passage, however, does not
necessarily indicate a textual dependence on
Deuteronomy by the grandson. The Shema was
undoubtedly familiar to Jews, and Ben Sira's
grandson could be expected to know a Greek form of
the passage. One might expect the Greek Sir to
reflect the OG of Deuteronomy, while not necessarily depending directly on the text itself.

A second problem concerns the order in which
the elements appear in the Hebrew and Greek. In
7.29, לב appears in the Hebrew where the Greek has
ψυχή, whereas Deuteronomy has καρδία. It appears
as if either a transposition took place between נפש
and לב in the Hebrew Sir, or the grandson, recognizing the allusion to the Shema, maintained the
order of the nouns as found in the OG. Which of
these explanations is the better is not clear.[77]

b. Sir 44.18 - באות עולם נכרת עמו (MS B) /
                לבלתי השחית כל בשר (MS B)
διαθῆκαι αἰῶνος ἐτέθησαν πρὸς αὐτόν /
ἵνα μὴ ἐξαλειφθῇ κατακλυσμῷ πᾶσα σάρξ

The beginning of this verse is problematic (MS
B has באות עולם נכרת; B(mg) has כרת instead of
נכרת). The story of Noah in Genesis actually has
two phrases that might be relevant here, אות הברית
(Gen 9.12, 13, 17) and ברית עולם (Gen 9.16). The
Greek, διαθῆκαι αἰῶνος, suggests that the grandson
may have had ברית עולם in his parent text.[78]
Reiterer has argued that the problem of singular-

plural differences between the Greek and the Hebrew
Sir is recurrent and should not materially affect
the evaluation here.[79] An allusion is probably
being made to the establishment of the rainbow as
the sign of God's covenant with Noah. The Greek Sir
reflects the translation of the OG, although the
translation equivalents are regular for Sir, and
the translator could have arrived at them
independently.[80]

Colon b of 44.18 may exhibit a clearer
influence of the OG than colon a. In this colon,
the Hebrew has the primary vocabulary of Gen 9.15.
The Hebrew Sir reads לבלתי השחית כל בשר, and Gen
9.15 has למבול לשחת כל בשר with the negative coming
in a previous sentence. The Greek Sir moves one
step further than the Hebrew and includes a
reference to the flood when it adds κατακλυσμῷ as
the means of destruction. The influence of the OG
on the Greek Sir can be seen in two ways. First,
only in Gen 9.15 does ἐξαλείφω render שחח in the
Pentateuch. The other occurrences of this equivalent in the OG are in unrelated contexts in Hosea
and Ezekiel. In the flood narrative ἐξαλείφω
renders מחה.[81] Second, the inclusion of
κατακλυσμῷ as the means of destruction parallels
the wording in Gen 9.15 where the Hebrew has למבול
and the OG has εἰς κατακλυσμόν. Thus, 44.18b
appears to be a clear case of the OG influencing
the translator of Sir.[82] The only ambiguity is that
κατακλυσμῷ could have a Hebrew parent text of
למבול. If this were the parent text then the Hebrew
Sir would demonstrate an even closer textual
dependence on the Hebrew scriptures than it does in
its extant form.

c. Sir 47.20 - וחחלל את יצועיך (MS B)
                καὶ ἐβεβήλωσας τὸ σπέρμα σου

A very interesting case is Sir 47.20, which
concerns Solomon. וחחלל את יצועיך is a close
reminiscence of Gen 49.4, אז חללת יצועי עלה, which
is part of Jacob's "blessing" to Reuben. The Greek
Sir, τὸ σπέρμα σου perhaps had זרעך in its parent
text instead of יצועיך.[83] The Greek translation of
the grandson, however, recalls very closely Lev
21.15, (οὐ) βεβηλώσει τὸ σπέρμα αὐτοῦ (= MT
ולא יחלל זרעו).

The context of the two verses suggests that
the Greek Sir (or its Hebrew parent text) may well
have been dependent on the Leviticus text. Sir
47.20 is part of a reproach against Solomon for
allowing his wives (presumably foreign) to "rule
over" his body. As a result, he has "defiled" his
seed. In Leviticus the same phrase immediately
follows an injunction that a priest must "marry a
virgin of his own people." Could the translator of
Sir be using this injunction against Solomon
because he had many foreign wives (cf. 1 Kgs 11.1-
8)? The use of σπέρμα as the object of βεβηλόω
only occurs in the OG in Lev 21.15, and although
the translation equivalents are fairly standard for
Sir, he may well be bringing this injunction
against Solomon despite its priestly connection in
Leviticus.[84]

3.2.1.3 HEBREW INDEPENDENCE / GREEK DEPENDENCE

There are three places that I have been able
to identify in which the Greek Sir shows a
dependence on the OG, but where the relationship of

Hebrew Sir to the Hebrew scriptural traditions is
questionable or unlikely.

a. Sir 8.3 - עץ שׁא על חתן ואל (MS A)
καὶ μὴ ἐπιστοιβάσῃς ἐπὶ τὸ πῦρ
αὐτοῦ ξύλα

This is one of the more interesting passages
in Sir from the perspective of the grandson's use
of the OG. The Hebrew of 8.3 has a certain
reminiscence of Lev. 1.7, 8, 12 where Aaron and his
sons prepare wood for the sacrificial fire. In
Leviticus, however, the verb ערכו is used, not נתן
as in Sir. Given the lack of stability in the
textual tradition of the Hebrew Bible at the time
of Ben Sira, this passage may be more suited to
section 2 above, but the fact that no text of
Leviticus survives with נתן instead of ערך leads me
to place it here.

As far as the Greek is concerned, the translator uses the verb ἐπιστοιβάζω, which seems to
appear for the first time in the Greek language in
the OG of Leviticus. Further, subsequent uses of
the term in Greek come in explicit connection with
the Leviticus passage except for the Greek of Sir
8.3.[85] The larger Greek phrase is the same as
Leviticus, that is, putting wood on the fire. The
grandson seems to have been reminded of the passage
by his grandfather's Hebrew and used the OG wording
in his translation. This is all the more remarkable
when one considers that the contexts of the word in
Leviticus and Sir are so completely different. The
translator does not normally use an OG passage in
such situations.

b. Sir 14.17 - וחוק עולם גוע גוע גועו (MS A)
ἡ γὰρ διαθήκη ἀπ᾽ αἰῶνος θανάτῳ
ἀποθανῇ

Eberharter lists גוע גוע יגועו in 14.17 as related
to Gen 2.17.[86] In fact, the phrase does not occur
in the Hebrew biblical traditions at all. The verb
גוע, however, is used elsewhere in Genesis,
although not with the infinitive absolute, and it
is usually translated by ἀποθνήσκω. The Hebrew
Sir is not borrowing from the story of God's
commandment to Adam and Eve in the garden, which
ends in the MT with מות תמות ("you will surely
die"), even though an allusion to the story may
have been Ben Sira's intent.

The use of the phrase in the Hebrew may well
have reminded the Greek translator of the Genesis
story of Adam and Eve because he uses the same
phrase as the OG for Gen 2.17. When God warns Adam
about eating from the tree of knowledge of good and
evil, he says, "In whatever day you eat from it,
you will surely die." The punishment of certain
death is rendered in the OG as θανάτῳ ἀποθανεῖσθε.
This is the same phrase used by the Greek translator of Sir. He appears to have interpreted the
whole half of 14.17 in light of Gen 2.17. Where the
Hebrew Sir says that the eternal decree is that
human beings will undoubtedly die, the grandson of
Ben Sira sees the story of Adam, Eve, and God in
the garden.[87]

c. Sir 36.26 - עזר ומבצר ועמוד משען (MS B)
βοηθὸν κατ᾽ αὐτὸν καὶ στῦλον
ἀναπαύσεως

This text is particularly difficult in that it
is contained in different forms in three of the

Geniza manuscripts. The problem here is the
beginning of the colon. MS B, given above, reads
עזר ומבצר, and B(mg), C and D have עיר מבצר. The
Greek throughout the verse agrees most closely with
MS B, and for this phrase it has βοηθὸν κατ'
αὐτόν. The Greek phrase is the same one used to
describe Eve in Gen 2.18 where the Hebrew is עזר
כנגדו, the phrase that most of the commentators,
except for Skehan and Di Lella, want to read as the
parent text of Greek Sir.[88] The Syriac has עדרא הי
גר אכותך, which reflects the Peshitta of Gen 2.18
and may offer some support for a Hebrew text which
had כנגדו. MSS B(mg), C, and D all have a text that
seems to have been harmonized to Jer 1.18, which
reads עיר מבצר.

There are three possible explanations for this
situation: (1) if one follows Skehan and Di Lella
in seeing עזר כעצמו as the original Hebrew, the
original עזר became corrupted to עיר, which
subsequently suggested מבצר due to the Jeremiah
passage;[89] (2) the Hebrew text of Ben Sira had
originally intended to make an allusion to Gen 2.18
in reference to a good wife and had עזר כנגדו,
which is reflected in Greek. כנגדו became corrupted
to ומבצר, which called to the mind of a scribe עיר
מבצר in Jer 1.18. This reading is reflected in MSS
B(mg), C, and D. (3) Ben Sira wrote עזר מבצר, which
later was corrupted to עיר מבצר under the influence
of Jer 1.18. The use of עזר to describe a wife
called to the mind of the translator the
description of Eve in Gen 2.18. He subsequently
used the Genesis text and ignored מבצר in his
parent text. In light of these three possibilities,
the presence of a Syriac text that has a text like

Gen 2.18 could be explained as either a translation
of כנגדו or a similar phrase in its parent text, an
independent harmonization to Gen 2.18, or a
reflection of the Greek of Sir, which occasionally
influences the Syriac translation. As far as a
judgment concerning the Greek text is concerned, it
seems likely that the translator drew on the
Genesis traditions about Eve in referring to wives
in general. Whether the Hebrew contained that
allusion is difficult to say with a high level of
confidence.[90]

3.2.1.4 PASSAGES IN HEBREW AND GREEK SIR THAT SUMMARIZE BIBLICAL TRADITIONS

As discussed above, a number of passages,
especially in the Praise of the Ancestors section,
show little clear textual dependence on either the
Hebrew scriptures or the OG, but have the same
traditions in common with them. A few examples are
discussed below.

a. Sir 16.7 – אשר לא נשא לנסיכי קדם (MSS A, B)
οὐκ ἐξιλάσατο περὶ τῶν ἀρχαίων
γιγάντων

In a short discussion centered around God's
anger against the wicked, Sir gives "historical"
examples. The first is the rebellion of the
"princes of old," a clear reference to the
tradition found in Genesis 6, Jubilees, and
1 Enoch, as well as other places. The language that
Ben Sira uses does not parallel the biblical
phraseology, nor for that matter does the Greek.
The only parallel in Greek is the reference to
γιγάντων, which is used in the OG of Genesis to
render גבורים and נפילים. The offspring of the

"sons of God" and the "daughters of men" are also
called "giants" in Jub. 5.1 and 1 Enoch 6.3 (cf.
also other texts from this period, such as Wis 14.6
and Bar 3.26, 28). To argue that all these texts
are dependent on Genesis 6 is really to beg the
question. They could easily be reporting similar
traditions to those found in Genesis, and Sir could
be using some source of the tradition other than
Genesis.[91] The major clue as to the exact identification of the event is its inclusion in a
larger list of events described by Ben Sira: (1)
the "princes of old;" (2) "the place where Lot
sojourned;" (3) "the nation accursed;"[92] (4) "the
six hundred thousand footmen." The "chronological"
list makes it probable that the "princes of old"
refer to the Genesis 6 tradition, but a textual
relationship with Genesis cannot be established.

b. Sir 45.18-19 (MS B)

     The story of the rebellion and subsequent
destruction of Korah, Dathan, Abiram, and their
followers is told in Num 16.1-35 and briefly
summarized in Num 26.9-10 and 27.3. The summary of
the story given in Sir has every appearance of
being based on the longer tradition of Numbers 16.
The only verbal similarities between Sir and
Numbers 16, however, are the phrase עדת קרח and the
verb אכל, which describes the action of the fire
that destroyed these people. None of the details of
the longer narrative are given in Sir. The verses
in Sir, then, serve a similar function to the
passages in Numbers 26 and 27 in that all three
give a short recounting of the opposition of Korah
along with God's anger and punishment.

The Greek Sir as well shows little connection
to the OG version of the story. The major similarity is the use of ἐπισυνίστημι at the beginning
of v 18. This verb is the same one used in Num 26.9
and 27.3 to describe the opposition of these people
to Moses and God. The verb in Numbers 16 is
συνίστημι. That ἐπισυνίστημι is used in various
summations of the longer story of Korah all with
different Hebrew parent texts (Num 26.9 has הצו and
בהצתם; Num 27.3 has הנועדים; and Sir 45.18 uses
ויחרו) points toward its inclusion as a standard
feature of the Greek tradition of the event and
does not prove to be clinching evidence for an
extensive textual relationship.[93] עדה is rendered
συναγωγή by Sir, and although this is the same
term used in Num 16.5, it is also the grandson's
favorite translation equivalent for עדה.[94] Finally,
Greek Sir renders ויאכלם בשבוב אש as καταναλῶσαι
ἐν πυρὶ φλόγος αὐτοῦ, whereas the OG uses τὸ
πῦρ κατέφαγεν. The Greek Sir thus appears to be
following its parent text independently of the OG
accounts.

c. Sir 45.23-24 (MS B)

A similar situation is found in Sir 45.23-24
concerning Phinehas. In these two verses, the basic
elements of the Num 25.6-13 story are present. With
the biblical story, Sir shares: (1) the report of
Phinehas's name as "Phinehas, the son of Eleazar;"
(2) his "zeal;" (3) his atonement for Israel; (4)
the covenant of peace;[95] (5) the reward of the
priesthood. The following additional elements are

also found in the Hebrew Sir: (1) Phinehas's
position in "might" (גבורה); (2) his standing "in
the breach" (בפרץ) for his people; (3) the
prompting of his heart (אשר נדבו לבו); (4) his
responsibility for the maintenance of the sanc-
tuary. The aspects of the biblical tradition found
in Sir would most likely find their way into a
traditional report concerning Phinehas. In fact,
Phinehas's zeal, the covenant, and the priesthood
are all reported in 1 Macc 2.54 in a discussion of
famous people.

The Greek of these verses follows the order of
the Hebrew Sir, if not in a word-for-word manner.
The translation of those elements that parallel the
biblical story is not decisive. בקנא is rendered
ἐν τῷ ζηλῶσαι αὐτόν. The קנא/ζηλόω equivalent
is found elsewhere in Sir (cf. 9.1; 30.26; 45.18),
however. Also the construction of a Hebrew
preposition with the infinitive is translated as a
Greek preposition with the infinitive elsewhere in
Sir (cf. 4.9; 40.14; 46.20; 50.11). כפר and
ἐξιλάσκομαι are also standard equivalents for
Sir, as are חק (ברית)/διαθήκη.[96] In Sir,
ἱερωσύνης is used to render כהנה (cf. 1 Macc
2.54), but ἱερετεία is used in Num 25.13. As a
result, the likelihood is that the grandson is here
following the Hebrew before him, which itself is
probably a composition of Ben Sira.[97] However, that
stories such as that of Phinehas were well known to
the grandson is probable, and some of the parallel
language, especially with the OG, may be the result
of the oral communication of these traditions in
Greek.[98]

d. Sir 45.1-5 (MS B, B[mg])

Perhaps the best example of a summarizing
tendency in Sir is 45.1-5, which deals with Moses.
At every turn the Hebrew Sir has summary forms of
what are longer stories about Moses and Israel
contained in the scriptural accounts. Vv 2 and 3
provide a very short summary of the contest between
Moses and Pharaoh. 45.3 has one parallel phrase to
Exodus, [העם] ל[א] ויצוהו, although even this
phrase is more general than the Exodus account,
which specifically refers to בני ישראל, a phrase
that will not fit in the lacuna in MS B at this
point. The Greek here uses a different term from
the OG of Exodus, ἐντέλλομαι rather than συντάσσω.
45.4 speaks of Moses' faithfulness, meekness, and
chosenness. In 45.5, a passage discussed above, Ben
Sira makes a reference to the cloud in which God
manifested himself, and it is only in this phrase
that one could argue for a textual dependence of
Ben Sira on the Hebrew scriptures in this material.
The general independence of the Greek Sir from the
OG in this passage makes it appear unlikely that
the grandson used the OG. Finally, the Hebrew Sir
refers to the giving of the Law to Moses and his
responsibility to teach it to Israel. Like the rest
of the passage, the language of this verse differs
from the longer accounts reported in Exodus. For
this verse, the Greek follows the Hebrew and does
not parallel the language of the OG. Viewed as a
whole, the entire section has the flavor of a
summary composition, which tells certain details
important to Ben Sira (or the tradition that he
inherited) about Moses' life and career. Direct

textual borrowing from the Pentateuch by Ben Sira or his grandson appears very unlikely.

3.2.1.5 LATER HARMONIZATION OF THE HEBREW SIR TO THE HEBREW BIBLE

Earlier in this chapter a caution was raised, namely, the possibility that during the transmission of the Hebrew Sir passages may have been revised to make them look more like passages from what, by the time of the copyist, had become a canon of scripture. There are a relatively large number of these passages, and I have not made any attempt to catalogue all of them. Each case needs to be judged on its own merits. In fact, some may not be as clear-cut as one might like. Some examples are given below.

a. Sir 15.14 – אלהים מבראשׁית ברא אדם (MSS A B[mg])
          הוא מראשׁ ברא אדם (MS B)
          αὐτὸς ἐξ ἀρχῆς ἐποίησεν ἄνθρωπον

The relationship of this verse to Gen 1.1 has been frequently noted.[99] Variant readings in the extant Hebrew manuscripts preclude any conclusions about textual dependence, however, and they indicate that מבראשׁית is a later harmonization toward Gen 1.1. Where MSS A and B(mg) read מבראשׁית ברא אדם, MS B has מראשׁ ברא אדם. The creation event is clearly being recalled, and the verb ברא is the one used in Genesis. The Greek ἐξ ἀρχῆς probably reflects מראשׁ in MS B, with the substitution of מבראשׁית in MSS A and B(mg) a result of familiarity with the creation story. A caution is provided by A. A. Di Lella who notes that "the מן with בראשׁית may, of course, be legitimate Hebrew, for the phrase בראשׁית (Gen 1.1) may have become by this

time such a stock phrase that it is taken for a
noun."[100] That the texts of MSS A and B(mg) have
been harmonized towards Genesis is supported by the
use of αὐτός, which reflects הוא in MS B and
shows אלהים in MSS A and B(mg) to be secondary. The
Hebrew that lay before the translator was not a
quotation from Genesis, but in words different from
Genesis, referred to the creation event. For their
part, MSS A and B(mg) have been harmonized to Gen
1.1 and 1.27 (ובּרא אלהים את האדם). The Greek has
translated the Hebrew of MS B, which has not
suffered the fate of MSS A and B(mg). Although it
is difficult to think that the translator did not
see the clear reference to the creation event, he
resisted any temptation to borrow the OG account,
and he remained faithful to his parent text.[101]

b. Sir 33.12 - השבח ראש פאתי מואב (MS B) /
                אויב   (MS B(mg))
        σύντριψον κεφαλὰς ἀρχόντων ἐχθρῶν

This text is one of the clearer examples of
harmonization toward the Hebrew biblical tradition.
The phrase פאתי מואב in MS B has been harmonized to
agree with Num 24.17 where the same phrase is used.
The Greek Sir has ἐχθρῶν, a reflection of the
textual tradition of MS B(mg), which has אויב
instead of מואב. The use of פאתי meaning "leader"
or "prince" reminded a copyist of the Numbers
passage, and he copied it in accordance with that
text.[102]

c. Sir 45.7 - ואזרהו בתועפות ראם (MS B)
              תואר (MS B(mg))
        καὶ περιέζωσεν αὐτὸν περιστολὴν δόξης

This text illustrates the difficulty of
deciding whether or not a passage in the Hebrew of
Sir has been harmonized to agree with a biblical
text. The Hebrew of MS B in 45.7 says that God
"girded" Aaron with תועפות ראם. The Hebrew phrase
itself is very difficult. In Num 23.22 and 24.8,
תועפות ראם describes the people Israel whom God has
brought out of Egypt, and it is often translated
into English as "strength of a wild ox" or
something similar. The Greek translator of Numbers
had some difficulty and rendered δόξα μονοκέρωτος.
For ראם, MS B(mg) has חואר ("outline, form") and
Smend, Box and Oesterley, and Skehan and Di Lella
regard it as the authentic text; they consider ראם
to be a correction toward the Numbers passage.[103]

Although this may be the case, some arguments
could be marshaled against the originality of חואר.
Why would a copyist take a phrase for which he
could seemingly derive some meaning (תועפות חואר)
and revise it to a phrase which is so inherently
difficult? One would have to argue that the
authority of the scriptural passage was great
enough to overcome the difficulty in meaning, or
perhaps that a copyist thought he knew what the
phrase meant. On the other hand, the Syriac of Sir
stands in the tradition of the Peshitta translation
of תועפות ראם and may indeed support the originality of that phrase.[104] The argument could also be
made that a substitution of חואר for ראם in Hebrew
would serve exactly the same purpose as the Greek
here; both are attempts to make some sense out of a
difficult Hebrew phrase.[105]

If the text of MS B is judged to be original,
the Greek translation must also be explained
because it does not use the OG translation of

ראם וחועפוח; it renders the phrase as περιστολὴν
δόξα. It is indeed interesting that δόξα appears
here as it does in the OG, and perhaps it is meant
to render וחעפוח. What appears to me to be the case
is that the translation of וזרהיו by περιέζωσεν
αὐτόν has determined the use of περιστολή.
δόξης probably renders וחעפוח and ראם is, for all
intents and purposes, ignored. Rather than a
harmonization, then, this text could represent a
use of the Hebrew scriptures by Ben Sira, but an
independence from the OG on the part of the
grandson. A high level of confidence for this
conclusion cannot be maintained.[106]

3.2.1.6 CONCLUSIONS CONCERNING THE USE OF SPECIFIC PASSAGES FROM THE GREEK PENTATEUCH

The overall data concerning the use of the OG
by the grandson of Ben Sira combined with the
discussion of the particular examples support
Reiterer's conclusions and show that the grandson
cannot be judged to be an uncritical imitator of
the OG of the Pentateuch. The places where he shows
a probable dependence on the OG do not indicate any
kind of consistency, certainly not the consistency
that Caird claims.[167] The clear impression that one
derives from this material is that the grandson,
when he recognizes familiar passages and contexts,
or when a particular Hebrew passage strikes a
familiar chord in him, may borrow from the OG
translations. In many cases, perhaps most, he may
be more dependent on oral traditions and formula-
tions that the OG may have spawned and would likely
be found in worship, liturgy, school, or home
contexts. His occasional use of specific vocabulary

in specific contexts indicates this kind of usage.
When one looks at the whole of the translation,
however, one finds that in the vast majority of
cases the grandson is translating the Hebrew that
his grandfather wrote independently of the
Pentateuch. The consistency of dependence that
Caird assumes and the picture that Smend paints of
a translator actively comparing the Hebrew
scriptures with their Greek translations and using
those translations as a basis for his work do not
appear warranted. If this situation obtains for the
Pentateuch, which seems to be an old and revered
fixture among Hebrew and Greek speaking Jews, one
can only wonder how much he excerpted passages from
the other portions of the Greek Bible.

3.2.2 LEXICAL EQUIVALENTS

Even if Ben Sira's grandson is not quoting
from the Greek Bible, he may still be using the
same lexical equivalents as those translations.
That is, he may well represent a similar tradition
of translation to that of the OG Pentateuch. The
extent of the similarity to the OG equivalents or
of the dissimilarity from them will affect, to a
great degree, the ability of scholars to retrovert
the lexical elements of the Greek Sir and reconstruct the Hebrew of Ben Sira in those places where
the Hebrew is not extant.

The criterion of lexical similarity is really
applied unevenly to the translation. I am not
concerned with those translation equivalents that
would be suggested automatically to the translator
or would be so common as to be irrelevant for

determining the grandson's relationship to OG
translations of the Bible. Translation pairs such
as אשה/γυνή, איש/ἀνήρ, בן/υἱός have little independent value for this kind of study, and there are
many such words in Sir. What needs to be considered
are rare or unusual words or words used in unusual
or special ways. The grandson's treatment of such
words should provide a striking indication of his
affinities with the OG. In this section the work of
two scholars, Emanuel Tov and Franz Reiterer, has
been utilized as a vehicle for examining this
issue.

3.2.2.1 THE WORK OF EMANUEL TOV

In an article entitled "The Impact of the LXX
Translation of the Pentateuch on the Translation of
the Later Books,"[108] Emanuel Tov has argued that
those who translated books of the Hebrew scriptures
subsequent to the Pentateuch often: (1) perpetuated
the vocabulary of the Greek Pentateuch in their
translations, and (2) looked to the Pentateuch for
assistance in translating difficult words. The
article largely consists of lists of words considered by Tov to have been perpetuated by later
translators, some of which he labels as septuagintal neologisms. In this section, I have taken
these lists, looked for those words that occur in
Ben Sira, and compared the translation equivalents
to those listed by Tov. Of the 46 OG words that
appear in Sir and are listed by Tov in his study,
17 do not render the Hebrew term given by him, 16
represent the Hebrew listed by him in some of their
occurrences, and 10 show complete agreement (of

these 10, 7 only occur one time in Sir). Three
cases are uncertain.

The examples discussed below have been divided
into the following types: (1) those that use only
the same equivalent as the OG; (2) those that use
the same equivalent as the OG as well as different
ones; (3) those that use a different equivalent in
every case. Within each category the examples are
listed in Greek alphabetical order followed by the
equivalent thought by Tov to be perpetuated later,
the chapter and verse of its occurrence(s), and
then any other equivalents used by the grandson. NE
(No Equivalent) signifies that the Greek has no
Hebrew equivalent; 0 indicates that the Hebrew
equivalent listed by Tov for the OG term does not
occur as an equivalent for the Greek term in Sir.
Those Greek words that have uncertain or ambiguous
Hebrew equivalents are marked with a question mark
(?). Presumed septuagintal neologisms are indicated
by an asterisk (*). The results can be charted as
follows:

TABLE 2 - TOV'S LISTS OF LEXICAL EQUIVALENTS

Total	100% = OG	Part = OG	None = OG	??
46	10	16	17	3

3.2.2.1a SAME EQUIVALENT AS THE OG

a. θυσιαστήριον* ("altar") = מזבח 50.11, 47.9(?);
   NE 35.8, 50.15

For none of the occurrences of θυσιαστήριον
are there any clear textual parallels with the OG.
50.11 has a clear correspondence with מזבח, and

למזבח is the most likely reconstruction of ל..ח in
47.9. מזבח also corresponds to βῶμος in 50.14.
κύριος is the formal equivalent of מזבח in 50.19
where the entire second half of the verse is
problematic. The commentators offer little more
than retroversions from the Greek here.[109]

b. καταπέτασμα ("curtain") = פרכת 50.5

The only occurrence of the Greek word in Sir
corresponds to the same Hebrew as the OG. The
phrase בית הפרכת, which refers to the temple or
perhaps the Holy of Holies, is not used in the
Hebrew scriptures at all, however. The phrase מבית
לפרכת ("within the veil") occurs a number of times
in the Hebrew scriptures and may have been the
origination point of the phrase in the Hebrew Sir.
The Greek Sir has οἴκου καταπετάσματος for בית
הפרכת.

c. κίδαρις ("headdress") = מצנפת 45.12

This noun describes the headdress that Aaron
was to wear. It reflects the same Hebrew as the OG
and is also used in the same general context of
Aaron's priestly garments. One would expect such
terms to become relatively fixed early in the Greek
tradition, although the grandson is not consistent
with the OG in his translation of all such terms
(see below under ἐπώμις).

d. παράδεισος ("garden") = גן עדן 0; עדן 40.17, 27

The Hebrew גן עדן does not occur in Sir, even
though the translator clearly takes עדן in that

sense while he ignores its general context. עדן is
a noun meaning "delight" or "luxury," and that
appears to be Ben Sira's intended meaning when he
uses it.[110] Thus one could translate 40.27a, "The
fear of God is a delight of blessing," not "Eden of
blessing," as Box and Oesterley have done. In
40.17, the Greek has παράδεισος where the Masada
text reads עד‎כ, and the grandson probably read
כעדן. These two places show that the grandson had a
fixed lexical equivalent for עדן, which seems
connected with the Genesis accounts about גן
עדן.[111]

e. σκληροτράχηλος* ("stiff necked") = ערף קשה 16.11

This equivalent is identical to that of the
OG, but the contexts are different. In the OG, the
word only occurs with reference to λαός, usually
meaning Israel.[112] In Sir, the reference is to any
obstinate person.

3.2.2.1b OG AND NON-OG TRANSLATION EQUIVALENTS

a. διαθήκη ("covenant") = ברית 41.19, 44.12,20,23,
   45.15,25; חק 11.20, 14.12,17, 16.22, 42.2, 44.20,
   45.5,7,17,24; NE 17.12, 24.23, 28.7, 38.33, 39.8

Of all the stereotyped renderings in the OG,
διαθήκη is the stereotyped rendering <u>par excellence</u>.
HR lists only one time in the Pentateuch where ברית
is not its equivalent, only five others in the
entire Greek Bible. On the other hand, HR does not
list even one occurrence of חק as an equivalent of
διαθήκη. This consistency in rendering does not

characterize the Greek Sir. Of the fifteen non-problematic occurrences of διαθήκη, seven render ברית and eight render חק.[113] In general, the Hebrew Sir makes a clear distinction between the two Hebrew terms. ברית is normally reserved for those covenant relationships into which God entered with specific figures. For example, Sir 44.23 refers to God's covenant with Abraham, which Isaac inherits.[114] In other places, the ברית/διαθήκη equivalence appears with famous people. In 44.20, the Hebrew refers to God's ברית with Abraham for which the translator uses διαθήκη. Immediately following, however, the Hebrew reads כרח לו חק, which is parallel to ברית. Here also the Greek has διαθήκη. If חק here means "covenant," it would be the only place in the Hebrew Sir that attests that meaning. Rather, חק refers here to the law of circumcision, and thus the phrase means, "He established with him a statute."[115] The Greek and Syriac translators both misunderstood this distinction and translated חק as synonymous with ברית (Greek = διαθήκη; Syr = קימה).

In 45.15, Ben Sira refers to a ברית עולם, which God made with Aaron. This phrase is translated διαθήκην αἰῶνος. The Hebrew phrase is never used of Aaron in those traditions that are preserved in the Hebrew Bible; there it usually is חק עולם (see below).

The covenant with David is mentioned in 45.25 where ברית is rendered διαθήκη.[116] The reference comes at the end of a section that deals with Phinehas in which ברית שלום (cf. Num 25.12) is rendered διαθήκη εἰρήνης. Here, חק appears adjacent to ברית, and it does not seem to be translated

into Greek. Smend, followed by Box and Oesterley,
argues that חק and ברית stand in an appositional
relationship in this place, and since the two words
are regularly rendered with διαθήκη, the translator wanted to avoid using the same word twice.[117]
The occurrence of both words here could also be
explained as an attempt to bring an original חק
שלום into conformity with the text of Numbers,
which has ברית שלום. The result is a doublet in
Hebrew.

Finally, two more general uses of ברית occur.
In 44.12, the introduction to the Praise of the
Ancestors section, the covenants are referred to as
the inheritance to their descendants, where ברית is
rendered by διαθήκη.[118] 41.19 uses the phrase פרר
ברית, which usually means "to break a covenant."
The grandson, who uses διαθήκη, has misunderstood
the larger context.[119]

All other occurrences of διαθήκη in Sir
render חק. This Hebrew word is used in a number of
different ways in Sir, but not to mean "covenant."
In the Hebrew scriptures, it usually means "decree,
statute."[120] Ben Sira's grandson, however, makes no
distinction between ברית and חק, and further, he
shows no knowledge of the renderings in the Greek
Bible for the the latter. For the grandson, חק and
ברית are synonymous.

In 14.12, the phrase חק שאול ("decree of
Sheol") is rendered διαθήκη ἄδου. The general
sense of חק as a decree is also found in 14.17 as
חק עולם, which is rendered διαθήκη ἀπ' αἰῶνος,
and in 16.22 where חק is translated διαθήκη. In
11.20, חק probably means "appointed task" as it
does in Exod 5.14. Box and Oesterley render the

phrase עמד בחוקך as "be steadfast in thy task." The
Greek renders the phrase στῆθι ἐν διαθήκῃ σου,
which seems to completely miss the intended meaning
of the Hebrew.[121]

In a number of places חק means "law," and in
each case again the Greek uses διαθήκη. Especially
interesting are two places where Israel is to be
taught the חקים. These occur in 45.5 with reference
to Moses, where חק is parallel to מצוה, תורת חיים,
and משפט, and also in 45.17 with respect to Aaron.
Here again חק is in parallel with מצוה and משפט.
The idea of teaching the commandments occurs in the
Greek Pentateuch, in Deut 4.14 and 6.1. In Deut
4.1, 5; 5.1; 6.1; etc., חק is found with משפט and
is consistently rendered by δικαίωμα. Finally,
Hebrew Sir, in 45.7 (cf. Exod 30.21; Lev 7.34;
etc.), refers to the eternal ordinance (חק עולם),
which is given to Aaron. This phrase appears in the
OG as νόμιμον αἰώνιον, whereas the grandson, possibly under the influence of Sir 45.15, translates
διαθήκην αἰῶνος.[122]

If the grandson had carefully worked his way
through the OG, one would expect that the uses of
חק would be more clearly defined by the translator.
As it stands, he has rendered ברית and חק alike as
διαθήκη where the Hebrew is clear as to the
difference.

b. νόμος ("law") = תורה 15.1, 32.19,28, 33.2,3,
41.8, 42.2, 45.5, 49.4; מצוה 44.20; דבר 33.3; ?
9.15, 45.17; NE 2.16, 17.11, 19.17,20,24, 21.11,
23.23, 24.23, 34.8, 35.1, 39.1

Like ברית/διαθήκη, תורה/νόμος is a lexical
correspondence that is very consistent in the OG,
and תורה is the most common equivalence of νόμος

for Sir when referring to the Law of God. Sir
evidences this equivalence nine times. Of these,
three are rendered νόμος ὑψίστου (חורת עליון),
one by νόμος ζωῆς (חורת חיים), and the others do
not appear in any distinct phrase. In one place,
44.20, the phrase שמר מצוח עליון is translated
συνετήρησεν νόμον ὑψίστου. שמר מצוה does occur
a number of times in the Hebrew Bible, but it is
translated φυλάσσειν τὰς ἐντολάς.[123] The verb
συντηρέω does not occur in this context in the OG.
One passage shows a rather unusual equivalent for
νόμος. 33.3 has דבר in parallel with חורה, and the
translator has probably rendered the word
exegetically. Here the "word" of God is taken as
synonymous with the Law and accordingly translated
νόμος.[124]

One occurrence of νόμος remains problematic.
45.17 has משפט corresponding to νόμος. This is a
case where it seems likely that the Greek had a
different parent text. Not only are the terms
different, the Greek has a prepositional phrase ἐν
νόμῳ αὐτοῦ while the Hebrew of MS B has ומשפט.[125]

חורה is found two times in the Hebrew of Sir
with Greek terms other than νόμος. In 32.21, חורה
occurs in a phrase where it could be interpreted
generally as law or more specifically the law of
God. In this case, the Greek has σύγκριμα, which
seems to interpret the word in a generic sense.[126]
For 41.4, MS B has the phrase חורת עליון, but the
Greek has εὐδοκίᾳ ὑψίστου. To judge from the
other occurrences of חורה עליון in Sir, the Greek
probably had a different parent text. The commentators suggest ברעוח (because of a certain graphic
similarity?) or ברצון.[127]

c. συναγωγή ("assembly") = עדה 4.7, 16.6, 41.18,
45.18, 46.14; לקבל 31.3; בעמד 43.20; NE 1.30,
21.9, 24.23

Of the five times where συναγωγή is found
corresponding to עדה, three instances refer to
unrighteous groups of people (16.6; 45.18; 41.18).
One especially interesting passage of these three
is 45.18, which speaks about עדת קרח (see above).
In the OG this phrase is rendered Κορε καὶ ἡ
ἐπισύστασις, whereas Sir has συναγωγή. In one
place, 46.14, συναγωγή renders עדה with reference
to Israel. Three passages in Sir refer to the "city
assembly" (4.7; 7.7; 42.11), once with עדה rendered
by συναγωγή (4.7) and twice with the phrase עדת
שער ("assembly of the gate"). In both of these
instances, the grandson uses πλῆθος for עדה. 7.7
has πολέως for שער, and 42.11 has πολλῶν, which
may be a corruption of πυλῶν or πολέως.[128] In
7.14, πλῆθος renders עדה in the phrase "assembly
of the elders." λαός is also an equivalent of עד,
and it refers to the people of Israel (44.15;
46.7).

One occurrence, 31.3, speaks of the gathering
of wealth. The Hebrew has לקבל, and the Greek has
συναγωγῇ. Smend and Peters argue for קבץ based on
the equivalence of συνάγω with this Hebrew verb in
14.4. Segal argues that the text should read קבל[129]
and that it makes the best sense this way.   I
think that in this verse the act of receiving
wealth could be construed as gathering it, and
there is no compelling reason to see a different
word in the parent text of the Greek. Finally, a

rather odd equivalence is found in 43.20 where
συναγωγὴν ὕδατος renders מעמד מים meaning "a
basin of water."

d. κατακλυσμός ("flood") = מבול 44.17; נהר 39.22;
   כלה(?) 40.10; NE 21.13, 44.18

Once in Sir, κατακλυσμός corresponds to מבול
as in the OG. This occurrence is in the story of
Noah, and it is the same term used in the Genesis
account of the flood (for discussion, see above).
In 39.22, κατακλυσμός translates נהר. Box and
Oesterly, Peters (cited in Box and Oesterly), Lévi,
and Segal all think that the Greek read מבול here.
Smend states that the Greek is rhetorical for
נהר.[130] What seems to me to have happened here,
though, is that the translator did not understand
the image of the verse. In the Hebrew, the verse
refers to the Nile and the Euphrates rivers.[131] The
grandson seems to have taken the Hebrew in a more
generic sense. Both ποταμός and κατακλυσμός are
without the definite article and could connote "a
river" and "a flood." Further, the image of
"saturating the world" in colon b of the verse may
have led the translator to see נהר in the sense of
a rushing river, and consequently, led him to
render נהר as κατακλυσμός.

Sir 40.10 presents another alternative equivalent. In this place κατακλυσμός formally represents כלה in MS B. MS B(mg) reads רעה and may be
evidence for a transposition of רעה in colon a and
כלה in colon b. If such a transposition took place,
and the translator read כלה as "all" in colon a,
the formal equivalent of רעה in MS B, ταῦτα
πάντα, makes sense. This would make κατακλυσμός

in colon b an exegetical rendering of רעה, perhaps
referring to the Noachic flood as the result of the
evil of humankind. Even if כלה were left in colon
b, one could still argue for an exegetical rendering, but ταῦτα πάντα in colon a would be
harder to explain.[132]

3.2.2.1c NON-OG TRANSLATION EQUIVALENTS

a. ἐπώμις ("breastplate") = אפוד 0; מעיל 45.8

The last phrase of Sir 45.8 gives three
articles of Aaron's priestly clothing, מכנסים
כתנות]=כתונת] ומעיל. Of these three, only one is
represented in Greek Sir as in the OG. מכנסים is
rendered περισκέλη as is always the case in the
OG. כתונת, however, is never rendered by ποδήρη in
the OG; it usually is χιτῶν.[133] Similarly,
ἐπώμις almost always renders אפוד, not מעיל as in
Sir 45.8 (διπλοίς is the major equivalent of מעיל
in the OG). On this passage, Smend argues that
כתונת is actually a corruption of כתפת and that
ἐπωμίδα is an inner-Greek corruption of διπλοίδα.
Smend's argument produces matching translation
equivalents between this verse and the OG. The
question must be raised, however, why the
translator could not simply have used different
equivalents from the OG here.[134]

b. σωτήριον ("thank offering") = שלם 0; תשועה
   39.18; מקדש 47.2; NE 35.2

Of the two occurrences of the neuter noun
σωτήριον in Sir, one occurs in 39.18 meaning
"deliverance." The rendering of the root ישע by

some form of σῴζω is usual in both Sir and the
OG. In the OG, however, σωτήριον is also a term
for a particular type of offering. In Sir 47.2, the
consonants מקדש correspond to the Greek noun.
Peters, Lévi, and Segal all suggest שלם here, and
indeed, some word for sacrifice or an offering
seems appropriate.[135] Smend calls the Greek a "free
translation," but gives no explanation for the
translation.[136] In fact, if the translator read the
word as a pual, מְקֻדָּשׁ, in the sense of "something
consecrated," this might have suggested σωτήριον.
The pual does occur in the MT in this sense
concerning priests (2 Chr 26.18; Ezek 48.11),
things (2 Chr 31.6), feasts (Ezr 3.5), and warriors
(Isa 13.3).[137]

3.2.2.1d SUMMARY

The foregoing evidence falls short of
establishing the translator's overall lexical
agreement with the Greek Pentateuch. It certainly
seems probable that some words that are unusual, or
even neologisms, in the OG would have become
standard Jewish-Greek vocabulary by the second
century BCE, and their use would not necessarily
indicate dependence on the OG, even though the
equivalents originally may have gained acceptance
in that translation. Further, it seems likely that
some of these words may have been used in liturgy
or school contexts and that the translator knew
this "translation vocabulary" (e.g., νόμος/תורה,
συναγωγή/עדה). It might be wondered, for some
words, how much latitude the translator had for
variety, and thus, some equivalents might only be

coincidentally the same as the OG. For the grandson, other words are used with slightly different
nuances from the OG. Finally, the context of a
passage may have reminded the grandson of familiar
passages, and consequently, the use of "biblical"
equivalents in such cases could represent true
dependence. It seems likely, for example, that the
translator of Sir would have known biblically based
Greek traditions about Noah from which the
κατακλυσμός/מבול equivalence may have derived. If
he did depend on the OG from time to time, he does
not appear to have done so consistently as evidenced by his use of ἐπώμις. The way the terms
listed by Tov in his study are used in the Greek
Sir indicates a clear flexibility of use relative
to the OG.

3.2.2.2 THE WORK OF FRANZ REITERER

In the concluding section of his study,
Reiterer lists Greek words in Sir that: (1) occur
in only one book of the OG; (2) occur in two books
of the OG; (3) occur in three books of the OG.[138]
These lists provide another basis from which to
examine the grandson's alleged dependence on these
Greek translations. If he used the OG as a dictionary, one might expect a large percentage of these
infrequent words to reflect the same Hebrew
equivalents as their OG counterparts. By the very
nature of Reiterer's study these lists include, on
the whole, fewer technical or special words than
did the study of Tov, and thus, the two works
complement one another on this issue. The format of
this section is the same as the preceding one. The
following chart gives a summary of the results.

TABLE 3 - REITERER'S LIST OF INFREQUENT WORDS IN SIR

Total	100% = OG	Part = OG	None = OG	??
45	15	2	25	3

3.2.2.2a SAME EQUIVALENT AS THE OG

a. γεώργιον ("field") = עבדה 27.6

The only occurrence of this word is in a verse
that the grandson has rendered in a slightly
different way from the intention of the Hebrew.[139]
In 27.6, the neuter γεώργιον, which usually means
"a field," seems to have the meaning "cultivation,"
which is the usual meaning of the feminine
γεωργία.[140] The Hebrew Sir has עבדה, meaning
"working" or "cultivation." In the Hebrew scriptures the root עבד also has the equivalent
γεώργιον in Gen 26.14. In that verse, however, BDB
takes the word to mean "household servants," even
though the context concerns Isaac who owns many
flocks and herds.[141] Perhaps the translator of
Genesis understood עבדה in this context in the
sense of "cultivation" and consequently used
γεώργιον "field." Apparently the grandson has
vocalized the word עֲבָדָה, as in Gen 26.14, and
rendered it the same way. Thus, this could be a
case where an unusual rendering of a word in the OG
is perpetuated in a later translation. The other
occurrences of γεώργιον in the OG are found in Jer
51.23 and often in Proverbs, none of which render

עבדה. There are no parallel contexts between them
and Sir. The feminine noun γεωργία does occur in
Sir 7.15 where it renders עבדה in parallel with
מלאכה and indicates some sort of labor.

b. γλύμμα ("engraved figure") = פתוחי 45.11; NE
   38.27

   In Sir, this term is used in the middle of the
description of the ephod and parallels its use in
Exodus 28. The phrase פתוחי חותם is rendered
γλύμματος σφραγῖδος in Sir just as it is in Exod
28.11. The contexts of Sir and Exodus are the same
and probably represent some sort of dependence on
the Hebrew and Greek traditions about Aaron.[142] In
the remainder of the Hebrew scriptures, γλύμμα
occurs in Isa 45.29 and 60.18 where the contexts
are totally unrelated to that of Sir.

c. ἐλευθερία ("freedom") = חופש 7.21; NE 33.26

   In only one place in Sir does the Greek term
occur with a corresponding Hebrew, and it reflects
the same Hebrew-Greek pair as in Lev 19.20. In both
instances, the context concerns the freeing of
slaves. The Hebrew of Leviticus has the feminine
noun חפשה, while Sir has the participle חופש. Even
though the contexts are similar, the use of
ἐλευθερία is natural, and it could have easily
been arrived at independently by the translator of
Sir and the translator of Leviticus. The word would
also be natural in ethical contexts concerning the
freeing or treatment of slaves. The grandson's
translation reflects the same translation
equivalents as the OG, but no clear decision can be
made as to dependence on the Leviticus passage.

d. κλώθω ("spin") = שזר 45.11

In a text concerning Aaron's priestly clothes,
the phrase חולעת שני is used to describe material
for making the ephod and the breastplate. There are
a number of places in the Pentateuch where this
Hebrew phrase occurs with specific reference to the
ephod and breastplate, although the word order is
reversed from that of Sir. In each instance in
Exodus and Leviticus, κεκλώσμενος corresponds to
שני as in Sir. As Reiterer observes, this translation places Sir in the tradition of the OG for
this term.[143] For חולעת, Sir uses the term κόκκος,
not κόκκινος, as in the translation of the
Pentateuch. κόκκος in the OG only appears in Lam
4.5, rendering חולעת. κλώθω is also used in the OG
to render משזר in the phrase שש משזר.

e. κλῶσμα ("cord") = פחיל 6.30

In Num 15.38, in a description of the tassels
on the corners of Israelite garments, we read,
"Throughout the generations to come you are to make
tassels on the corners of your garments with a blue
cord on each tassel. You will have these tassels to
look at and so you will remember all the commandments of the Lord. . . ." In Sir 6.30, Ben Sira has
deliberately chosen פחיל תכלח to describe the bonds
with which wisdom binds her adherent. The OG phrase
κλῶσμα ὑακίνθου has also been used by the
translator, who successfully transfers the image
into Greek. As Snaith comments about the Hebrew,

"it is difficult to find any other reason for the
use of this phrase in this particular context other
than that Ben Sira is using a quotation to point
out the close link between Wisdom and the
requirements of Torah." The same could likely be
said of his grandson.[144]

3.2.2.2b OG AND NON-OG EQUIVALENTS

In the lists of terms that Reiterer gives,
there are only two cases from the Pentateuch that
have both OG and non-OG equivalents. Both are given
here.

a. συμβολοκοπέω* ("given to feasting") = חמב? 9.9;
   זולל 18.33

Only three occurrences of συμβολοκοπέω are
given by Liddell and Scott; the occurrences in Sir
are not listed.[145] Apparently, it was coined by the
translator of Deuteronomy who, in 21.20 of that
book, uses the term to translate זולל ("glutton").
Philo, in On Drunkenness 1.14(1.359), cites the
Deuteronomy passage and then etymologizes the word.

The only other occurrences of this term are
Sir 9.9 and 18.33. In Sir 9.9, a caution is given
about relationships with married women. The Greek
συμβολοκοπέω stands in place of חמב in MS B, but
could possibly render חמם.[146] In that case, the
Greek would somewhat loosely render the idea of
mixing wine. In 18.33, the Hebrew Sir uses the same
phrase as Deut 21.20, זולל וסובא. The OG has
συμβολοκοπῶν οἰνοφλυγεῖ. Sir, however, renders the
phrase πτωχὸς συμβολοκοπῶν ἐκ δανεισμοῦ. Smend
argues that the additional πτωχός comes from the

idea of poverty in the previous verse and that ἐκ
δανεισμοῦ is an addition. Thus, the translator
took זולל and טובה as synonyms, and he rendered
them by one word.[147] Consequently, even though the
זולל/συμβολοκοπέω equivalence is the same as Deut
21.20, it is difficult to accept that the translator
of Sir depended on the Deuteronomy passage for his
translation of 18.33.

b. χολέρα ("cholera") = צער? 31.23; זרא 37.30

צער ("pain") is probably the equivalent of
χολέρα in Sir 31.23. As many of the commentators
point out, the colon containing χολέρα appears too
long, especially since חשניק ("choke") has no
equivalent in Greek. Smend suggests that perhaps
the Greek read both words as χολέρα, but he leans
toward חשניק as an addition to the phrase. Segal
suggests that צער is a corruption of זרא, which is
the equivalent of χολέρα in Sir 37.30 and Num
11.20.[148] צער seems to fit well here, however, and
I am reluctant to accept a change in the parent
text of the Greek. In 37.30, זרא ("loathsome") is
the equivalent of χολέρα, as it is in Num 11.20,
but the two contexts are different, and no longer
parallel exists.

3.2.2.2c NON-OG TRANSLATION EQUIVALENTS

A large number of terms listed by Reiterer do
not use the OG equivalent at all in Sir. Some
examples are discussed below.

a. ἀποτίνω ("repay") = משלם 8.13; NE 20.12

Sir 8.13 comes in the middle of a discussion
concerning lending and borrowing. Here משלם, ("one
who pays") is very appropriately translated by
ἀποτίνω. In the OG, this verb in the middle voice
renders חטא in the piel meaning "to bear a loss"
(Gen 31.39), and in Ps 68(69).5, also in the middle
voice, it corresponds to אשיב ("I will give back").
There are no contextual parallels between the OG
and Sir, and the conclusion is that the grandson
used this term independently of any specific OG
influence.

b. ἐπίχαρμα ("malignant joy") = שמחה 6.4, 42.11?;
   NE 18.31

The only occurrence of the Greek word in the
OG is Exod 32.25 where שמצה, a hapax legomenon in
the MT, is its Hebrew equivalent. BDB defines שמצה
as "whisper, derision."[149] The phrase שמצה בקמיהם
is rendered ἐπίχαρμα τοῖς ὑπεναντίοις in Exodus.
Greek Sir uses a similar phrase, ἐπίχαρμα τῶν
ἐχθρῶν, three times. In 6.4, the phrase is שמחת
שונא in MS A. In 18.31, only שונא is visible in MS
C at the end of the verse. ἐπίχαρμα τῶν ἐχθρῶν
σου leads Segal to reconstruct שמחה here on the
basis of 6.4.[150] In 42.11, there seem to be two
different traditions preserved in the manuscript
witnesses. MS B and one of the marginal corrections
read פן תעשך שם סרה (B[mg] סרח). Masada preserves
only the ו of פן and the ח of תעשך. A second
marginal correction in MS B has a number of
abbreviations and reads פ'. תעי' שׁ' לא'.[151] This set
of abbreviations can be reconstructed with the help
of the Greek ἐπίχαρμα ἐχθροῖς, as well as the

other occurrences of ἐπίχαρμα, as פן חעשך שמחה
לאויבים.[152] In no case does the Greek phrase equal
that of Exod 32.25, and there does not seem to be
any influence of that passage on the grandson's use
of ἐπίχαρμα.

c. σκληροκαρδία ("hard hearted") = לב זדון 16.10

In 16.10, Ben Sira gives "arrogance of heart"
as the reason that an entire generation of
Israelites died without entering the promised land.
He also refers to this generation in 46.8 by his
reference to the 600,000 foot soldiers and a land
"flowing with milk and honey." Of this number, only
Joshua and Caleb remained to enter the promised
land. The Greek word in 16.10 is σκληροκαρδία.[153]
In Deut 10.16 and Jer 4.4, this term renders the
phrase ערלת לב ("uncircumcised of heart"). זדון לב
does occur once in the Hebrew scriptures, in Jer
49.16(30.10), where it is rendered ἰταμία καρδίας.

3.2.2.2d SUMMARY OF REITERER'S LISTS

The words examined from Reiterer's lists total
45. Of this number, 25 do not use the same
equivalent as the Greek Pentateuch; 15 use only the
OG equivalent; 2 use the OG equivalent for some,
but not all of their occurrences. Three cases were
too questionable to be decided. With respect to
lexical similarity, one cannot stop at the mere
listing of statistical agreement and disagreement.
As we noted with Tov's lists, there are some
equivalents, which, though the same, may only be so
coincidentally due to the fact that the lexical

choices available to the translators may have been
limited enough to cause them to use the same word.
For example, a word such as ἐλευθερία, which renders the Hebrew root חפש, could have been suggested
to the translator without any reference to the OG.
Also the context of the term plays an important
role in its analysis. Of the words discussed above,
two come from a description of Aaron's priestly
clothing (γλύμμα, κλώθω), and they have the same
equivalents as the description in Exodus. Terms of
this sort might be expected to become fixed early
in the Greek tradition, perhaps because of their
use in the OG. Yet, in the Greek of Sir different
equivalents from the OG are sometimes used for such
words (for example, see above under ἐπώμις). When
these variables are considered, the number of
agreements that genuinely indicate a similarity
with the tradition of translation of the OG is
further reduced.

3.2.3 CONCLUSIONS CONCERNING THE USE OF THE GREEK
      PENTATEUCH

    All the general statistics and examples given
above lead to the general conclusion that the
grandson was not overly dependent on the OG
Pentateuch. He certainly does not appear to use it
as a dictionary. His use of specific OG passages
indicates that when a particular passage in his
grandfather's Hebrew reminded him of some Greek
scriptural passage he was likely to use it in his
translation. This seems to be the most probable
explanation for his use of ἐπιστοιβάζω in Sir
8.3, where no clear contextual parallel to
Leviticus exists in the Hebrew. Further, the

grandson probably knew Greek traditions about the
ancestors of old which informed some of his
translations in the Praise of the Ancestors
section. This explanation helps to account for his
inconsistent use of OG terminology throughout this
section. If he were attempting to use the OG
consistently, his frequent departures from the
language of the OG in the Praise of the Ancestors
section would be difficult to explain. The almost
unanimous assumption by previous scholarship that
Ben Sira and his grandson had to be using textual
sources has colored the evaluation of the Hebrew
and Greek of Sir on these matters. In fact, the
evidence suggests that they were probably not using
written biblical sources exclusively in contexts
dealing with "biblical" subject matter.

On the more general issue of lexical equivalence, there is no consistent use of OG lexical
equivalences in the grandson's work. The most that
can be said is that sometimes he uses the same term
as the OG Pentateuch and sometimes he does not.
This lack of consistency is found for various types
of terms. His translation of cultic and technical
vocabulary, for example, shows no significant
difference in consistency from his renderings of
more general terms. Much of the similarity between
the OG and the Greek of the grandson could be
accounted for by a number of possibilities such as:
(1) the simple independent use of terms; (2) the
embedding of certain Greek terms in traditions
about certain figures, such as Phinehas; (3) the
influence of the OG within Alexandrian Jewish
circles, which resulted in words that were rare or
unusual when the OG translations were made becoming

more and more used in synagogue or worship contexts, or even in everyday speech; (4) the existence, by the time of the grandson, of a sort of
translation language perhaps derived from the OG,
which he knew and sometimes used. In any event, it
seems clear that the grandson was not a mechanical
imitator of the OG translations of the Pentateuch;
nor did he even fall consistently within the
tradition of translation of those books.

The results of the preceding examination of
lexical equivalents parallel those reached above
concerning the grandson's textual dependence on
specific passages from the OG Pentateuch. When one
considers the high regard in which the Pentateuch
was held in Jewish communities, his overall
inconsistent and comparatively infrequent use of
specific passages and lexical equivalents does not
make one optimistic about discovering any more
thorough or consistent use of non-Pentateuchal or
post-Pentateuchal translations for which
scholarship possesses less certain knowledge about
their dates and locales.

3.3 THE "FORMER AND LATTER" PROPHETS

3.3.1 INTRODUCTION

In contrast to the Pentateuch, there is much
less certainty concerning the makeup of the
category "Prophets." No canonical lists survive
from Ben Sira's time, nor are there writings that
give clear indications as to what books were
considered authoritative in that period. Thus, the
degree to which, during Ben Sira's time, this group

contained all the books of the נביאים as they were
later constituted in the Hebrew Bible is problematic.[154] Which books were in Greek translation and
available to Ben Sira's grandson is even more of a
problem. For the purposes of this section, the
question is held somewhat in abeyance by the fact
that I have looked for evidence of dependence on
the OG of all these books without making judgments,
such as Caird tried to do, concerning how any
demonstrable dependence impacts on the question of
the availability and canonicity of these books in
Greek at the time of the grandson. Included in this
section are the books of Joshua, Judges, 1 and 2
Samuel, 1 and 2 Kings, Isaiah, Jeremiah, Ezekiel,
and the Twelve (the so-called Minor Prophets).

The procedure used here is identical to that
used above for the Pentateuch. The same relationships have been explored, and the same criteria
have been used here as above. The overall figures
for this section can be charted as follows. (For an
explanation of the columns in the chart, see above
section 3.2.1, p. 144).

TABLE 4 - THE USE OF THE PROPHETS BY BEN SIRA AND HIS
         GRANDSON

Author	A	B	C
Schechter/Taylor	109	28	10
Eberharter	213	31	10
Middendorp[155]		22	6
Gasser	130	27	8
Total Number of Different Texts		40	14

The figures in this chart give the same
general results as we saw for the Pentateuch. They
cannot be taken with as much certainty, however.
If, for example, Ben Sira was dependent on a Hebrew
scriptural book which was not available in a Greek
translation to the grandson, then the numbers
listed above become slightly misleading. Therefore,
caution needs to be exercised when dealing with
these figures, but the examples discussed below do
point to the same general conclusions reached
previously for the Pentateuch.

In this section, there are many more problematic "dependences" of Ben Sira on the Hebrew
scriptures due to one major factor, difference in
context. Often a phrase that is rare in the Hebrew
scriptures is used by Ben Sira in a context
different from the scriptural context. Thus, some
ambiguity is present due to this difference. This,
of course, makes the conclusions in this section
generally less firm than above in section 2.

3.3.2 INFORMAL CITATIONS AND ALLUSIONS

3.3.2.1 HEBREW DEPENDENCE / GREEK INDEPENDENCE

Twenty-five passages fall into this category.
Of this number, 13 are outside the Praise of the
Ancestors section (6.4?; 6.9?; 11.1; 11.12; 13.12;
16.6?; 16.19?; 35,23?; 35.25?; 36.8; 40.9?; 40.27;
43.30?), and 12 are within this section (44.21;
45.11; 46.1?; 47.4; 47.18?; 47.24; 48.1; 48.18?;
48.24?; 49.7; 50.10; 50.13). Some selected examples
are discussed below.

a. Sir 11.1 ובאין נדיבים חשיבנו (MSS A, B)
   καὶ ἐν μέσῳ μεγιστάνων καθίσει αὐτόν

In the Hebrew Sir and 1 Sam 2.8, the hiphil of
ישׁב is used with נדיב. The contexts are also very
similar. 1 Sam 2.8 is part of the prayer of Hannah,
who, while blessing God, extols him as one who
"raises the poor. . . lifts the needy . . . and
makes them sit with nobles (נדיבים)." In Sir 11.1,
it is the wisdom of the poor person that enables
one to sit among princes (נדיבים). Thus, the Hebrew
Sir seems to be an informal citation of the Samuel
passage.[156]

The Greek of Sir is different from 1 Samuel in
the translation of נדיבים. The OG has δυναστῶν,
while Sir uses μεγιστάνων. The translation of ישׁב
by καθίζω is not unexpected and has no influence
on judgments about influence of the OG. If the OG
was available to the grandson, he shows no
dependence on it here.[157]

b. Sir 16.6 ובגוי חנף נצתה חמה (MSS A, B)
   καὶ ἐν ἔθνει ἀπειθεῖ ἐξεκαύθη ὀργή

The phrase גוי חנף appears only once in the
Hebrew scriptures (Isa 10.6). The verse in Sir
precedes a chronological list of wicked people whom
God punished. Ben Sira seems deliberately to have
borrowed this phrase from Isaiah as a general
description of wicked people.[158]

If the Hebrew is dependent on Isaiah, the
Greek is not. The OG of Isaiah has the phrase
ἔθνος ἄνομον, but Sir has ἔθνει ἀπειθεῖ. Of
the examples that were given for the Pentateuch,
only a very few of such short phrases were
translated in the same way as the OG, and the
conclusion seems likely that the grandson was not

even aware that they were derived originally from
scriptural texts.

c. Sir 40.27 ועל כל כבוד חפחה (MS M)
   καὶ ὑπὲρ πᾶσαν δόξαν ἐκάλυψεν αὐτοῦ

The Masada scroll represents the best form of
the text since it has ועל at the beginning of the
verse, which corresponds to καὶ ὑπέρ. The
reading וכן of MS B in place of ועל may well have
originated under the influence of the following
כל.[159] The entire phrase is almost a verbatim
parallel of Isa 4.5, כי על כל כבוד חפה. Although
the contexts are different, the closeness of the
wording between Sir and Isaiah point to Isa 4.5 as
the source of the phrase in the Hebrew Sir.

The Greek of Isaiah reads חפה as a form of the
verbal root חפה, and the translator rendered the
whole phrase as πάσῃ τῇ δόξῃ σκεπασθήσεται. Interestingly, the grandson also took חפחה as a form
from חפה, but translated ἐκάλυψεν αὐτόν.[160] He
apparently did not recognize the connection between
his grandfather's Hebrew and Isa 4.5.

d. Sir 47.24 ולכל רעה התמכר (MS B)
   καὶ πᾶσαν πονηρίαν ἐξεζήτησαν

The use of the phrase וכל רעה התמכר is
reminiscent of the similar phrases in 1 Kgs 21.20,
25 and 2 Kgs 17.17. In each place, the noun רעה is
used with the hithpael of מכר. The biblical passages, however, additionally have the infinitive
לעשות. The context also helps to establish the
connection between the Hebrew Sir and the Hebrew
scriptures. In 1 Kings 21 and Sir, the phrase is in
a context connected with Elijah. In the biblical

narrative, the phrase occurs in the story of
Naboth's vineyard. In 2 Kgs 17.17, it appears in
the context of the Israelites who gave their
children as offerings to Baal. The phrase occurs in
Sir directly before the section about Elijah (48.1-
11), and it serves as a sort of introduction to the
section. The arrival of the prophet in 48.1 (עד אשר
קם נביא) is necessitated by the people "selling
themselves to every evil thing."[161]

The Greek translation treats the phrase
differently from the OG. In the OG, πεπράσκω is
used in 1 Kgs 21.20 and 25, whereas Ben Sira's
grandson has ἐξεζήτησαν. There is no apparent
textual dependence of the Greek Sir on the OG of 1
Kings.

e. Sir 48.24 ברוח גבורה (MS B)
           πνεύματι μεγάλῳ

The use of ברוח גבורה in connection with
Isaiah makes it hard to resist the conclusion that
Ben Sira took this phrase from Isa 11.2. In the MT,
Isaiah speaks about the "shoot from the stem of
Jesse." He says that "the spirit of counsel and
might" (רוח עצה וגבורה) will be upon him. This is
the only occurrence in the Hebrew scriptures where
the terms רוח and גבורה are used in combination.
Although in the MT Isaiah does not use the phrase
of himself, in this instance it seems clear that
Ben Sira borrowed the phrase and applied it to the
prophet.

As far as the Greek is concerned, the translator of Isaiah has rendered גבורה by ἰσχύος.[162]
Ben Sira's grandson uses μεγάλῳ, treating גבורה
as an adjective rather than a noun. Where he does

treat גבורה as a noun, μεγαλεῖον is one of his
translation choices (cf. 42.21; 43.15). It appears
unlikely that the grandson is at all dependent on
the OG of Isaiah here.

f. Sir 49.7 לנחוש ולנחוץ ולהאביד להרס (MS B) /
ובן לבנת לנחע ולהשיב (MS B)
ἐκριζοῦν καὶ κακοῦν καὶ ἀπολλύειν
ὡσαύτως οἰκοδομεῖν καὶ καταφευτεύειν

The textual situation in Sir 49.7 is both
interesting and difficult. It is also very
characteristic of many of the texts found in this
section. The Hebrew text as it is extant in MS B
concerns the prophet Jeremiah, and the list of
infinitives is very close to that found in his call
(Jer 1.10). The only difference consists of an[163]
additional infinitive at the end of the list.
When compared to the Greek, it seems likely that
some harmonization toward the Jer 1.10 passage has
taken place during the course of the textual
transmission of the Hebrew. The Greek lacks any
equivalent for להרס, and the presence of this
infinitive probably is the result of harmonizing
activity.[164] Further, there is no corresponding
Greek for [להש]יב, which may indicate that it too
is a gloss, perhaps intended to fill out the structure of the verse.[165] Beyond these two "glosses,"
the Hebrew Sir still has five infinitives in common
with Jer 1.10: לנטע; לבנת; להאביד; לנחוץ; לנחוש.

The Greek Sir also shows some elements in
common with the OG of Jeremiah. As a translation of
לנחוש, the grandson has ἐκριζοῦν as does
Jeremiah. In Sir 3.9, however, נחש is used in the
Hebrew, and it is also represented by ἐκριζόω.
ἀπολλύειν is the translation להאביד as in

Jeremiah, but this pair also occurs elsewhere in
Sir (41.2). Finally, לנטע is rendered
καταφευτεύειν in Sir and Jeremiah.

Some differences also exist between the two
Greek texts. For לבנה, the grandson has the simplex
οἰκοδομεῖν, whereas Jeremiah has the compound
ἀνοικοδομεῖν, although this difference is somewhat mitigated by the fact that some manuscripts of
Jeremiah have the simplex. For לנחוץ, where
Jeremiah has ἀκατασκάπτειν, the grandson has
κακοῦν.[166] The disparity in meaning between לנחוץ
and κακοῦν has led some commentators to reject
לנחוץ as the Hebrew of Ben Sira and to reconstruct
להרע on the basis of its equivalence in Jer
31.28.[167] κακοῦν indeed seems to reflect a
different parent text from that extant in MS B. I
can see no clear exegetical reason for the grandson
to translate לנחוץ as κακοῦν unless he simply did
not know the word and was guessing at its meaning.

One further complication needs to be noted
here. In 49.7, where the Hebrew has והוא מרחם נוצר,
an allusion to the call of Jeremiah, the Greek has
καὶ αὐτὸς ἐν μήτρᾳ ἡγιάσθη. ἡγιάσθη is the
same verb used in Jer 1.5 to translate הקדשׁתי,
and thus, it may show an awareness on the part of
the grandson of Jeremiah 1. The use of ἁγιάζω to
render קדשׁ would be expected, however, and these
two roots are equivalents elsewhere in Sir.

This argument might have further bearing on
the text under discussion, in that one could argue
that the grandson was following his grandfather's
Hebrew in 49.7 and used the OG equivalents for
those infinitives that his grandfather's Hebrew had
in common with Jer 1.10. Those that were not in

common he simply translated independently, in this
case using κακοῦν (to render להרע[?]).[168]

This situation makes a firm decision on this
verse very difficult. It may well be that the
grandson was familiar with the call of Jeremiah,
and consequently, he used ἡγιάσθη, but translated
the infinitives without resorting to the OG. As I
noted, ἐκριζοῦν and ἀπολλύειν are used elsewhere
in Sir with the same Hebrew as 49.7. The use of
κακοῦν still remains the fly in the ointment. In
the end, I included this verse in this category
because: (1) even excepting the glosses, the Hebrew
Sir does seem to demonstrate a clear dependence on
Jer 1.10, and (2) even leaving out κακοῦν, the
relationship between the Greek of Sir and the OG of
Jeremiah is simply not unequivocal. I lean toward
the conclusion that the grandson was not dependent
on the OG here, although I do not hold this
position with a high level of confidence.

3.3.2.2 HEBREW DEPENDENCE / GREEK DEPENDENCE

Of the fourteen passages included in this
section, eight fall outside the Praise of the
Ancestors section (6.3, 7.11?, 14.17, 33.13?,
36.4?, 36.5, 36.8, 36.13?), and six are inside that
section (46.4?, 46.9, 48.10; 48.15, 48.20, 48.24?).
The evaluation of the texts included in this
section has one major difficulty. The possible ways
of construing the evidence for these passages does
not permit a high level of confidence in their
evaluations. The way that the grandson translates
many of the relevant Hebrew terms elsewhere in his
work suggests that some of these passages may be
independent translations that look similar to

passages in the OG. Other passages seem to be the
types of passages that might have come to the
grandson from contexts other than contact with the
written text. One possible example of this kind of
passage is Sir 36.5, כי אין אלהים זולחך, which
occurs in the MT in 2 Sam 7.22 and 1 Chr 17.20. The
Greek, ὅτι οὐκ ἔστιν θεὸς πλὴν σοῦ, could well have
been very familiar to the grandson from its use in
liturgy or worship, or some other similar context.
Furthermore, the translation equivalents used in
this phrase are not unusual for the grandson, and
they could have been used independently of the
Greek scriptural passages.[169] As a result, the
uncertainty accompanying judgments about passages
such as this one will necessarily be reflected in
the discussion of each example.

a. Sir 6.3 כעץ יבש (MS A)
       ὡς ξύλον ξηρόν

The phrase "as a dried up tree" is only used
once in the Hebrew scriptures (Isa 56.3) with the
meaning "lacking children" or "sexual impotence."
In Isaiah, the phrase refers to eunuchs who bemoan
their sexual inabilities.[170] Ben Sira has probably
gotten the phrase in its sexual connotation from
Isaiah, though a more general euphemistic use of
the phrase cannot be discounted.

The Greek translation in both Isaiah and Sir
is ξύλον ξηρόν. The context in Sir is not the
same as Isaiah, and the identical wording of the
grandson's Greek might seem to contradict the
general finding above that the he uses the OG when
he recognizes a phrase or verse in his grandfather's Hebrew as coming from the scriptures. In

this case, three different scenarios could explain
the situation: (1) the grandson recognized the
passage as coming from scripture; (2) he was aware
of some cliché or euphemistic use of the phrase;
(3) he independently translated the phrase the same
way as the translator of Isaiah.[171] The most that
can be said is that he uses the same Greek as
Isaiah.

b. Sir 14.17 כל בשׂר כבגד יבלה (MS A)
πᾶσα σὰρξ ὡς ἱμάτιον παλαιοῦται

Ben Sira's statement that "all flesh grows old
like a garment" is very similar to Isa 50.9 and
51.6.[172] In Sir, the phrase is an analogy to the
inevitability of death, whereas in Isaiah it refers
first to the demise of the prophet's opponents
(50.9) and then as an illustration of the end of
the earth (51.6).[173] With respect to this statement, there is some ambiguity about the relation of
the Hebrew to the Hebrew scriptures. The phrase
seems to be just the sort of saying that could
easily have become proverbial, and thus, it would
not prove a dependence on the Hebrew scriptures.
Therefore, it is not certain that the Hebrew Sir
shows dependence on Isaiah; the phrase may well
have derived from a proverb that originated in the
Isaiah passages, or even gave rise to them.

The grandson renders the Hebrew in the same
way as the OG of Isaiah, using ἱμάτιον for בגד
and παλαιόω for בלה. The other uses of the words
in the Greek Sir do not provide any additional
assistance.[174] This situation for the Greek
presents the same options here as for Sir 6.3
discussed above.

c. Sir 36.8 שפך חמתך (MS B)
    ἔκχεον ὀργήν

In the prayer for Israel contained in 36.1-17,
Snaith argues that there are a number of passages
taken from the Hebrew Bible.[175] One of these
phrases, שפך חמתך, is found in Jer 10.25. In both
Sir and Jeremiah, the plea is for God to pour out
his anger on the nations who are against Israel.
The likelihood, based on terminology and context,
is high that Ben Sira borrowed this phrase from
Jeremiah.

The Greek of the grandson is a little more
difficult to evaluate. He translates the phrase
ἔκχεον ὀργήν, which is the same as in Codex
Alexandrinus for Jer 10.25. Thus, the Greek of Ben
Sira's grandson could reflect a tradition of the OG
of Jeremiah. On the other hand, the Greek equivalents for this phrase are fairly standard for the
grandson. שפך is rendered by either ἐκχέω or χέω
in all its occurrences in Sir (see 20.13; 30.18;
43.19), and ὀργή is used along with θυμός as a
term translating Hebrew terms for anger.[176] Thus,
this translation could represent an independent
translation on the part of the grandson. In
addition, if שפך חמתך is part of a larger standard
prayer as Snaith and Lehmann suggest, then its
translation may also have gained some currency in
Jewish communities and exercised an influence on
the grandson's rendering.

d. Sir 46.9 להדריכם על במתי ארץ (MS B)
    ἐπιβῆναι αὐτὸν ἐπὶ τὸ ὕψος τῆς γῆς

In its context in the Hebrew Sir, this phrase
refers to Caleb and implies that God caused him to

be dominant over the land of Israel. The phrase דרך
על במתי ארץ occurs twice in the Hebrew scriptures,
in Amos 4.13 and Mic 1.3, with reference to God.
The similarity of the phrase in the Hebrew Sir to
Amos and Micah may well have been an attempt on the
part of Ben Sira to bring the image of God's
dominion over creation into a connection with God
giving lasting strength to Caleb. It seems likely
to me that Ben Sira borrowed the scriptural phrase
in this verse.[177]

The Greek of Sir uses the same translation
equivalents in 46.9 as does the translator of the
Minor Prophets. The two key pairs are להדריך/
ἐπιβῆναι and במתי/τὸ ὕψος. A similar phrase
to 46.9 occurs in Sir 9.2 where the Hebrew has
להדריכה על במותיך and comes in the context of a
woman "treading on your high places." In this
instance, ἐπιβαίνω translates להדריך as in
46.9.[178]   The grandson, in 9.2, uses ἰσχύς for
במות and seems to have rendered the Hebrew
exegetically.[179]

The possibility remains then that the grandson
was familiar with the rendering of להדריך על במתי
ארץ in Amos and Micah and that he relied on it for
his translation. It may be equally as likely that
he has translated independently of the OG. The fact
that ὕψος is used elsewhere for מרום in Sir (see
16.17; 43.1, 8) may, on the one hand, push one
toward the latter conclusion. On the other hand,
the use of ἰσχύς for במתי in 9.2 rather than
ὕψος mitigates this leaning somewhat. No high
level of confidence is possible here.

e. Sir 48.10 להשיב לב אבות על בנים (MS B)
            ἐπιστρέψαι καρδίαν πατρὸς πρὸς υἱόν

In his section on Elijah, Ben Sira uses a
phrase that is very close to Mal 3.24, a verse that
also concerns Elijah. The passage in Sir has an
eschatological thrust just as in Malachi where
Elijah waits to return in order to still God's
anger. Sir 48.10 begins with the participle הכתוב,
which some scholars argue is a formula citandi that
refers explicitly to Malachi.[180] Beentjes, however,
convincingly argues that הכתוב is not an introductory formula, but part of the longer structure
of the Elijah section.[181] Each verse in the section
from v 5 through v 10 begins with an articulated
participle that describes Elijah. הכתוב is part of
this series. The Greek, ὁ καταγραφείς, clearly
takes the participle as referring to Elijah. The
Hebrew here is not a formula, but part of the
continuing description of the prophet and might be
translated, "who was surely appointed for the
time."[182] Thus, it is accurate to say that Ben Sira
contains no explicit citations of the Hebrew
scriptures. This conclusion does not mean, however,
that . . . להשׁיב is not dependent on Malachi. I
would argue, based on similarity of context and
wording, that it is, in fact, dependent on Mal
3.24; it simply is not quoted explicitly by Ben
Sira.

The major difference between Greek Sir and the
Greek Malachi is the use of a different verb to
translate להשׁיב. The grandson has chosen
ἐπιστρέψαι, whereas the OG has ἀποκαταστήσει.
The grandson does use καταστῆσαι in the next
colon, but there it renders להכין. Both Sir and
Malachi have καρδία in the singular and πρὸς
υἱόν. The context of the passage, which deals

with Elijah, and the similarity of the wording may
indicate a dependence of the grandson on the
Malachi passage. If this is the case, the
difference in verbs may suggest that the grandson[183]
knew a variant form of the Malachi passage.

3.3.2.3 HEBREW INDEPENDENCE / GREEK DEPENDENCE

As was the case with the Pentateuch, there are very
few passages that reflect the grandson's use of the
OG while the Hebrew shows no corresponding dependence on the Hebrew scriptures.

a. Sir 37.10 אל תועץ עם חמיך (MS D)
                μὴ βουλεύου μετὰ τοῦ ὑποβλεπομένου σε

This verse is a good example of how difficult
these passages are to evaluate. The Hebrew of the
colon is very difficult to understand because of
חמיך. Box and Oesterley adopt Lévi's suggested
emendation to קמיך, "those opposed to you." Skehan
and Di Lella, as well as other commentators, resist
the effort to emend the text and try to make sense
of it as it stands. Two possibilities seem the most
likely. First, the Latin cum socero tua reflects an
understanding of "father-in-law." The Hebrew could
be read in this way, and this is the sense that
Skehan and Di Lella give in their translation.
Second, the Greek translation τοῦ ὑποβλεπομένου
indicates that the grandson read the word from the
Aramaic root חמא or חמי, "to see," and that he
understood the word as "to look askance." This
interpretation parallels the מקנא in the second
colon of the verse.[184]

The use of ὑποβλέπω is interesting when one
attempts to understand any possible relation of the

grandson's Greek translation to the OG. The verb
itself only occurs one time in the OG (1 Sam 18.9)
where Saul is said to "look upon David with
suspicion" (ὑποβλεπόμενος τὸν Δαυιδ). If the grandson read חמי֫ך from the Aramaic חמא, ὑποβλέπω may
have been suggested to him as meaning to view
someone with evil intent. If, in addition, he knew
the story of David and Saul, he could have used the
word purposely to bring in the image of Saul's
suspicion of David. The grandson would be subtly
giving an injunction against taking counsel with an
untrustworthy person like Saul who sought David's
life. Though one cannot be certain here, the rarity
of the Greek word in the OG suggests a conscious
use of the biblical image of David and Saul. On the
other hand, the word itself is not so rare in Greek
literature outside of the OG, and it could have
been used independently of the OG.

b. Sir 48.21 ויהמם במגפה (MS B)
      καὶ ἐξέτριψεν αὐτοὺς ὁ ἄγγελος αὐτοῦ

This text is interesting for the range of
possibilities that it demonstrates. Ben Sira, in
his description of Hezekiah, clearly refers to
Sennacherib's siege of Jerusalem and the tradition
of his army's defeat by the God of the Israelites
when he says, "And he (God) confused them by the
plague." The Hebrew Sir, however, does not reflect
the story as it is found in either 2 Kgs 17.35 or
Isa 37.36. In both of those places the Hebrew is
ויצא מלאך יהוה ויך במחנה, and no מגפה is mentioned.
      The Greek, for its part, in the place of במגפה
has ὁ ἄγγελος αὐτοῦ, which clearly reflects the
2 Kings/Isaiah tradition. The verb in the grand-

son's translation, ἐξέτριψεν, does not appear in
the scriptural tradition of the story. Is the
grandson using the OG here or not?

The story of Sennacherib's retreat from
Jerusalem was undoubtedly well known and popular.
It is reviewed in brief in 1 Macc 7.41 and 2 Macc
8.19.[185] Both passages refer to the "angel of the
Lord." It could well be that Ben Sira's grandson
knew this story and substituted the crucial element
ὁ ἄγγελος αὐτοῦ for במגפה.[186] Box and Oesterley
state that the Greek of the grandson is "the better
reading," and they suggest that he had מלאך in his
parent text.[187] I consider this unlikely. First,
the Syriac מחוחה, "wound," seems to presuppose a
parent text like מגפה.[188] Second, if מלאך were the
original Hebrew, I find it difficult to understand
how the alternative במגפה arose. It is not widely
used in the Hebrew scriptures. In fact, I would
expect the process to go in the reverse direction,
from מגפה to מלאך. By this argument, however, I do
not mean to suggest that the grandson is relying
specifically on the text of the OG, but only that
he knows the story with the angel as a critical
component. Whether he took it from 2 Kings/Isaiah
or learned it in some other context is impossible
to say.

3.3.2.4 PASSAGES IN HEBREW AND GREEK SIR THAT
        SUMMARIZE BIBLICAL TRADITIONS

a. Sir 47.12-22

This section, which treats Solomon, is a
litany of his deeds and their consequences. Ben
Sira shows practically no textual dependence on the

Hebrew scriptures at all in this section. Nonethe-
less, he knows many of the traditions reported
about Solomon in 1 Kings. He mentions: Solomon's
dwelling in safety; the building of the temple; his
wisdom and subsequent fame; his wealth; his wives;
the splitting of the kingdom under Rehoboam. In
only one case, 47.18cd, does Ben Sira use any
language that is even close to the Hebrew
scriptural traditions about Solomon.[189]

The grandson's Greek translation for these
verses, although exhibiting some exegetical
tendencies, follows the Hebrew Sir and does not use
terminology from 1 Kings. As we saw above, this
summary technique was used by Ben Sira for
pentateuchal figures as well, and in those cases,
the grandson used few if any pentateuchal texts in
his translation. This tendency continues in the
prophetic materials, and it is a characteristic of
both Ben Sira and his grandson throughout the
Praise of the Ancestors section.

3.3.2.5 LATER HARMONIZATION OF THE HEBREW SIR TO THE HEBREW BIBLE

a. Sir 16.19 קצבי הרים וימודי חבל (MS A)
τὰ ὄρη καὶ τὰ θεμέλια τῆς γῆς

In this text, the Hebrew of MS A has an
additional word when compared to the Greek. As it
is extant, קצבי הרים has only τὰ ὄρη as an
equivalent. The phrase occurs in the Hebrew
scriptures in Jonah 2.7 as part of the phrase לקצבי
הרים ירדתי. Some commentators seem to accept the
originality of the phrase due to its occurrence in
Jonah; others do not comment on the phrase at
all.[190]   One explanation for the extra Hebrew phrase

might be that since קצב only occurs three times in
the entire Hebrew Bible, the grandson did not
understand its meaning and did not render it. The
fact, however, that the Syriac has a translation of
קצבי and that the parallel phrase ויסודי תבל has
two nouns in construct may argue for the originality of קצבי. Yet, as H. P. Rüger has argued,[191]
the Syriac often translates a younger form of the
Hebrew, a form in which the harmonization could
have already taken place. Therefore, the evidence
of the Syriac is not convincing in and of itself.
As far as rare or difficult words are concerned,
the grandson does not hesitate to attempt translations of them elsewhere. We saw in Chapter 2
concerning quantitatively shorter translations that
the Greek Sir represents a rather free approach,
which certainly increases the uncertainty
surrounding this example, in that, the grandson
does translate two Hebrew words by one Greek word
in other places.[192]

The argument that the parallelism between קצבי
and ויסודי supports the originality of קצבי may
have some validity, but that parallel structure
could have been created by a scribe who was
familiar with Jonah and who was uncomfortable with
the structure of the verse as it stood. The image
of Ben Sira's text, that of God shaking the
mountains and the foundations of the earth, could
well have suggested the phrase to a scribe who knew
the Hebrew Bible well. All these reasons indicate
that for this passage the possibility of a
harmonization can be raised with some legitimacy.

b. Sir 40.30 ובקרבו כאש תבער (MS M) /
             וקרבו תבער כמו אש (MS B)
             καὶ ἐν κοιλίᾳ αὐτοῦ πῦρ καήσεται

The discovery of the Masada scroll clarified
the textual situation of this verse considerably.
The reading of MS B, ‏וקרבו חבער כמו אש‎, has a word
order different from the Greek, but similar to the
wording of Ps 79.5 and Ps 89.47 where God's
jealousy (79.5) and his wrath (89.47) burn like
fire. The text of MS B(mg), ‏כאש בערת‎, is close to
the Masada reading and is the same phrase found in
Jer 20.9. MS B(mg) differs from the Greek in that
the participle ‏בערת‎ modifies ‏אש‎, whereas the Greek
has a finite verb καήσεται. The Masada text is the
closest to the Greek, and it shows that only two
consonants had to be displaced (the placing of ‏ב‎ at
the beginning of the word and the change of ‏ת‎ to ‏י‎)
in order for the text to read like Jer 20.9 (MS
B[mg]). The Masada text itself is the same as Ps
83.15, which speaks of a burning forest (‏יער‎).

The question then arises, if the Greek is a
translation of the Masada text, is the Masada text
already itself a harmonization to an MT text? The
Greek has no ὡς in place of ‏ב‎ , and it seems to
concretize the simile of the Hebrew. The existence
of ‏ב‎ in all the extant Hebrew texts leads me to
believe that it was original, which suggests the
possibility that the original Hebrew of Ben Sira
was dependent on Psalms for this verse.[193]

c. Sir 42.6 ‏ידים רבות‎ (MS M) /
             ‏ידים רפות‎ (MSS B, B[mg])
             χεῖρες πολλαί

In this phrase, πολλαί clearly reflects the
‏רבות‎ of the Masada scroll. ‏ידים רפות‎ ("feeble
hands") is most likely a harmonization to Isa 35.3
(cf. also Job 4.3) where the strengthening of weak

hands is mentioned. The graphic similarity of ס and
ב seems to have been the reason for this harmonization. Almost all of the commentators prior to the
discovery of the Masada scroll correctly reconstructed רבוח in this place.[194]

3.3.2.6 SUMMARY

The picture given above confirms the picture
that emerged for the Pentateuch with the additional
factor that there is more uncertainty in this
section regarding decisions concerning both the
Hebrew and Greek of Ben Sira. Many of the passages
discussed above illustrate the often ambiguous
relationship between Ben Sira's Hebrew and the
scriptural prophetic corpus. Oftentimes, it seems
that Ben Sira may have been drawing on traditional
material that was acquired through means other than
dependence on written scriptural accounts. The
Greek of the grandson also reflects the OG wording
of the prophetic books infrequently, and in those
cases where it does have similar wording, other
possible explanations of the evidence increase the
uncertainty as to the relationship between the OG
and the grandson's translation.

3.3.3 LEXICAL EQUIVALENTS

As with the Pentateuch, we also need to
examine the vocabulary of the grandson's translation to see if he has any general reliance on the
translation equivalents found in the OG translations of the prophetic corpus. In this section, I
will continue to use Reiterer's work as a basis for

discussion. Since Tov's study specifically targeted
the Pentateuch, it has no bearing on the discussion
of these materials. The following chart summarizes
the data for Reiterer in this section.

TABLE 5 - REITERER'S LIST OF INFREQUENT WORDS IN SIR

TOTAL	100% = G	Part = OG	None = OG
42	13	3	26

3.3.3.1 SAME EQUIVALENT AS THE OG

a. ἀλισγέω ("pollute") = מעגל (מגעל) 40.29

The commentators unanimously agree that a
metathesis of the ג and ע has taken place, and the
Hebrew should read מגעל. In Sir, the word refers to
the soul that indulges in luxurious foods (מטעמים).
The Greek rendering ἀλισγήσει is somewhat
unusual. The term means "pollute," but it is
exceedingly rare. Liddell and Scott list it as only
in Jewish-Greek.[195] It occurs in Mal 1.7, 12, in
reference to defiled bread that has been placed
upon the altar. There it translates the root גאל,
related to the root געל, which also means "pollute,
defile."[196] Both געל and גאל are rendered by a
number of different Greek words in the OG so that
the use of this rare Greek word is notable.[197] This
commonality may mean nothing more, however, than
that ἀλισγέω, due to its use in the OG, has
gained greater currency in the language. The
contexts of Sir and Malachi are different, and I do
not think that the case can be made for any wider
textual dependence on the OG.

b. ἀντίζηλος ("rival") = צרתה 37.11; NE 26.6

The sense of the Hebrew word "rival" here
clearly concerns a woman taken as a second wife,[198]
and it is probably a technical term. In the MT, it
only occurs in 1 Sam 1.6, where it refers to
Peninnah, the wife of Elkanah, who is the "rival"
of Elkanah's other wife, Hannah, the mother of
Samuel. The Greek translations of 1 Samuel and Sir
use the term ἀντίζηλος. The related verb צרר,
which occurs in Leviticus, is broken up in the OG
into a verb and object, λήμψῃ ἀντίζηλον, and thus,
shows the technical use of the noun. Its continued
use as a translation of צרה in 1 Samuel and Sir is
not surprising and would argue against broader
textual dependence of the grandson on the biblical
passages.[199]

c. ἄτιμος ("dishonor") = נקלה 10.19

The use of ἄτιμος as a translation of נקלה
is only found once in the OG. The translator of
Isaiah uses the Greek term twice, once for נקלה
(3.5) and once for בזה (53.3). Isa 3.5 has no
relation to the text of Sir; Isaiah is speaking of
a dishonorable person, whereas Sir refers to a
dishonorable race (זרע). The noun ἀτιμία is by
far the most frequent equivalent for קלון in the
MT,[200] but the clear need for an adjective in this
passage may have occasioned the use of ἄτιμος by
the grandson. As a result, no clear dependence on
the OG of Isaiah by the grandson can be
demonstrated.[201]

d. ὄναγρος ("wild ass") = פרא 13.19

ὄναγρος, a shortened form of ὄνος ἄγριος,
occurs twice in the OG where it renders פרא as here
in Sir.[202] The longer ὄνος ἄγριος is the more
frequent form in the OG.[203]

This Greek term probably represents a standard
Greek equivalent for פרא, even though it is less
common than the longer form. The context of the
passage in Sir differs from the OG texts that use
ὄναγρος, and thus, it probably does not represent
textual dependence on the OG.

e. σπινθήρ ("spark") = נצוץ 11.32, 42.22

The occurrence of נצוץ in Sir 11.32 is
relatively unproblematic, and it is translated
σπινθῆρος πυρός ("spark of fire"). This rendering
is the same as that found in Isa 1.31, but the
contexts are different. Isaiah concerns the works
of God; Sir refers to villains.[204]

The second occurrence is a little more
problematic. The Hebrew text is extant only in the
Masada scroll. In the scroll, ניצוץ is spelled
plene and corresponds to σπινθῆρος. The difficulty
concerns the meaning of the phrase that Yadin
reconstructs, עד ניצוץ וחזות נראה.[205] John
Strugnell, in his review of Yadin, observes that
ניצוץ is not parallel to colon a, which speaks of
the loveliness of God's works, and it does not fit
the general context. He proposes to divide the
letters and to read עדני צוץ, "delightful to gaze

upon."[206] This may well fit the context better, but
as both Strugnell and G. Prato note, the word
division עד ניצוע is evidenced at an early stage,
namely, in the Greek.[207] Yet, there is no clear
indication that this translation is dependent on
the passage from Isaiah.

f. ὕαινα ("hyena") = צבוע 13.18

Although the biblical Hebrew term צבוע means
"variegated" or "colored," it clearly comes to
refer to a hyena or leopard in post-biblical
Hebrew,[208] and that is the way both the translator
of Jeremiah and the grandson of Ben Sira understood
it. In Jeremiah, עיט צבוע seems to refer to some
type of bird of prey. In the Hebrew Sir, however,
the use of צבוע with כלב indicates something more
on the order of a hyena or leopard, consistent with
post-biblical usage. Clearly, by the time of the
Greek translations of Jeremiah and Ben Sira, צבוע
was more specific than "spotted" or "variegated;"
it referred to a particular animal, which was
ὕαινα in Greek. As a result, the two translations
were probably using standard equivalences rather
than the grandson being dependent on the OG of
Jeremiah.

g. φυσάω ("blow") = נפוח 43.4; NE 28.12

This entire verse is difficult, as Lévi
noted,[209] but we are primarily concerned with the
two opening words, נפוח כור ("a furnace that is
blown upon"). The Hebrew Sir is here likening the
sun's rays to a hot furnace (cf. 43.3b and 4b) that

is continually kept hot by blowing. The grandson
has apparently taken the word in the active voice,
נופח, and translated φυσῶν (perhaps meaning
"glowing"?). This same translation equivalence only
occurs once in the OG, in Isa 54.16. The Hebrew of
Isaiah, נפח באש פחם, refers to a smith who blows
over coals.[210] Although the agreement in translation equivalence between Isaiah and Sir coincides
in an unusual pair, the use of compounds of φυσάω
elsewhere in the OG to translate נפח also permits
the conclusion that the simplex was used
independently by the two translators.[211]

3.3.3.2 OG AND NON-OG EQUIVALENTS

a. παρθενία ("virginity") = נעורים 15.2; בחוליה
42.10

In Jer 3.4, the translator uses παρθενία to
translate נערים. The grandson does the same thing
in Sir 15.2. In Jeremiah, אלוף נערי אחה, which
refers to God, is translated ἀρχηγὸν τῆς παρθενίας
σου. The word in Sir refers to a wife, and it was
most likely intended to mean "virginity." This
meaning is confirmed by the grandson's use of the
word in 42.10, where, speaking of daughters, Ben
Sira writes בבחוליה פן תחל ("in her virginity lest
she be defiled"). In addition, נעורים is used
elsewhere in Sir in a more generic sense meaning
"youth." None of these cases is connected with
wives or sexual relations, and in each case,
νεοτής is the translation.[212] This internal
coherence of the uses of παρθενία and νεοτής
combined with the difference in context between
Jeremiah and Sir make it unlikely that the grandson
was using the Jeremiah passage here.

3.3.3.3 NON-OG EQUIVALENTS

a. θυμώδης ("hot-tempered") = בעל אף 8.16; NE 28.8

The Greek word only occurs once in Sir with a
Hebrew equivalent, in 8.16, as part of an admoni-
tion not to fight with a wrathful person. It also
appears infrequently in the OG. It occurs in Jer
30(37).23 as a rendering of חמה, and the phrase
ἀνὴρ θυμώδης appears a number of times in
Proverbs as a translation of איש חמה. Given the
contextual differences, there is probably no
connection between Sir, on the one hand, and
Jeremiah and Proverbs, on the other.

b. καρτερέω ("restrain") = יתכלכל 12.15

In 12.15, Ben Sira warns about impious people
and remarks that "as long as you stand, he [the
impious person] does not reveal himself, but if you
fall, he will not restrain himself." The word that
means "restrain oneself" is יתכלכל, which is
translated as κατερήσῃ. The Greek word is used
only once in the OG translations with the meaning
"to restrain oneself." In the OG of Isa 42.14, God
says that he has restrained himself for a long
time. The MT has אתאפק. There is no contextual
similarity between Sir and Isaiah, and no[213]
relationship is apparent between the two.

c. τρυφάω ("live luxuriously") = התבעבע 14.4

The hithpalpel of the verb בוע ("swell") does
not occur in the Hebrew Bible, although a noun

derivative does.[214] τρυφάω occurs one time, in Isa
66.11, apparently with the meaning "be satisfied or
delighted," and it renders התענג. This particular
place in Sir shows no dependence on the Isaiah
passage. The grandson seems to have extended the
meaning of "swell, rejoice" to "be satisfied" or
"live luxuriously."[215] Although the verbal
equivalence is not the same as the Isaiah passage,
the noun τρυφή frequently renders תענוג in Sir.[216]

d. περίμετρον ("circumference") = המון 50.3

The word περίμετρον appears twice in the
Jewish-Greek scriptures outside of Sir. In 1 Kgs
7.15, it translates חוט, which was a thread used
for measuring length, and there it refers to the
circumference of the pillars in Solomon's temple.
In Sir, it translates המון, a term used to mean
"abundance."[217] How the grandson meant περίμετρον
is unclear. The adjective περίμετρος can mean
"very large," and perhaps the grandson transferred
this meaning to the noun, which usually means
"circumference." In 50.3, Ben Sira refers to a
large reservoir built by Simeon the high priest as
having "the vastness of the sea."[218] The grandson
perhaps used περίμετρον as a way of transferring
the image of the large pool of Simeon into Greek.
Peters comments that περίμετρον is "a moderating
explanation of the hyperbolic המון."[219] I am not
sure, however, that the pool being like the
circumference of the sea is any less of a hyperbole
than saying, as does Ben Sira, that it was like the

sea "in its abundance." At any rate, in this
instance the grandson does not demonstrate any
dependence on a specific OG passage.

3.3.4 CONCLUSIONS CONCERNING DEPENDENCE ON
THE PROPHETS

When one considers the lexical evidence given
here, the same situation obtains as above for the
grandson's use of pentateuchal vocabulary. The
overall data show no predominant use of Greek terms
that were used by the translators of the prophetic
books. When one looks more deeply, the general
indications of these numbers are reinforced. Many
of the terms that the grandson uses for the same
Hebrew words as the OG are likely to be used
independently by him. It seems certain that
ὄναγρος and ὕαινα fit this category, and other
terms, such as σπινθήρ, probably presented a
limited number of lexical choices to the translator. Finally, an equivalent like צרה/ἀντίζηλος
could be an example of dependence on the OG, but
the use of the term in a technical sense could
constitute evidence for the opposite conclusion. No
unambiguous picture emerges from the lexical
equivalents presented in this section, and the
earlier conclusions, drawn from the evidence of the
Pentateuch, seem to be supported.

3.4 THE WRITINGS

Two very knotty problems hinder any examination of the reliance of the grandson on the wisdom
materials. The first involves the Hebrew; the

second concerns the Greek. Regarding the Hebrew, did Ben Sira rely on specific wisdom texts for his work, or did he know wisdom traditions that find their way into his work as well as into other Hebrew wisdom books? Ben Sira's knowledge and use of Proverbs seems certain. Further, it seems certain that Ben Sira would have known at least some corpus of Psalms. In general, the Hebrew Sir contains many words, phrases, and even parts of verses, which are very similar to elements in the wisdom literature of the Hebrew scriptures. These similarities sometimes occur in contexts parallel to the biblical materials, and sometimes they are quite removed from those biblical contexts. Yet, much of the material is clearly proverbial in nature and could have circulated in forms independent of the Hebrew scriptures. These variables lead me to be much more pessimistic about being able to demonstrate clearly any thoroughgoing textual dependence of Ben Sira on books such as Proverbs, Psalms, or Job, even though I think that Ben Sira must have used these books.

On the Greek side, it is totally unclear which books comprise the group that the grandson calls "the other books." He gives no explicit indications, and his translation provides precious little help as well. Some of the operative questions here are similar to those raised above for the Hebrew. He probably knew some corpus of Psalms in Greek, but did he know them in homogeneous textual forms or through their possible use in worship or school traditions? The same holds true of more proverbial material. In light of these problems, I have conducted some initial investigations on Psalms,

Job, and Proverbs, based largely on the studies of
Schechter and Taylor and Eberharter, for informal
citations and allusions, and on Reiterer for
translation vocabulary. I have not examined all the
writings in this section, but have chosen the three
books that seem most clearly to have been known by
Ben Sira: Proverbs, Psalms, and Job. A more
complete investigation would include books like[220]
Song of Songs, Qoheleth, and Lamentations. The
results are summarized below.

TABLE 6 - POSSIBLE USES OF PSALMS, JOB, AND PROVERBS
          BY BEN SIRA AND HIS GRANDSON

PSALMS

Author	A	B	C	??
Schechter/Taylor	50	17	4	6
Eberharter	211	42	12	4

Author	Total	100% = OG	Part	None	??	NE
Reiterer	47	9	1	15	2	20

JOB

Author	A	B	C	??
Schechter/Taylor	26	7	0	3
Eberharter	32	7	0	

Author	Total	100% = OG	Part	None	NE
Reiterer	29	6	0	10	13

PROVERBS

Author	A	B	C	??
Schechter/Taylor	44	10	0	6
Eberharter	92	16	0	

Author	Total	100% = OG	Part	None	NE
Reiterer	63	9	6	32	16

These summaries leave the general impression
that if the grandson knew Psalms, Job, and
Proverbs, he did not draw on them very often for
his own translation. The clearest indications are
that he probably knew Psalms and used them. It must
be emphasized, however, that these charts represent
initial investigations, and that to understand
fully the relationship of the Hebrew of Ben Sira
and the Greek of his grandson to these materials,
more extensive and detailed studies need to be done
than are possible within the present framework.
Further, in light of the difficulties in knowing
just what material was available to the grandson in
translation, the numbers contained in the charts
above may well be skewed by the fact that he did
not have certain translations to use, even if he
would have used them were they available.

3.5 CONCLUSIONS CONCERNING DEPENDENCE ON JEWISH-
    GREEK BIBLICAL TRANSLATIONS

The results of the examinations conducted
above lead to several related conclusions. First,
the general statement that Ben Sira himself knew
and used the Hebrew scriptures is confirmed. The

key question, however, is how Ben Sira used the
material from the Hebrew scriptures. Although the
main focus of this study lies elsewhere, the
impression is certainly present that Ben Sira
integrated the biblical material quite thoroughly
into his work. Even in the Praise of the Ancestors
section considerable independence from the wording
of the Hebrew Bible is characteristic. This raises
the question of the degree to which Ben Sira
actually took material from written biblical texts,
or from other textual sources, or even from other
non-textual sources. The high degree of integration
of these materials by Ben Sira into his work makes
a firm conclusion difficult.

An examination of the grandson's translation
raises similar issues, but it seems unlikely that
the grandson depended heavily on the OG for his
translations. There is no clear pattern of a
recognition on his part of associations between his
grandfather's Hebrew and the Hebrew scriptures, and
of a subsequent use of portions of the OG or OG
equivalents to render those sections into Greek. In
fact, the conclusion reached by Reiterer, that the
grandson did not depend very much on the OG
Pentateuch for the beginning of the Praise of the
Ancestors section (44.16-45.26), seems more than
supported here regarding his possible dependence on
the Law and Prophets for the entire translation.[221]
When the grandson does use OG terminology, it seems
more likely that this use results from familiarity
with the material in contexts such as worship or
school than from written texts. Indeed this is not
entirely unexpected. If he were familiar with the
material from these kinds of sources, sporadic
terminological parallels would be likely.

In addition, the integration of biblical
passages into another work in forms that do not
constitute quotations per se is not unique to the
Wisdom of Ben Sira. One example is the use of the
OG in the Wisdom of Solomon. In this book, there
are many parallels to the OG that are worked into
the text and used to express the particular ideas
of the author. C. Larcher describes the use of the
OG by the Wisdom of Solomon by saying,

> We sum up then the dominant traits of this use
> of the biblical sources in Wisdom. Although
> they are abundant and reveal an author
> familiar with the language of the Greek Bible,
> implicit citations are the exception and very
> few of the texts are given literally. As a
> general rule, the author treats his sources
> with a great liberty and the expression of the
> rest of his thought is his own: he does not
> want to compose a clever mosaic of biblical
> words and expressions. . . .[222]

One could easily expect that this kind of usage
would be widespread throughout the literature of
Early Judaism, both in its Semitic and Greek forms.
The biblical traditions seem to have been well
known by these authors, and its seems somewhat
naive to describe the authors as if they produced
catenae of biblical quotations. The reality seems
much more subtle and sophisticated.

CHAPTER 4

CAN THE PARENT TEXT OF THE GREEK TRANSLATION OF BEN SIRA BE RECOVERED?

4.1 INTRODUCTION

In Chapters 2 and 3, I discussed two areas crucial for any attempt to reconstruct the parent text of the grandson's Greek translation. One issue, translation technique, has rarely been discussed at all by those who propose to reconstruct the Hebrew parent text, except perhaps very briefly and in generalizing terms.[1] The second, the use of the Jewish-Greek translations by the grandson, has only been addressed in one study limited to a short section.[2] In this concluding chapter, I will briefly try to assess the impact of the conclusions reached in Chapters 2 and 3 on the enterprise of recovering the Hebrew parent text of the Greek Sir.

A major reason that no adequate discussion has as yet appeared is that it is usually assumed that the parent text of a Greek translation can, in fact, be reconstructed, and when one compares most of the OG translations to the MT, that assumption usually appears to be correct, with the possible exceptions of translations such as Proverbs or Job. For Sir, the situation is quite different, as we saw above. The Hebrew of Sir is not complete for the entire book, and the manuscripts of the Hebrew that are available present an often bewildering text-critical puzzle that is difficult to sort out. In addition, even though the Greek translation of Ben Sira's grandson is the primary text used for reconstructing the "original" Hebrew, it is virtually certain that the Hebrew text of the book

231

that the grandson used already contained some
corruptions and textual problems. Thus, before the
"original" Hebrew of Ben Sira can be reconstructed
these problems need to be resolved. They do not,
however, seem to be insurmountable. In some
instances, data that would help with such solutions
are already available. For example, Segal provides
a detailed list of passages that he believes are
the product of an already corrupt Hebrew text that
came to the grandson.[3]

Also, any attempt to reconstruct the Hebrew of
Ben Sira must of necessity take into account the
Latin and Syriac translations, which have unique
problems of their own.[4] Consequently, the question
that needs to be asked intitially does not get
asked. Rather than make the assumption that the
Hebrew parent text of the Greek, and concurrently
the Hebrew of Ben Sira himself, can be reconstructed, the question that should be asked,
especially with the material in Chapters 2 and 3 in
view, is if the parent text can be reconstructed at
all, and if it can, what aspects of that parent
text can be recovered with any degree of
confidence?

Based on the conclusions reached in the
previous two chapters, I tend to be pessimistic
about the prospect of recovering the Hebrew parent
text of the grandson's Greek in general. This
pessimism, it must be emphasized, pertains to the
possibility of reconstructing the complete, running
text of the Hebrew that the grandson translated.
Certainly in individual passages various aspects of
the Hebrew may be recovered with a degree certainty, but that is different from arguing that the

entire Hebrew text that the grandson used can be
pieced together based on his translation.

4.2 RECONSTRUCTING THE HEBREW PARENT TEXT OF THE GREEK SIR

The pessimism expressed above derives from the
general conclusions reached in Chapters 2 and 3. In
Chapter 2, I argued that when one considers certain
general features of the way in which the grandson
represents several formal aspects of his parent
text, he is not very consistent. Of the four
aspects treated, word order, segmentation, quantitative representation, and lexical choice, one
sees a variation in the consistency of the translation from aspect to aspect.

For word order, although Ben Sira fell near
the bottom of the table, there was still some
distance between the grandson's translation and
those of Proverbs, Esther, and Job, all of which
were much less consistent than the grandson in
their representations of the Hebrew word order. A
large portion of the translation's inconsistency is
due to the existence of many syntactic word-order
deviations, deviations that are easy to treat when
reconstructing the Hebrew parent text. The large
percentage of word-order deviations that are
syntactic, although they point to the grandon's
stylistic variation, lessen the degree to which the
translation contains displacement variations, which
are the more difficult to evaluate. The Greek of
Sir was shown to be somewhat consistent when it
came to the quantitative representation of its
parent text, at least when compared to the other

translations studied. This relative consistency
pertained to longer quantitative texts rather than
to shorter, but there were special problems with
the shorter texts.[5] Segmentation, however, was an
area where the Greek of Sir showed little overall
consistency when compared to other translations,
even though it was more consistent than both
Proverbs and Job. Finally, in the area of lexical
representation, Sir was the least consistent of all
the translations studied. When using nouns and
verbs, the grandson did not seem to be at all
concerned about using the same Greek rendering for
each occurrence of the same Hebrew word.

Consequently, when one attempts to reconstruct
those aspects of the Hebrew parent text of the
Greek Sir represented by segmentation, shorter
quantitative translations, and lexical representation, little confidence is warranted. Segmentation is especially difficult to judge because
many of the elements of the Hebrew that are subject
to segmenting by the translator, such as conjunctions and pronominal suffixes, present difficulties
in general throughout the OG translations and might
be expected to suffer in the course of the transmission of the text.[6] With respect to lexical
representation, the results obtained in this study
indicate that even a careful examination of each
use of a particular word in the Greek Sir may not
bring one closer to a confident reconstruction. By
contrast, the grandson does follow the Hebrew word
order fairly well, and he does not tend to add
words in his translation that are not already in
the Hebrew. Although caution must be excercised,
these two aspects of translations can be expected
to yield better results than the other three.

The preceding discussion needs to be qualified
somewhat. Simply because the Greek of Sir is judged
to be inconsistent in certain aspects of translation, the entire endeavor of attempting to
determine its parent text is not vitiated. For
example, the fact that the Greek of Sir was the
least consistent in its representation of lexical
elements in the Hebrew means that the reconstruction of these elements will often remain very
uncertain, unless a pattern of use or a specific
context can be demonstrated for the word or words
being reconstructed. The characterizations of the
grandson's translation for these aspects of
translation were meant as general indications of an
approach to translation. They are more specific
than blanket characterizations of entire translations, but they are not made on narrow aspects
either. Each individual case still must be
evaluated individually, but the knowledge of how
woodenly a translator represented certain elements
of the Hebrew parent text provides useful guidance
to the scholar attempting to reconstruct the
Hebrew. Indeed, many specific elements of the
parent text may be reconstructed in spite of the
grandson's general lack of consistency in some of
these areas.

The conclusions reached in Chapter 3 complement those in Chapter 2, and they also provide
important indications for reconstructions of the
Hebrew parent text of the Greek Sir. The two areas
examined in that chapter indicate that Ben Sira's
grandson was far less dependent on the OG translations of the Bible than has been previously thought

and that he did not necessarily fall into the same
tradition of the translation of lexical elements as
the OG. These conclusions also complicate the
reconstruction process. One cannot take, as a
standard practice, OG/MT lexical equivalents as
normative for the Greek and/or Hebrew of Sir
because, especially in the case of the grandson,
they do not seem to have been frequently utilized.
As a result, any attempt to retrovert Greek words
that have no Hebrew counterparts anywhere in Sir on
the basis of OG/MT equivalents is fraught with
uncertainty. Nor does the grandson appear to have
any general program in his translation for drawing
on the OG for specific passages; on the contrary,
he most often translates quite independently. Even
if one is relatively sure that Ben Sira's grandson
was aware of some biblical tradition, the comparison of his Greek in relation to the OG and MT
passages for the reconstruction of the Hebrew
parent text may not be warranted. The lines of
clear dependence simply cannot be drawn closely
enough between the grandson's translation and the
Jewish-Greek translations.

These uncertainties can perhaps be best seen
when examining a particular attempt at reconstruction. As an example, I have examined one specific
reconstruction, that of Sirach 24 by Patrick W.
Skehan,[7] in relation to those elements that were
studied in the two preceding chapters. Skehan's
article is primarily an attempt to demonstrate the
Hebrew strophic arrangement of this poem, but he
retroverts the entire poem into Hebrew in order to
do this. The poem is also a good candidate for this
kind of exercise because there are no great textual

problems in the Greek, and on the whole, the Syriac
does not seem to diverge greatly from the Greek,[8]
which gives a certain unanimity to the evidence.
It is important to remember that Skehan has used
all the available evidence, including both the
Greek and the Syriac translations.

In the examples given below, I have used
Skehan's reconstruction simply as a heuristic
device that helps to point out where the use of the
Greek alone is inadequate to the task of reconstructing the Hebrew. The discussions are in no way
intended to be a critique of Skehan's choices in
his reconstruction. In many of these cases Skehan's
Hebrew reconstruction is dependent on the Syriac
rather than the Greek. The importance of the Syriac
evidence notwithstanding, in the following
examples, I have commented on Skehan's Hebrew
reconstruction in its relation to the Greek
translation <u>as if</u> it had been taken from the Greek
alone. A more complete and detailed look at the
non-Greek evidence can be found in the notes to the
individual passages discussed.

4.2.1 THE RECONSTRUCTION OF LEXICAL ELEMENTS

Probably the most pervasive and recurring
difficulty concerns what Hebrew lexical items
should be selected for the reconstruction of the
parent text. In many cases, the Greek simply cannot
be used as decisive evidence, and the Syriac gives
the better clues. Skehan, of course, recognizes the
difficulty of choosing vocabulary for the retroversion, and the Syriac, because of its numerous
cognates with Hebrew, often serves as his basis for

the lexical reconstructions. Yet, the comparison of
Skehan's lexical choices with the grandson's
translation illustrate very well the difficulties
of trying to rely on the Greek Sir.[9]

Skehan also looks to other passages in Sir for
the use of lexical equivalents, although when
different Hebrew words are found in different
places as equivalents of the same Greek word, it
sometimes is not clear, on the basis of the Greek
translation, how one should choose one word over
another. In places where no Hebrew equivalents
occur elsewhere in Sir, Skehan sometimes looks to
the OG materials for assistance. His awareness that
this poem seems to have some relationship with the
poem to Wisdom in Proverbs 8 also appears to
influence his choice of lexical elements for the
Hebrew. Some examples of the lexical problems
follow.

24.1	ובתוך עמה תתפאר	חכמה תהלל נפשה
24.2	ונגד צבאו תתהלל	בקהל עליון תפחח פיה

In both of these verses, the Greek translation
ends with the verb καυχάομαι. In v 1, Skehan's
reconstruction has תתפאר, and in v 2, תתהלל. The
use of the same verb in Greek creates some problems
for reconstruction of the Hebrew. In all its
occurrences in Greek Sir where there is Hebrew
available, καυχάομαι is used for the hithpael of
פאר, and based on that usage one might propose פאר
in both places. The primary reason, based on the
Greek, for the reconstruction of different verbs
would be to avoid the same word at the end of each
verse. In that case[16] the Greek Sir would provide no
decisive evidence.

חוג השמים הקפתי לבדי   ובמעמקי תהומות התהלכתי 24.5

The reconstruction of these two cola depends
on the Greek, since the Syriac says something
entirely different. The reconstruction of חוג is
mainly conditioned by the imagery of the verse,
which is very similar to Proverbs 8.28 where this
word is used. γῦρον occurs only here in Sir and
not at all in the Greek Proverbs. The verb γυρόω,
however, does occur in 43.12, and it corresponds to
חוג in the Masada scroll. Thus, the combination of
similar imagery to the Proverbs passage and a
similar equivalent elsewhere in Sir provides the
basis for this reconstruction.

24.8   ועושני הניח משכני   אז צוני יוצר הכול
          ובישראל התנחלי   ויאמר ביעקב שכני

In 24.4, Wisdom says of herself, "In the
heights I dwelt (κατεσκήνωσα)." In 24.8, the verb
κατασκηνόω ("to dwell") corresponds to Skehan's
reconstruction, שכנתי. The reconstruction of שכנתי
seems plausible enough, even though the Greek verb
only occurs here and in 24.4. The reconstruction of
the verb, however, seems to condition the reconstruction of the noun σκηνή as משכן in v 8. In
this verse, σκηνή seems to have a different use
from its other uses in vv 10 and 15 where it
clearly refers to the Tabernacle, and where
Skehan's reconstruction of משכן is a more probable
lexical choice. A parallel idea to that of v 8 is
found in Sir 14.25, the only occurrence of the
Greek noun in Sir where a Hebrew equivalent is

extant. This verse refers to the one "who pitches
his tent beside her [Wisdom]." In this case,
στήσει τὴν σκηνὴν αὐτοῦ renders ונטה אהלו. The
idea in 24.8 is also that of fixing or pitching a
tent. Based on a similar context and the correspondence of אהל and σκηνή in 14.25, the Greek
evidence might suggest אהל as the parent text.[11]

   Where the grandson's Greek has καὶ ὁ κτίσας
με, Skehan's Hebrew has עושי in 24.8. Although
this is the only use of κτίζω as a participle in
Sir, none of the other occurrences of this verb
render the Hebrew verb עשה. The participle of עשה
with a pronominal object is translated elsewhere by
the grandson with the verb ποιέω.[12] κτίζω with a
pronominal object is also used in v 9, where Skehan
reconstructs בראני, undoubtedly due to the use of
the phrase ἀπ' ἀρχῆς immediately preceding it (see
Gen 1.1). Again the Greek evidence appears ambiguous, and Skehan has probably based his reconstruction on the Syriac.[13]

24.12   בחלק יהוה נחלתי   ואשריש בעם נכבד

   The reconstruction of אשריש in colon a appears
to be a literal retranslation from ἐρρίζωσα in the
grandson's translation. Elsewhere in Sir, the simplex ῥιζόω is used to translate נטע, and the
compound ἐκριζόω renders נחש. The two occurrences
in Sir of the verb שרש (6.3; 10.16) have the
connotation "destroy," and the Greek has ἀπόλλυμι
in both places.[14]

24.29   ועצתה מתהום רבה   כי מים עצמה מחשבתה

The reconstruction of מחשבתה is a good
illustration of the problems that are sometimes
encountered when using both the Greek and the
Syriac translations. The Greek term, διανόημα,
does not render מחשב elsewhere in Sir; it is
translated as διαλογισμός (13.26; 33.5) and
λογισμός (43.23). The Syriac in this place, חכמה,
also does not render מחשב, but most frequently
renders its cognate in Hebrew. תרעיתא translates
מחשב in Sir (13.26; 33.5). Since διανόημα renders
חכמה in 32.22 and חכמה is by far the most common
equivalent of the Syriac term, perhaps consideration should be given to using it here.

24.33   והשארתיה לדר דרים   עוד לקח כנבואה אשפך

In this verse, Ben Sira says that he intends
to "leave behind" his teaching for future generations. The Greek verb used by the grandson is
καταλείπω. Skehan's reconstruction in this place
has the verb שאר. This word appears one other time
in Sir as an equivalent for καταλείπω (48.15). A
number of other Hebrew verbs, however, are rendered
by this Greek word, the most frequent being עזב
(11.19; 14.15; 47.23; 49.4). Four other verbs, חמל,
נטש, עבר, and נוח, are also rendered by καταλείπω.
What criteria does one use in making a decision as
to which Hebrew verb the Greek translator had in
front of him? This text illustrates the difficulty
of such decisions in Sir.[15]

4.2.2 THE RECONSTRUCTION OF SEGMENTS OF HEBREW WORDS

When one approaches the issue of segmentation, the lack of consistency that was demonstrated above for the Greek Sir casts uncertainty on the reconstruction of affixed elements. In the extant Hebrew manuscripts, there are many places where these elements are present in Hebrew and missing in Greek.[16] Thus, for example, in 24.7 where in Greek Wisdom says, "μετὰ τούτων πάντων ἀνάπαυσιν ἐζήτησα," should ἀνάπαυσιν be reconstructed as simply "a resting place" (מנוחה), or should it be, "Among all these I sought my resting place?"[17] In v 30, where Ben Sira's grandson translates, "καὶ ὡς ὑδραγωγὸς ἐξῆλθον εἰς παράδεισον," should παράδεισος remain simply "a garden" (לגן), or perhaps "my garden" in consonance with the following nouns that are qualified with a genitive case pronoun? Based solely on the patterns found in the Greek translation, these problems remain insoluble.

4.2.3 THE RECONSTRUCTION OF QUANTITATIVE ELEMENTS

Skehan's reconstruction also follows the quantitative form of the Greek translation fairly closely. Yet, whereas the grandson seems to have refrained, for the most part, from adding elements that were not in the Hebrew, his translation was last among those studied when it came to the leaving out of Greek words that were in the Hebrew, which results in a translation that is quantitatively different from the parent text. Might there be such cases in Sir 24? Skehan's reconstruction contains some interesting examples.

24.23   מורשה קהלת יעקב   כל זאת ספר ברית עליון
                                        תורה צוה לנו משה

In the discussion of longer translations, a
number of them were excluded because they probably
did not represent a variant Hebrew parent text.
This verse contains a good example. The Greek ὃν
ἐνετείλατο has almost certainly been correctly
reconstructed as צוה. The relative pronoun in Greek
most likely does not represent אשר in the Hebrew.

Sometimes possible quantitative differences
can be isolated despite the difficulty of the
analysis. In 24.23, the grandson uses the phrase
διαθήκης θεοῦ ὑψίστου. Skehan in his Hebrew
reconstruction has only ברית עליון. This reconstruction may well reflect a similar situation to
that found in 41.8 where νόμον θεοῦ ὑψίστου
corresponds to תורת עליון in the Masada scroll.
What complicates matters, however, is the occurrence of the same Hebrew phrase, תורת עליון, in
42.2 and 49.4, and of the similar phrase, מצות
עליון, in 44.20, all translated by the grandson as
νόμος ὑψίστου. Further, in 47.5, the phrase
κύριον τὸν ὕψιστον renders אל עליון. Does this
evidence indicate that there was a Hebrew word in
the grandson's parent text that corresponded to
θεός in 24.23 and 41.8, or for some reason did the
grandson simply add θεός to these two phrases? How
should this evidence be evaluated in light of the
data on quantitative representation presented in
Chapter 2?[18]

In 24.33 (see above p. 241 for Skehan's Hebrew
reconstruction) again a Greek phrase occurs that is
close to some others in Sir. Here the verse ends

with εἰς γενεὰς αἰώνων, which is retroverted as
לדר דרים. Unfortunately, the exact Greek phrase
occurs only here in Sir; the closest to it is εἰς
γενεὰς αὐτῶν in 16.27 and 45.26. In two places
(44.14, 16), Hebrew Sir uses the phrase לדור ודור
when speaking of many generations. The Greek
renders these with the plural of γενεά only.
Interestingly, in 45.26, MS B has לדורות עולם,
precisely what one might expect as the parent text
here in 24.33. The Greek in that passage, however,
is εἰς γενεὰς αὐτῶν, leading one to suspect that
the grandson read לדורותם in his parent text.

What results from this confusing evidence is
more uncertainty and another possible solution. One
could argue that αἰώνων in 24.33 is actually an
inner-Greek corruption from αὐτῶν, perhaps as a
result of the use of abbreviations for these words
in Greek manuscripts (something like αων?), although no evidence exists that these words were
subject to abbreviation. Perhaps the confusion
resulted from the use of an exemplar that had been
damaged at this place or whose writing had faded
and was difficult to read. The Latin of this verse
hints that something like this might be the case.
It reads for colon b, <u>et relinquam illam</u>
<u>quaerentibus sapientiam et non desinam in progenies</u>
<u>illorum</u> (=? εἰς γενεὰς αὐτῶν) <u>usque in aevum</u>
<u>sanctum</u> (=? εἰς γενεὰς αἰώνων).[19] Thus, one
could argue that in 24.33 and 45.26 the original
Greek translation is εἰς γενεὰς αὐτῶν, which
rendered לדורותם. αὐτῶν became corrupted to read
αἰώνων, which resulted in a doublet in the Latin
translation. In both instances (24.33 and 45.26),
the result is a quantitatively equal translation in

contrast to 44.14, 16 where the translations of
לדור ודור are not quantitatively equal. Again the
Greek translation, even though it provides the
basic evidence, is not sufficient by itself to
solve the problem.

4.2.4 THE RECONSTRUCTION OF THE HEBREW WORD ORDER

We found in Chapter 2 that the Greek Sir stood
with the majority of the OG translations in that
the grandson followed the word order of his Hebrew
fairly closely. In Skehan's reconstruction of
Sirach 24 both syntactic and displacement differences are present. The syntactic word-order
differences are easy to recognize and to
reconstruct. In Sirach 24, the Greek shows these
changes in v 7, where μετὰ τούτων πάντων must be
something like Skehan's בכל אלה. This same order of
demonstrative followed by a form of πᾶς also
occurs in v 23 where the same type of reconstruction is necessary. Sirach 24 contains only one
occurrence of a postposition conjunction. In v 20,
τὸ γὰρ μνημόσυνόν μου has been retroverted by
Skehan as כי זכרי, which, if Ben Sira indeed used a
conjunction here, is probably correct.[20] In two
cases in v 31, the possessive pronoun precedes the
noun it governs, and thus, it is easily retroverted
into Hebrew.[21]

Skehan has two places where he reconstructs
displacement differences between the Greek
translation and its Hebrew parent text (vv 2 and
31). The reasons for these word-order differences
do not seem to concern the Greek, but rather they
involve Skehan's analysis of the poetic structure

and the evidence of the Syriac. The analysis of
poetic structure is an important aspect of understanding Ben Sira's work, one that I cannot treat
here, but it may very well be that the inner
structure of the bicola and the parallelism in Ben
Sira's poetry, as it comes into the Greek and
Syriac translations, may give important clues as to
certain elements of his work.[22]

At the end of the first colon of 24.2 (see
above, p. 238 for Skehan's Hebrew reconstruction),
where the Greek has στόμα αὐτῆς ἀνοίξει Skehan has
פיה תפתח. This change in word order makes v 2a
parallel to v 1a, which has the verb-object order,
while both v 1b and v 2b end with a verb, which
produces the parallel structure, verb-object,
prepositional phrase-verb, verb-object, prepositional phrase-verb.[23]

24.31   וארוה ערוגתי   אמרתי אשקה גנתי
         ונהרי היה לים   והנה יובלי היה לנהר

Similarly, in 24.31c, ἐγένετό μοι ἡ διῶρυξ
is retroverted by Skehan as יובלי היה. This
reconstruction brings colon c into parallel with
colon d, which has the word order noun-verb-
prepositional phrase. Based on the Greek translation alone, however, one could postulate that the
word order of the second colon should be changed in
order to preserve the parallel structure. The
Syriac word order, which Skehan's reconstruction
reflects, helps to solve the problem, whereas the
Greek does not provide any decisive evidence.

The examples given above help to demonstrate
that it is often difficult, based on the Greek

translation of the grandson alone, to have any firm
understanding of what variations existed between
the translation and its Hebrew parent text. What
the analyses of translation technique in Chapter 2
indicate is the relative confidence with which
these reconstructions can be made. Sometimes
parallels from elsewhere in a translation may be of
help, but often there are no parallels to be found,
and one must make the best possible guess. In the
case of Sirach 24, a number of words are used that
appear nowhere else in Sir. How should they be
reconstructed? A large number of possessive pronouns are used. Do they all represent pronouns in
the parent text? Unfortunately, these questions and
other similar ones cannot always be answered with
the degree of confidence that one might desire when
one attempts reconstructions. This uncertainty is
especially acute when one is faced with a situation
like that of Sir, where, for large portions of the
text, no Hebrew text at all has survived to use as
a basis for comparison.

4.2.5 THE USE OF GREEK BIBLICAL TRANSLATIONS IN
RECONSTRUCTIONS

When one comes to the issue of dependence on
the biblical traditions, Sirach 24 stands with the
Praise of the Ancestors section as having clear
roots in the Hebrew scriptures. In this instance,
those roots can be traced primarily to Proverbs
8.[24] Despite the fact that Proverbs 8 has
influenced the Hebrew of Sirach 24, the analysis
done in Chapter 3 should perhaps caution one about
finding an extensive literary dependence by Ben
Sira or his grandson on a written form of that

wisdom poem. There are certainly reminiscences of
and allusions to the Proverbs 8 material, but given
the paucity of what I have called informal citations of the biblical materials in Sir generally,
and in places such as the Praise of the Ancestors
in particular, a great number of informal citations
should not expected here either. On the whole, it
appears clear that Skehan has been careful not to
rely on the Greek translation of Proverbs 8 for his
reconstruction, although some Hebrew elements seem
to fit well once they have been reconstructed.

The best example of this tendency is Skehan's
retroversion of the Greek of v 10b, καὶ οὕτως
ἐν σιων ἐστηρίχθην, as החיצבח בציון ובכן. In
his brief remarks on this verse, Skehan writes,
"The החיצבח of 10b reflects נצבה of Prov 8:2."[25]
His reconstruction, however, does not seem so much
based on the exact text from Proverbs as this
statement might imply. The primary factor in the
reconstruction of החיצבח seems to be the grandson's choice in Sir 39.32 of ἐστηρίχθην for the
same Hebrew verb. As a secondary benefit, this
reconstruction coincides with the use of יצב in
Prov 8.2. The only place where Skehan directly
invokes the authority of the OG/MT lexical
equivalents is in vv 13-15 for the names of the
plants. These lexical equivalences are probably
justified, although Skehan's reference to them
being "guaranteed" may be too strong in light of
the conclusions reached in Chapter 3 and possible
evidence from elsewhere in the book.[26]

Skehan does not make any remarks about the
relationship of the Greek translation to that of
Proverbs 8, but it seems clear that no close

relationship exists, and the data provided at the
end of Chapter 3 give a strong indication that a
close relationship between the two Greek
translations should not be expected.

4.3 GENERAL CONCLUSIONS AND FURTHER RESEARCH

The brief examination in the previous sections
of Skehan's reconstruction of Sirach 24 provides
examples of some of the complicated problems
connected with reconstructing the Hebrew text of
Ben Sira from its Greek translation. The analyses
carried out in this study have only been able to
sketch the barest outlines of the translation
technique of Ben Sira's grandson. These outlines,
however, do suggest that the grandson was not
usually concerned to give a word-for-word translation of the Hebrew, nor did he usually resort to
using existing OG translations as helps in his
work. The recognition by the grandson of the
differences between the Greek translations and
Hebrew "originals" of the biblical books perhaps
points in this direction. Here was a translator
concerned to give a _translation_ of his grandfather's wisdom, not a mechanical _reproduction_ of
his grandfather's Hebrew. Only by concerning
himself with the message and intent of his grandfather could the grandson fulfill his grandfather's
desire to make wisdom generally accessible, in
order that those who so desired would be able "to
live their lives according to the standard of the
Law."

In order thoroughly to define the prospects
for reconstructing the Hebrew of Ben Sira, the

Greek should be studied in far greater detail than
has been possible here. In Chapters 2 and 3, I
outlined in various places some of the possibilities for further study of this book. These and
other studies should be taken up in the future in
order to make the results of this study more
complete. Other aspects of the grandson's
translation technique need to be studied, such as
the representation of the various modes of the
Hebrew verbs, the appreciation and representation
by the grandson of the poetic structure of the
Hebrew, as well as other detailed elements. The
continued accumulation of knowledge about the way
in which Ben Sira's grandson rendered the many
different elements of his Hebrew text can only
bring us closer to as full a recovery as possible
of Ben Sira's original text.

APPENDIX

COMPUTER APPLICATIONS:
ELECTRONIC DATA, HARDWARE, SOFTWARE

The textual analyses conducted in this study have relied on the use of the computer as a tool for storing, gathering, and organizing the large amounts data required. In some ways this tool is no different from index card systems or printed tools; in other ways the traditional tools of scholarship do not compare with it. The collection, identification, and retrieval of large amounts of data has been hampered by the limitations of printed books and certain technical inconveniences. Most scholars who have studied translation technique have recorded data on index cards for storage in some pre-determined order. The recording and locating of data stored in this way can be quite cumbersome and time consuming. Information stored in some pre-determined form might not allow the flexibility of changing one's mind or looking for different kinds of information.

The limitations of the existing scholarly tools for collecting certain specific types of data further impede research. The deficiencies of works such as E. Hatch's and H. A. Redpath's <u>A Concordance to the Septuagint</u> are well known, and they affect the scholar's ability to have access to certain types of information.[1] The ability of the computer, however, to isolate, excerpt, and format data rapidly and to maintain that data in forms that permit a great flexibility allow the scholar to go beyond many of the limitations of older tools and methods. Some of the aspects of the use of the computer in this study illustrate the situation.

251

A.1 THE ELECTRONIC DATA

Increasingly, more and more texts are being
put into "machine-readable" form. With the
development of optical scanning and CD-ROM (compact
disc) technology, the traditional problems of
inputting and storing large amounts of data are
more and more readily overcome. Through the efforts
of a number of projects, Greek, Latin, and Hebrew
texts are becoming more generally available for use
on the computer.[2] Not only must the texts be put
into an electronic form, they must further be
formatted in ways that will be useful to scholars.
For the Jewish-Greek translations this is being
done by the Computer Assisted Tools for Septuagint
Studies (CATSS) project based at the University of
Pennsylvania and at the Hebrew University of
Jerusalem. The texts contained in that data bank
form the textual basis for the present study.

The inception and development of the CATSS
project have been chronicled in a number of publications and need not be repeated here.[3] The project
was conceived as a means for developing tools, with
the assistance of available computer technologies,
that would facilitate the production of a lexicon
of "Septuagint" Greek, as well as other tools for
the study of the OG translations and other cognate
literature.[4] The project's data bank has three
major components: the morphological analysis of the
OG, the parallel alignment of the OG and MT, and
the textual variants to the OG.[5] At present, the
morphological analysis of the Greek and the
parallel alignment have been completed, in at least

provisional forms, whereas full work on the textual variants is still in the initial stages. In this study, both the morphological analysis and the parallel alignment have been utilized, and thus, they require more detailed description.

The morphological analysis of the OG (including the Apocrypha) was accomplished by using a program written by David Packard, which automatically parses classical Greek words. This program was adapted for use on the OG translations, and the resulting files contain each word of the OG on a line with its location in the text (chapter and verse) and the parsing information for that word (part of speech, parsing of the particular word, and dictionary form). For example, the morphological analysis for the word ἀγρῷ in Ruth 1.1 looks as follows:

RT 01 01 ἀγρῷ   N2   DSM   ἀγρός

In this case the text word, ἀγρῷ is a second declension noun (designated N2), dative, singular, masculine (DSM), from the word ἀγρός. Each word of the OG is analyzed in this fashion. In the studies undertaken above, the morphological data were often used in conjunction with the parallel alignment in order to produce alphabetized concordances, which could be searched and manipulated to produce easy access to the desired features of translation technique.[6]

By far the most important part of the data bank for the present study is the parallel aligned MT and OG. In this component of the CATSS data, the MT and OG are listed vertically in parallel columns

with a variety of notations. The initial alignment
was performed automatically using a program written
by John R. Abercrombie.[7] The subsequent corrections
and notations were done by a team working in
Jerusalem using an interactive correction program
written by E. Manzury. The resulting text then
shows, as clearly as possible, the Hebrew-Greek
equivalents of the MT and OG. The following sample,
Ps 63(62).1, shows the alignment in its least
complicated form, where all the elements of the
Hebrew and Greek match one another in the same
order:

p	63	1	מזמור	ψαλμὸς [62.1]
p	63	1	ל/דוד	τῷ δαυιδ [62.1]
p	63	1	ב/הי/ות/ו	ἐν τῷ εἶναι αὐτὸν [62.1]
p	63	1	ב/מדבר	ἐν τῷ ἐρήμῳ [62.1]
p	63	1	יהודה	τῆς ιουδαίας [62.1]

In those cases where the texts do not line up so
easily a system of notations was devised to alert
the user to the problems.[8] Each constituent element
of a Hebrew word is divided using a slash ("/") so
that prefixes and affixes may be easily distinguished. In more complicated cases, where the
Hebrew parent text is suspected as having been
different from the MT, a second column has been
added, which follows an equal sign ("="), where
notations are made concerning the conjectured
differences.

    Included in this parallel alignment is Sir,
which is a special case. Since there is no MT for
Sir, all of the available Hebrew manuscripts of Sir
were used in the alignment.[9] Each Hebrew manuscript
was assigned a single digit number, which accompa-
nied each reading taken from that manuscript. Since
the available Hebrew evidence sometimes preserves

variants to the same passage, there is often more
than one Hebrew word aligned with the Greek. This
situation facilitates the textual criticism of the
Hebrew. In addition, where more than one Hebrew
manuscript is extant in one place, if one reading
clearly agrees more closely with the Greek than the
other, the number representing the manuscript whose
reading is the closest to the Greek has been set
off with curly brackets ("{}").

I produced the initial alignment of Sir in
Jerusalem. Since there was no machine-readable form
of the Hebrew texts available, the first alignment
was done manually on paper. This "hardcopy" alignment was then typed into the computer where further
corrections and changes could be made with the
interactive correction program in use in Jerusalem.
The Greek text is the GKI of Ziegler's Göttingen
edition. The Hebrew text used is that of the Hebrew
Language Academy, which contains all the manuscripts of the Hebrew Sir that were known in
1973.[10] All of the Hebrew doublets are marked as
such with the siglum {d}, and they were not counted
in the analysis in Chapter 2. Unfortunately, since
not all of the second Hebrew recension can be
identified with certainty, there is no sign
indicating a second Hebrew recension reading. These
readings need to be identified on a case by case
basis. All the other procedures for this alignment
follow those for the other books.[11] A brief sample
of the alignment follows (Sir 37.16):

```
si 37 16                    125 ראש  ἀρχή
si 37 16                    125 כל   παντὸς
si 37 16                  125 מעשה   ἔργου
si 37 16          1 דבר 25 מאמר     λόγος
si 37 16    1 ו/ראש {25} י ל/פנ    καὶ πρὸ
si 37 16                    125 כל   πάσης
si 37 16        12 פועל 5 פעל      πράξεως
si 37 16                   125 היא  ---
si 37 16                 125 מחשבת   βουλή
```

The numbers 1, 2, and 5 represent MSS B, B(mg), and D from the Cairo Geniza. In one place the curly brackets are used to indicate that one of the alternative Hebrew readings agrees more closely with the Greek. This alignment forms the textual basis for the studies conducted above in Chapters 2 and 3.

In Chapter 2, where the most extensive use is made of automatic data collection, all the programs were run on the parallel alignment and the morphological analysis files. Although the complicated programming required for Chapter 2 was not required for the analysis performed in Chapter 3, the parallel alignment of Sir served as the base text from which I worked, and a number of search programs were utilized to locate important elements in Sir and the other OG translations.

A.2 HARDWARE AND SOFTWARE

Not only must formatted electronic data be available for use on the computer, but software must be available that will perform the necessary tasks of data gathering and data manipulation. For work on personal computers a growing number of programs that are designed to be used for textual analysis is available from commercial vendors.[12]

Since the investigations conducted here used a
number of different OG translations in conjunction
with Sir, some of which were quite large, the data
were gathered from the morphological analysis and
parallel alignment files stored on the IBYCUS mini-
computer at the University of Pennsylvania, a
system developed by classicist David Packard for
use with ancient Greek and Latin texts and the
primary computer used by CATSS in Philadelphia.
This computer uses the programming language IBYX,
also designed by David Packard for use on this
machine, and all the programming necessary for this
study was done in that language. Since there is no
commercially available software for IBYCUS, all
special software applications were developed "in
house" by me and other members of the CATSS staff.

A number of complicated tasks needed to be
accomplished so that all the important data could
be collected. One of the most important was the use
of the parallel alignment and the morphological
analysis files in conjunction with one another. In
some instances, the dictionary forms needed to be
taken from the morphological files and linked with
the parallel alignment in order to produce alphabetized lists. For the study of lexical consistency, it was necessary to excerpt all nouns and
verbs from the parallel alignment, and the part of
the morphological files containing information
concerning the part of speech of the word was the
primary focus. An initial program, which allowed
the two files to be linked, was written by Walter
Mankowski and was developed further by Jay Treat at
the University of Pennsylvania. I did other
additional special utility programming. I was also

able to utilize extensively the rather large
library of IBYX utility programs written by various
members of the CATSS staff for use with the CATSS
data bank.

Programs were written specifically for each of
the different sections in Chapter 2. For word
order, the data gathering was relatively easy.
Since differences between the sequences of the
Hebrew and Greek are marked in the CATSS files with
a unique symbol, I wrote a short program that
selected each line containing that symbol. The
output files were then manipulated to isolate the
units of word-order deviation and to arrive at the
overall number of sequence differences between the
Hebrew and Greek.

For the section on segmentation, several
programs were used to excerpt the data. The most
important of these programs took each line of the
computer file and first examined the Hebrew side to
determine the number of segments contained in the
Hebrew. This could be done easily because in the
CATSS files each element of a Hebrew word is
separated by a slash ("/"). For example, the word
ובב׳חו would appear in the CATSS file as ו/ח׳ב/ב/ו.
After counting the number of Hebrew segments, the
programs counted the number of Greek words on the
Greek side. If the number was the same, the line
was marked with an "equals" sign ("="), and if they
were not the same the mark was a "greater than"
sign (">"). Occurrences of the preposition ל were
marked with an upper case L, while all occurrences
of את were tagged with a right parenthesis (")"),
the transliteration used for א. Special consideration was given to the occurrence of the definite

article in Greek, since its presence could result
in an artificial discrepancy between the number of
elements on the Hebrew and Greek sides. Subsequently, these markers were sorted into separate
groups, and the data was output to hard copy and
examined line by line in order to be certain that
each line tagged by the program was appropriate for
segmentation.

The programs written for the section on
quantitative representation are comparable to those
used for segmentation. A series of programs was run
that identified possible instances of quantitatively unequal translations. Each of these possible
occurrences was tagged as being one of two basic
types: (1) those where the Greek is longer than the
MT or extant manuscripts of Sir, and (2) those
where the Greek is shorter than the Hebrew. Each
instance was then examined to be certain that it
belonged in this category.

Finally, for lexical representation, the
morphological analysis and the parallel alignment
were used. A program was written that matched the
parsing data and the dictionary form from the
morphological analysis with the corresponding word
or words contained in the parallel alignment. A
subsequent program excerpted the nouns and verbs
into separate files. The files were then sorted
into alphabetical order using the dictionary form.
From these sorted files, the data for the analysis
of lexical consistency were easily obtained.

The use of the computer as a tool for
addressing traditional scholarly problems does not
eliminate the need for close scrutiny of the texts
themselves. Especially in the investigations

conducted in Chapter 2, where intensive computer
use was necessary, the machine functioned as a data
gatherer and data manipulator. As the introductions
to the individual sections of each chapter show,
the methodological difficulties in treating these
issues remain, and they must be resolved independently of the computer. For every aspect of
translation technique, each passage that was output
automatically was examined individually in order to
ensure its suitability for the issue under study.
This process involved a great deal of time, but
were it not for the fact that the computer could be
used to locate, excerpt, and format the texts in
ways that were easy to use, the investigations
themselves would not have been feasible. The fact
that these investigations could be undertaken at
all indicates the tremendous possibilities that
this technology offers for scholarly research.

[1]For a discussion of the name of the author of the book and the traditions concerning the book's title, see Rudolph Smend, Die Weisheit des Jesus Sirach erklärt (Berlin: Georg Reimer, 1906) XIV-XV, and the newly published Anchor Bible Commentary by Patrick W. Skehan and A. A. Di Lella, The Wisdom of Ben Sira, Anchor Bible 39 (New York: Doubleday, 1987) 3-4.

[2]All translations are made by the author unless otherwise noted.

[3]For a discussion of the types of wisdom materials as well as other literary genres utilized by Ben Sira, see Skehan and Di Lella, 21-39.

[4]The exact form of the so-called Praise of the Ancestors section is a matter of some dispute and has recently been discussed at length in two books: Burton L. Mack, Wisdom and the Hebrew Epic: Ben Sira's Hymn in Praise of the Fathers, Chicago Studies in the History of Judaism (Chicago: University of Chicago, 1985); and Thomas R. Lee, Studies in the Form of Sirach 44-50, SBLDS 75 (Atlanta: Scholars, 1986).

[5]For a much more detailed explanation of the background of the book, see the introductory chapters of Skehan and Di Lella. On the transmission and medieval discovery of the Hebrew text, see A. A. Di Lella, The Hebrew Text of Sirach: A Text-Critical and Historical Study (The Hague: Mouton, 1966).

[6]For a detailed narrative of this discovery, see Solomon Schechter, "A Fragment of the Original Text of Ecclesiasticus," Expositor 5th ser. 4 (1896) 1-15.

[7]Until a short time ago portions of five Hebrew manuscripts of Ben Sira were known from the Geniza. They were individually published in a variety of places: E. N. Adler, "Some Missing Chapters of Ben Sira [7,29-12,1]," JQR 12 (1899-1900) 466-480; A. E. Cowley and A. Neubauer, eds., The Original Hebrew of a Portion of Ecclesiasticus (Oxford: Clarendon, 1897); M. Gaster, "A New Fragment of Ben Sira [parts of chaps. 18, 19 and 20]," JQR 12 (1899-1900) 688-702; I. Lévi, "Fragments de deux nouveaux manuscrits hébreux de l'Ecclésiastique," REJ 40 (1900) 1-30; idem, "Un

nouveau Fragment de Ben Sira," REJ 92 (1932) 136-
145; Marcus, J., The Newly Discovered Original
Hebrew of Ben Sira (Ecclesiasticus xxxii,16-
xxxiv,1): The Fifth Manuscript and a Prosodic
Version of Ben Sira (Ecclesiasticus xxii,22-
xxiii,9) (Philadelphia: Dropsie College, 1931)
[This volume is a revised version of Marcus's
article that originally appeared in JQR n.s. 21
(1930-1931) 223-240.]; G. Margoliouth, "The
Original Hebrew of Ecclesiasticus XXXI.12-31, and
XXXVI.22-XXXVII.26," JQR 12 (1899-1900) 1-33;
Schechter, "A Fragment of the Original Text of
Ecclesiasticus;" idem, "A Further Fragment of Ben
Sira [MS C; parts of chaps. 4, 5, 25, and 26]," JQR
12 (1899-1900) 456-465; idem, "Genizah Specimens:
Ecclesiasticus [original text of 49:12-50:22]," JQR
10 (1897-1898) 197-206; Solomon Schechter and C.
Taylor, The Wisdom of Ben Sira: Portions of the
Book Ecclesiasticus from the Hebrew Manuscripts in
the Cairo Genizah Collection Presented to the
University of Cambridge by the Editors (Cambridge:
Cambridge University, 1899); J. Schirmann, "דף חדש
מחוך ספר בן-סירא העברי," Tarbiz 27 (1957-1958) 440-
443; idem, " בן-סי'ראי'דפים נוספים מחוך ספר,'" Tarbiz
29 (1959-1960) 125-134. In 1982, A. Scheiber ("A
New Leaf of the Fourth Manuscript of the Ben Sira
from the Geniza," Magyar Könyvszamle 98 [1982] 179-
185) published two new fragments, one of MS C and
one he identified as MS D. In the Anchor Bible
Commentary on Ben Sira, A. A Di Lella has
challenged Scheiber's identification of the leaf
that he called MS D. Di Lella believes this to be a
fragment of an altogether different manuscript that
he has called MS F. Di Lella's transcription and
analysis of the fragment can be found in "The Newly
Discovered Sixth Manuscript of Ben Sira from the
Cairo Genizah," Biblica 69 (1988) 226-238. See
also, on MS F, Skehan and Di Lella, 51-52. For the
scraps from Qumran, see M. Baillet, J. T. Milik,
and R. de Vaux, Les "Petites Grottes" de Qumrân,
DJD 3 (Oxford: Clarendon, 1962). The chap. 51
material was published by J. A. Sanders, The Psalms
Scroll of Qumrân Cave 11 (11QPs^a), DJD 4 (Oxford:
Clarendon, 1965). The Masada Scroll can be found in
Yigael Yadin, The Ben Sira Scroll from Masada
(Jerusalem: Israel Exploration Society, 1965) while
valuable corrections to Yadin's text are given in
J. M. Baumgarten, "Some Notes on the Ben Sira
Scroll from Masada," JQR 58 (1968) 323-327 and John
Strugnell, "Notes and Queries on 'The Ben Sira

Scroll from Masada,'" in W. F. Albright Volume, ed.
A. Malamat, Eretz Israel 9 (1969) 109-119.

[8]The most vocal proponent of this theory was
D. S. Margoliouth. See primarily "The Destruction
of the Original of Ecclesiasticus," ExpTim 16
(1904-1905) 26-29, and The Origin of the "Original
Hebrew" of Ecclesiasticus (London: Parker, 1899).
For other objections to the authenticity of the
Hebrew of the Geniza manuscripts, see C. C. Torrey,
"The Hebrew of the Geniza Sirach," in Alexander
Marx Jubilee Volume (New York: Jewish Theological
Seminary of America, 1950) 585-602, and H. L.
Ginsberg, "The Original Hebrew of Ben Sira 12 10-
14," JBL 74 (1955) 93-95.

[9]Yadin, The Ben Sira Scroll, 5-11 (English)
and 5-13 (Hebrew).

[10]Although Di Lella's book was published two
years after the discovery of the Masada scroll, the
scroll had not yet been published at the time the
book was written. Di Lella knew of the discovery,
but did not yet know the details of the text. See
pp. 80-81. In his book, Di Lella treats in detail
all the major arguments against the authenticity of
the Geniza Hebrew, especially the theory of
retranslation from Syriac. See also John
Strugnell's review of Di Lella's book (CBQ 30
[1968] 90) where he remarks, "Of DiL.'s conclusions, the statements that the doubters are clearly
wrong and the Cairo texts substantially authentic
are true beyond doubt." A brief, but detailed
synopsis of the history of scholarship on Ben Sira
including the arguments over the authenticity of
the Hebrew can be found in Milward Douglas Nelson,
"The Syriac Version of the Wisdom of Ben Sira
Compared to the Greek and Hebrew Materials" (PhD.
diss., UCLA, 1981) 10-23.

[11]On the second Hebrew recension, see C.
Kearns, "Ecclesiasticus, or the Wisdom of Jesus the
Son of Sirach," in New Catholic Commentary on Holy
Scripture, eds. R. D. Fuller, et al. (New York:
McGraw-Hill, 1969) 547-550, and Skehan and Di
Lella, 57-58, who rely primarily on Kearns's
analysis. See also in this regard M. H. Segal, "The
Evolution of the Hebrew Text of Ben Sira," JQR n.s.
25 (1934-1935) 91-149 and C. Kearns, "The Expanded
Text of Ecclesiasticus" (S.S.D. diss., Pontifical
Biblical Commission, 1951).

[12]This list of passages of the extant Hebrew
manuscripts was taken from Skehan and Di Lella, 52-
53. There are some additional citations of Ben Sira
in various places in rabbinic literature. These
citations, however, are frequently quite different
from the forms of the text as they are extant in
the Hebrew Ben Sira manuscripts. For a list of
these "quotations," see Solomon Schechter, "The
Quotations from Ecclesiasticus in Rabbinic
Literature," JQR 3 (1890-1891) 682-706; Cowley and
Neubauer, xix-xxx; Smend, XLVI-LVI.

[13]Ziegler's Origenic group includes MS 253-
Syrohexapla, and often the uncials V and S^c, the
Armenian, and Latin versions. The main Lucianic
group consists of MSS 248-493-637 and sometimes the
Armenian, Old Latin, and Syriac translations. The
Lucianic subgroup consists of MSS 106-130-545-705.
He includes the GKII additions in the running text
of his edition, but they are set in smaller type so
that they can be distinguished readily.
For Ziegler's arguments concerning these
groups, see Sapientia Iesu Filii Sirach, Septuaginta 12/2 (Göttingen: Vandenhoeck & Ruprecht,
1965) 58-69; Joseph Ziegler, "Hat Lukian den
griechischen Sirach rezensiert?" Bib 40 (1959) 210-
229; idem, "Die hexaplarische Bearbeitung des
griechischen Sirach," BZ N.F. 4 (1960) 174-185;
idem, "Die Vokabel-Varianten der O-Rezension im
griechischen Sirach," in Hebrew and Semitic Studies
Presented to Godfrey Rolles Driver, ed. D. Winton
Thomas (Oxford: Clarendon, 1963) 172-190.

[14]For Ziegler's reconstruction of the relationship between GKI, GKII, and the two Hebrew
versions, see Ziegler, Sapientia Iesu Filii Sirach,
81-84.

[15]H. B. Swete, The Old Testament in Greek, 3rd
ed., vol. 2 (Cambridge: Cambridge University, 1907)
vi-vii.

[16]Skehan and Di Lella, 56-57.

[17]See Skehan and Di Lella, 57, who cite
Kearns, "Ecclesiasticus," 547, in making this
judgment.

[18]Ibid., 60.

[19]This is the thesis of M. M. Winter in "The
Origins of Ben Sira in Syriac," VT 27 (1977) 237-

253 and 494-507. For a summary of the other
positions, see Nelson, "The Syriac Version of the
Wisdom of Ben Sira," chapter II.

[20]Nelson, "Syriac Version," 152; Skehan and Di
Lella, 57.

[21]Winter, "Origins," 238-251; Skehan and Di
Lella, 59. Besides the Peshitta, Sir is also found
in the Syrohexapla, which, according to Ziegler
(Sapientia Iesu Filii Sirach, 31), is an important
witness to the Origenic recension.

[22]I. Lévi, L'Ecclésiastique ou la Sagesse de
Jésus, fils de Sira, 2 parts (Paris: Leroux, 1898,
1901); Norbert Peters, Das Buch Jesus Sirach oder
Ecclesiasticus, EHAT 25 (Münster i. W.: Aschendorff,
1913); Smend; M. H. Segal, ספר בן-סירא השלם, 2nd
ed. (Jerusalem: Bialik Institute, 1958); G. H. Box
and W. O. E. Oesterley, "Sirach," in APOT 1, ed. R.
H. Charles (Oxford: Clarendon, 1913).

[23]A great impetus for the study of translation
technique came from the work of Dominique
Barthélemy on the Greek Minor Prophets scroll from
Nahal Hever (Les devanciers d'Aquila, VTSup 10
[Leiden: E. J. Brill, 1963]). See also the section
entitled "Translation-technique" in Sidney
Jellicoe, The Septuagint and Modern Study (Oxford:
Clarendon, 1968), and the bibliography contained in
the section entitled "Translation technique" in
Sebastian Brock, Charles Fritsch, and Sidney
Jellicoe, A Classified Bibliography of the
Septuagint, Arbeiten zur Literatur und Geschichte
des hellenistischen Judentums 6 (Leiden: E. J.
Brill, 1973).

[24]Arbeiten zu Text und Sprache im Alten
Testament 12 (St. Ottilien: EOS, 1980).

[25]Reiterer, 242-249.

[26]Raymond Martin, for example, (Syntactical
Evidence of Semitic Sources in Greek Documents, SCS
3 [Cambridge, Mass.: Society of Biblical Literature,
1974]), along with other matters, counted the
occurrences of prepositions in the OG based on HR.
Simply counting all the occurrences of prepositions
like ἐν must have demanded a great amount of time,
let alone any attempt to check the passages in

which these prepositions were found. For a comparison, based on Rahlfs' Septuaginta, using the computer to do the counting, see Benjamin G. Wright, "A Note on the Statistical Analysis of Septuagintal Syntax," JBL 104 (1985) 111-114. Other attempts to gather similar types of data, such as N. Turner's ("The Relation of Luke I and II to the Hebraic Sources and to the Rest of Luke-Acts," NTS 2 [1955-56], 101-109) figures for καί and δέ, must have encountered similar difficulties.

[27]Although Reiterer does not explicitly formulate the issue in these terms, on the whole, he resists making generalizing claims about the entire translation.

[28]See, for example, I. Soisalon-Soininen, Die Infinitive in der Septuaginta, AASF B 132.1 (Helsinki: Suomalainen Tiedeakatemia, 1965); idem, "The Rendering of the Hebrew Relative Clause in the Greek Pentateuch," Proceedings of the Sixth World Congress of Jewish Studies I, ed., Avigdor Shinan (Jerusalem: World Union of Jewish Studies, 1977) 401-406; Raija Sollamo, Renderings of Hebrew Semiprepositions in the Septuagint, AASF 19 (Helsinki: Suomalainen Tiedeakatemia, 1979); Anneli Aejmelaeus, Parataxis in the Septuagint: A Study of the Renderings of the Hebrew Coordinate Clauses in the Greek Pentateuch, AASF 31 (Helsinki: Suomalainen Tiedeakatemia, 1982).

[29]Detailed descriptions of the technical issues involved with the use of the computer have been kept to a minimum in the analyses of translation technique. Information concerning hardware, software, and the data files used in this study can be found in the Appendix.

[30]In many cases, both in Greek Sir and the OG, a Greek manuscript may have a textual variant that more closely represents the Hebrew text. For Sir, I have operated on the principle that Ziegler's critical Greek text is as close to that of the grandson as is obtainable at this time. The results of this study, however, may assist in the textual criticism of the Greek Sir. In some cases, where Greek manuscripts of Sir preserve a reading that is closer to the Hebrew texts, it is noted. A study of the Greek variants in Sir that bring the translation into closer conformity with one or more of the extant Hebrew texts would be valuable. For the

Greek scriptural traditions, the textual variants
are more carefully scrutinized. If the grandson
depended on Greek translations, they may not
necessarily have been the original OG, but perhaps
an early revision or corruption of the OG. This
problem is most acute for the examination of books
such as Samuel-Kings. Where variants exist that
show a similarity to what is in the grandson's
translation, they are noted. In the majority of
cases, however, there is little textual variation,
and the Greek variants play only a small part in
the analysis.

[31]For more extensive examples of the problems
connected with formal equivalence, see Emanuel Tov,
Computerized Data Base for Septuagint Studies: The
Parallel Aligned Text of the Greek and Hebrew Bible,
CATSS 2, Journal of Northwest Semitic Language
Supplementary Series 1 (Stellenbosch: Journal of
Northwest Semitic Languages, 1986) 26-30, and idem,
"Computer Assisted Alignment of the Greek-Hebrew
Equivalents of the Masoretic Text and the
Septuagint," in La Septuaginta en la Investigacion
Contemporanea (V Congreso de la IOSCS), ed. Natalio
Fernandez Marcos, Consejo Superior de Investiga-
ciones Cientificas (Madrid: Textos y Estudios
"Cardenal Cisneros" de la Biblia Poliglota
Matritense Instituto "Arias Montano" C.S.I.C.,
1985) 221-249.

[32]These emendations are few, however, and do
not seem to move the statistical data in one
direction or the other. From a practical standpoint, it is simply not feasible to make these
kinds of decisions for all of the books that are
treated below. The compilation of such emendations
for the Greek translations of the Bible is being
done by the CATSS team working in Jerusalem,
however. The computer files of the Hebrew-Greek
parallel texts have a separate column where this
data is recorded. Thus, studies of these books can
make full use of similar data for books other than
Sir. For more details on the computer text files,
see the Appendix.

CHAPTER 2: NOTES

[1]See above Chapter 1, nn. 8-10.

[2]For some recent studies, see M. Delcor, "Le
texte hebreu du cantique de Siracide 51.13 et ss et

les anciennes versions," Textus 6 (1968) 27-47; A.
A. Di Lella, "Sirach 10.19-11.6: Textual Criticism,
Poetic Analysis, and Exegesis," in The Word of the
Lord Shall Go Forth: Essays in Honor of D. N.
Freedman in Celebration of His Sixtieth Birthday,
ed. C. L. Meyers and M. O'Connor (Winona Lake,
Ind.: ASOR-Eisenbrauns, 1982) 157-164; M. Fang Che-
yong, "Sir 7,36 (Vulg 7,40) iuxta hebraicum
veritatem," VD 40 (1962) 18-26; Ph. B. Payne, "A
Critical Note on Eccl. 44.21's Commentary on the
Abrahamic Covenant," JETS 15 (1972) 186-187;
Benjamin G. Wright, "Ben Sira 43.11b - 'To What
Does the Greek Correspond?'" Textus 13 (1986) 111-
116; Roy K. Patteson Jr., "A Study of the Hebrew
Text of Sirach 39:27-41:24" (Ph.D. Diss., Duke
University, 1967).

[3]The Syriac, for its part, is not complete for
the entire book. The Old Latin, translated from
Greek, is a valuable witness to the GKII recension.
On these two versions, see Smend, CXVIII-CXXIX (Old
Latin), and CXXXVI-CXLVI (Syriac). Only Smend
includes any discussion of reconstructing the
Hebrew of Sir, and his discussion revolves, for the
most part, around the worth of the different
versions rather than around issues of translation
technique. See Smend, CIL-CLIX.

[4]Skehan and Di Lella, 132.

[5]Ziegler, Sapientia Iesu Filii Sirach, 83.

[6]Patteson, "A Study of the Hebrew Text of
Sirach 39:27-41:24," 36.

[7]Th. Middendorp, Die Stellung Jesu ben Siras
zwischen Judentum und Hellenismus (Leiden: E. J.
Brill, 1973) 37.

[8]Box and Oesterley, 279; Smend, LXIII; Peters,
LXX-LXXII.

[9]Reiterer, 241-249. In the first section of
the book, he examines a number of areas: word
order, differences in singular and plural, Greek
texts longer than the Hebrew, Greek texts shorter
than the Hebrew, verbal usage, the representation
of the Hebrew construct relationship, the use of
the article, the representation of the Hebrew
preposition ל, the treatment of את, and sentence

formation. For a more detailed assessment of the
book, see my review in JQR 75 (1984) 182-185.

[10]Tov, The Text-Critical Use of the Septuagint.

[11]For some studies of particular aspects of
translation technique, see the sections entitled
"Translation technique" in Brock, Fritsch, and
Jellicoe, A Classified Bibliography, and Emanuel
Tov, A Classified Bibliography of Lexical and
Grammatical Studies on the Language of the
Septuagint and Its Revisions (Jerusalem: Akademon,
1982).

[12]For more detail on this issue, see Emanuel
Tov, "The Nature and Study of the Translation
Technique of the LXX in the Past and Present," in
Cox, 337-359.

[13]I. Soisalon-Soininen, Die Infinitive in der
Septuaginta; Emanuel Tov, "The Representation of
the Causative Aspects of the Hiph'il in the LXX - A
Study in Translation Technique," Bib 63 (1982) 417-
424. A number of other studies of this type have
been done. For other studies by Soisalon-Soininen,
see Anneli Aejmelaeus and Raija Sollamo, eds.,
Ilmari Soisalon-Soininen: Studien zur Septuaginta-
Syntax, AASF B 237 (Helsinki: Suomalainen
Tiedeakatemia, 1987), and for Tov, see Emanuel Tov,
A Classififed Bibliography of Lexical and
Grammatical Studies. For other studies of specific
techniques of translation, see Jellicoe, The
Septuagint and Modern Study, under "Translation-
technique," and Brock, Fritsch, and Jellicoe, A
Classified Bibliography, under "Translation
technique."

[14]H. St. John Thackeray, A Grammar of the Old
Testament in Greek According to the Septuagint I,
Introduction, Orthography, and Accidence
(Cambridge: Cambridge University, 1909) 12-13.

[15]The practical aspects of the problem are
illustrated well by the work of Soisalon-Soininen
and his students, R. Sollamo and A. Aejmelaeus. All
three have produced excellent detailed studies of
one aspect of translation technique (Soisalon-
Soininen, among other things, on the infinitive,
Sollamo on the semiprepositions, and Aejmelaeus on
parataxis) and, except for Sollamo, have confined
themselves to the Pentateuch.

[16]This problem has also been discussed in
Emanuel Tov and Benjamin G. Wright, "Computer-
Assisted Study of the Criteria for Assessing the
Literalness of Translation Units in the LXX,"
Textus 12 (1985) 151-154.

[17]Barr and Tov, The Text-Critical Use of the
Septuagint. For other, less comprehensive
discussions of the literal approach of the biblical
translators, see E. J. Bickerman, "The Septuagint
as a Translation," PAAJR 28 (1959) 1-39; Sebastian
Brock, "The Phenomenon of the Septuagint," OTS 7
(1972) 11-36, and "Aspects of Translation Technique
in Antiquity," GRBS 20 (1979) 67-87; H. M.
Orlinsky, "The Septuagint as Holy Writ and the
Philosophy of the Translators," HUCA 46 (1975) 103-
114; C. Rabin, "The Translation Process and the
Character of the Septuagint," Textus 6 (1968) 1-26.

[18]Barr, 281. Tov (The Text-Critical Use of the
Septuagint, 53), for his part, wants to start from
criteria for literalness, "not because literalness
formed the basis of most translations, but rather
because these criteria can be defined more easily
than those for free renderings."

[19]Barr, 294; Tov, The Text-Critical Use of the
Septuagint, 54-59.

[20]For a similar discussion of what literalness
measures, see Benjamin G. Wright, "The Quantitative
Representation of Elements: Evaluating 'Literalism'
in the LXX," in Cox, 311-314.

[21]I. Soisalon-Soininen, "Methodologische
Fragen der Erforschung der Septuaginta-Syntax," in
Cox, 431-435.

[22]Tov and Wright, 153.

[23]For a similar description of the terms
"literal" and "free," see Tov and Wright, 152-154,
and Wright, "Quantitative Representation," 311-314.

[24]See, for example, Soisalon-Soininen, Die
Infinitive in der Septuaginta, Introduction, and
idem, "Methodologische Fragen."

[25]Ep. LVII 5,2, "ego enim non solum fateor,
sed libera voce profiteor, me in interpretatione
graecorum absque scripturis sanctis, ubi et

verborum ordo mysterium est, non verbum e verbo,
sed sensum exprimere de sensu" (quoted in Brock,
"The Phenomenon of the Septuagint," 21, n. 4). I do
not know of any studies of the extent to which
Jerome followed the word order of his source texts.
One need not assume that it was only sacred
writings that were treated thus. The need for
translation of documents of various kinds, legal
and business, for example, necessitated close if
not overly literal translation. On this issue and
the work of the so-called dragoman, see Bickerman,
"The Septuagint as a Translation," 16-17; and
Rabin, "The Translation Process and the Character
of the Septuagint," 19-26. On attitudes towards
translation in general in the ancient world, see
Brock, "Aspects of Translation Technique in
Antiquity."

[26]Brock, "Aspects of Translation Technique,"
81. He argues that the motivation for such a
correspondence is the high value that the
translator places on the text of the parent text.
J. M. Rife ("The Mechanics of Translation Greek,"
JBL 52 [1933] 245) calls word-order correspondence
the "basic characteristic" of Greek that translates
a Semitic original. In contrast, Barr, 300, argues
that adherence to the Hebrew word order "is
probably to be attributed to habit and the quest
for an easy technique rather than to any literalist
policy." In response to this argument, Galen
Marquis ("Word Order as a Criterion for the
Evaluation of Translation Technique in the LXX and
the Evaluation of Word-Order Variants as
Exemplified in LXX-Ezekiel," Textus 13 [1986] 61)
properly notes that Barr's position assumes a
conscious, deliberate choice of literalism as a
philosophy of translation.

[27]Hebraisms can result from different
processes within the act of translating. They can
be caused, for example, by certain lexical choices
made by the translator or, in the case of word-
order differences, syntax. Thus, I accept Tov's
definition of Hebraisms as "Greek words, phrases or
constructions which transfer certain characteristic
Hebrew elements into Greek in disregard of Greek
idiom" (Tov, The Text-Critical Use of the
Septuagint, 56).

[28]Rife, "Mechanics," 247. Since Rife is not
concerned with translation technique, but with

detecting Greek that has translated a Semitic
document, the second category, displacement
differences, plays no part in his analysis.

[29]Shemaryahu Talmon, "The Textual Study of the
Bible - A New Outlook," in Qumran and the History
of the Biblical Text, eds. Frank Moore Cross and
Shemaryahu Talmon (Cambridge: Harvard University,
1975) 359. Talmon examines Isa 28.7, where the OG
makes the Hebrew A-B // B-A chiastic structure into
an A-B // A-B pattern, in order to show the
difficulty of determining whether this is a problem
of a differing parent text, or whether the
translator simply exercised "literary license."

[30]See above Chapter 1 on formal
representation.

[31]This same point is made and is explained in
greater detail by Marquis, "Word Order," 62.

[32]Ibid., 64.

[33]For investigations of the relationship of
καί to δέ in Greek literature, see N. Turner, A
Grammar of New Testament Greek, III, Syntax
(Edinburgh: T & T Clark, 1963); idem, "The Relation
of Luke I and II to the Hebraic Sources, 107-109;
Martin, Syntactical Evidence, 16-20.

[34]In his summaries, Marquis counts all word-
order changes together. Since he argues that word-
order differences that result from "linguistic or
grammatical limitations or conventions" ("Word
Order," 61) should be considered, I presume that he
has included items such as the occurrence of δέ in
his statistical summaries.

[35]Marquis, besides giving a good theoretical
discussion of the problem of word-order differences, has given some indications of this type of
variation for the OG of Ezekiel. See "Word Order,"
12-13.

[36]Certain allowances are made for problems
found in individual books. For all the books,
doublets have been disregarded because each doublet
would need to be studied individually in order to
determine which part of the doublet was original,
or whether the original translator created the
doublet. For Sir, only the lines of text for the

two-thirds of the book for which Hebrew is
available are counted. Other special cases are
Daniel and Esther for which the lines constituting
the Greek additions were discounted, Jeremiah for
which the number of lines had to be reduced by
approximately one-seventh in order to take account
of the presumed shorter Hebrew parent text of that
book, Job for which the Theodotion lines were
disregarded, and the Minor Prophets, which are
treated as one translation, since they likely were
translated by the same person. The data for each
individual book of the Minor Prophets are presented
in a separate table. The books of Samuel and Kings
will be divided into H. St. John Thackeray's
translation sections: α = 1 Samuel, ββ = 2 Sam 1-
11.1, βγ = 2 Sam 11.2-1 Kgs 2.11, γγ = 1 Kgs 2.12-
21.43, γδ = 1 Kgs 22.1-2 Kgs. See H. St. John
Thackeray, "The Greek Translators of the Four Books
of Kings," JTS 8 (1907) 262-278, and Dominique
Barthélemy, Les devanciers d'Aquila, 36. Ezekiel is
broken into three sections as delineated by Leslie
John McGregor (The Greek Text of Ezekiel: An
Examination of Its Homogeneity, SCS 18 [Atlanta:
Scholars, 1985] 95). They will be designated here
as, Ezek(α') (chaps. 1-25), Ezek(β') (chaps. 26-39)
and Ezek(γ') (chaps. 40-48).

With regard to the method of counting, some
slight imprecision is introduced by the fact that
if a word-order deviation takes three lines, it has
a statistical value of one, while each of the three
lines is counted individually in the total number
of lines. This problem, however, exists for all the
translations studied, and, since the percentages
are used as means of comparison between translations, this imprecision should not affect the basic
relationships. Further, in the CATSS computer files
there are a number of irrelevant lines. For
example, some lines simply indicate that a Greek or
Hebrew word is found elsewhere in the file. These
lines have been eliminated as far as possible.

[37]Marquis, "Word Order," 64.

[38]Ibid., 64, n. 17.

[39]Although one Hebrew word per one computer
record is the general rule in the CATSS parallel
aligned texts, there are cases in every book where
more than one Hebrew word occurs on one line. For
example, the Greek μακρόθυμος translates the
Hebrew words ארך אפים, and they are on one line in

the CATSS files. Hence, I have used the number of
lines in the file as the basis for the percentages.

[40]Barr, 281.

[41]The persistent use of δέ in Genesis is
probably due to the fact that the book is mostly
narrative and requires numerous coordinators, while
Job and Proverbs, at least, are mostly poetry and
require fewer paratactic conjunctions. On the use
of parataxis in the Pentateuch, see Aejmelaeus,
Parataxis in the Septuagint. Ruth is one other book
whose position relative to the other translations
changes dramatically when δέ is excluded from
consideration (from 27th position on Table 2 to
20th). When δέ is included, Ruth falls close to
Daniel o' and Isaiah, but when δέ is excluded,
Ruth stands close to the Pentateuch, Jeremiah, and
Ezek(α'). The Minor Prophets show a similar
movement up the scale (from 15th position to 10th),
as does Psalms (from 19th to 14th).

[42]Reiterer, 60, notes the relative latitude
that the grandson takes in the section comprising
Sir 44.16-45.26, although this is in particular
contrast to the Syriac, which, Reiterer notes,
follows the Hebrew more closely.

[43]The frequency of γάρ for כי is only matched
in Proverbs. For statistical data on γάρ as a
lexical equivalent of כי, see Tov and Wright, 164-
165.

[44]This type of deviation is most frequent
elsewhere in Proverbs where the possessive
adjective is used rather than the independent
personal pronoun. See, for example, Prov 1.23; 3.1;
3.5; 3.26. In Sir, see 8.19.

[45]See, for example, Sir 5.15; 7.11; 8.8;
11.12; 16.1; etc.

[46]Marquis, "Word Order," 66.

[47]For detailed discussions of these translations, see Sollamo, Renderings, 280-287, and Tov
and Wright, 181-187. The criteria used by Tov and
Wright basically focus on the representation of the
Hebrew preposition ב, the conjunction כי, the
addition of prepositions, and the frequency of
post-position particles.

[48]Sollamo, Renderings, 284-286.

[49]Tov and Wright, 182, 185-187. The translations belonging to this last group are Sirach, Psalms, Lamentations, 1 Samuel, Ezekiel, and the Minor Prophets.

[50]Barr, 294. For Barr's complete discussion of segmentation, see Barr, 294-303. For Tov's discussion, see The Text-Critical Use of the Septuagint, 57-58. Some of the introductory discussion in this section is also presented in my paper "The Quantitative Representation of Elements: Evaluating 'Literalism' in the LXX."

[51]Barr, 295.

[52]Ibid.

[53]The treatment of the definite article is a problem that threatens to undermine any statistical analysis of data on segmentation. In this section it is treated in the following ways: (1) if the noun has no prepositional prefixes and no definite article in Hebrew, the addition of the in Greek article is not counted, but it is considered part of the noun; (2) if the noun has some prepositional prefix or other prefix that would require the definite article to be represented in the vocalization, the presence of the article is taken as part of the noun (it is for this reason discounted as a quantitative plus in the following section of this chapter); (3) if the noun has the definite article ה prefixed, the article is counted as a segmentable part of the Hebrew word, and its absence in Greek is considered an example of a nonsegmented word. The use of the definite article in these different instances could form the basis for a useful study. Unfortunately, the scope of this dissertation does not allow for such an undertaking.

[54]Barr, 298.

[55]Ibid., 300.

[56]Sollamo, Renderings, 1. She uses the term "semipreposition" for lack of a better term. She notes that this English term is actually a translation of the German "Halbpraeposition" used by Carl Brockelmann in Grundriss der vergleichenden

Grammatik der semitischen Sprachen II (Berlin, 1913).

[57]Ibid.

[58]Ibid., 282.

[59]For the list of semiprepositions in the Jewish-Greek translations, see Sollamo, Renderings, 2. Some of the most frequently occurring words, other than the semiprepositions are: מעל, מנגד, מאח, לבלתי, לבד, בעבור, בגלל, מזה, משם, כאשר, מחחח, מעם.

[60]The Masada scroll has [..]מי, which is apparently the same as MS B.

[61]For generalizing characterizations of the translations of the canonical corpus, see H. St. John Thackeray, A Grammar of the Old Testament in Greek According to the Septuagint I, 12-13, and R. A. Kraft, "Septuagint," in The Interpreter's Dictionary of the Bible: Supplementary Volume (Nashville: Abingdon, 1976) 807-815. Some studies have attempted to characterize certain translations on the basis of specific criteria. See Soisalon-Soininen, Die Infinitive in der Septuaginta, 177-178, 186, 189; Sollamo, Renderings, 280-289; Tov, The Text-Critical Use of the Septuagint, 63; Tov and Wright, 181-187; Wright, "Quantitative Representation," 331-332; Marquis, "Word Order," 63-66; idem, "Consistency of Lexical Equivalents as a Criterion for the Evaluation of Translation Technique as Exemplified in the LXX of Ezekiel," in Cox, 416-417.

[62]Of the biblical translations selected for use in this section, all are OG except for Qoheleth, which may be the work of Aquila, and if it is not, it is at least a very wooden translation of the MT. The books, however, were not necessarily selected because they represent the OG, but because they represent a wide range of approaches to the Hebrew by the translators. Such a wide range of approaches helps to provide a clear basis against which to judge Sir. On the translation of Qoheleth, see Barthélemy, Les devanciers, 21-30.

[63]One particular type of problem may skew some of the statistics somewhat. It may occasionally happen that the Greek by coincidence has omitted an

element in the Hebrew and translated another
element by more than one word, thus producing
"equal" segmentation. Any instance such as this
would be accidental, since I checked each passage
that the computer output in order to make sure that
problems such as these did not find their way into
the final tallies.

[64]Sollamo, Renderings, 285-286. For a list of
the translations that she studied and their
groupings, see above p. 53.

[65]Tov and Wright, 181, 185. For the groupings
delineated by Tov and Wright, see above p. 54.

[66]Barr, 303-315; Tov, The Text-Critical Use of
the Septuagint, 58-59.

[67]Barr, 305, makes this claim, and the initial
studies carried out here bear it out.

[68]Wright, "Quantitative Representation," 315.
Much of what follows in this introduction and in
the section on longer quantitative additions has
been adapted from this paper.

[69]The material in this section, except for the
data on Qoheleth, is a summary of my paper
"Quantitative Representation."

[70]For discussions regarding the types of
elements that can and cannot be reconstructed with
certainty, see Tov, The Text-Critical Use of the
Septuagint, 217-228, and Tov, A Computerized Data
Base for Septuagint Studies, 102-103.

[71]σημεῖον is the reading of Ziegler's
edition. A. A. Di Lella, in his review of Ziegler
(CBQ 28 [1966] 540), argues that the grandson
mistranslated אוֹיָ֑ה. The grandson read אוֹנָ֑ה, and
consequently, the original Greek translation was
σημεῖα. This Greek reading appears in MSS 248-672.

[72]As in the previous two sections doublets
have not been considered in the final tallies. For
Sir, only those places for which a Hebrew text is
extant are counted.

[73]Tov and Wright, 181-186.

[74]Sollamo, Renderings, 184-186. The groups in
which she places Numbers and Amos are not given

specific descriptive names. They do, however,
correspond to the groups that Tov and I called
relatively literal and relatively free.

[75]For כל, see Prov 1.13; 1.17; 1.25; 1.30;
7.26; 16.11. For גג, see Prov 14.13; 14.20; 17.15;
17.26, 28; 26.4.

[76]See, for only one of several examples, Ezra
(II Esdras) 10.2.

ועתה יש מקוה לישראל על זאת
καὶ νῦν ἔστιν ὑπομονὴ τῷ ισραηλ ἐπὶ τούτῳ

[77]For examples of this situation, see Sir 5.11
where MS A has טובה and MS C and Greek have
nothing. See also Sir 41.3 where Ms B has כֹ', but
the Masada scroll and Greek lack any parallel. Some
other places where this occurs are Sir 4.30; 7.1,
23; 10.25, 29, 30; 15.19; 16.3, 7; 31.9; 35.14;
37.3, 28, 29, 31; 38.12; 40.14; 41.3, 6; 42.8;
44.2, 3, 16; 51.15, 18, 19.

[78]The term "stereotyping" is used by a number
of scholars, and, according to Tov (The Text-
Critical Use of the Septuagint, 54), the term seems
to have originated with M. Flashar ("Exegetische
Studien zum Septuagintapsalter," ZAW 32 [1912]
105). "Verbal linkage" is used by Rabin ("The
Translation Process and the Character of the
Septuagint," 8); "concordant relationship" by E.
Nida (Towards a Science of Translating [Leiden: E.
J. Brill, 1964] 156); and the phrase "regular
lexical correspondence" is used by Brock ("Aspects
of Translation Technique in Antiquity," 67-87).
"Lexical equivalency" appears as a synonym for
these other terms in Marquis ("Consistency of
Lexical Equivalents"). I consider all of these
terms to be synonymous, and mostly for the sake of
convenience, the term stereotyping is used
throughout this section.

[79]A number of studies treat the idea of
stereotyping in general. Most predominant among
these are Barr, Tov, (The Text-Critical Use of the
Septuagint) and Brock, "Aspects of Translation
Technique in Antiquity." Some studies go farther
and attempt to give some data on stereotyping. See,
for example, Sollamo, Renderings, Tov and Wright,
and Marquis, "Consistency of Lexical Equivalents."

[80]There is evidence that certain glossaries or word lists did exist and that they were used, mostly by the professional translator, the so-called dragoman. On the function of this translator and the evidence for these lists, see Rabin, "The Translation Process and the Character of the Septuagint," 23-24, and Bickerman, "The Septuagint as a Translation," 13-16.

[81]See above n. 61.

[82]Marquis, "Consistency of Lexical Equivalents," 410.

[83]Ibid., 412.

[84]Ibid., 412.

[85]Sollamo, Renderings, 13.

[86]Ibid., 283.

[87]Marquis, "Consistency of Lexical Equivalents," 410.

[88]Some studies have already treated certain aspects of this area. See, for example, Soisalon-Soininen, Die Infinitive in Der Septuaginta, and Tov, "The Representation of the Causative Aspects of the Hiph'il in the LXX," 417-424. For Sir, see Reiterer, Chapter 3, where some of these aspects are examined for 44.16-45.26.

[89]The only word not included that occurred more than 5 times was the Greek verb εἰμί. This word has such a wide variety of possible uses and is so flexible that in every case its stereotyping tendency would fall below 50 percent.

[90]The second two limits were not chosen entirely arbitrarily. They were chosen so that there would be a wide enough range of percentages to handle words that occur only a few times. Thus, for example 4/5 = 80%; 4/6 = 66.66%; 3/5 = 60%. If the limits were drawn higher, some of these percentages would be included together and others excluded, although no possibilities existed for occurrences in the middle.

[91]The only real problem comes with Song of Songs in Table 11, where the stereotyping tendency

is only 80 percent. The reason for this relatively low figure when compared to its stereotyping tendency in the other tables is that only 5 nouns fall into this category, and 4 of them have individual stereotyping tendencies of over 75 percent.

[92]For a detailed treatment of διαθήκη in Sir, see below Chapter 3.

[93]Smend, LXIII, in fact does make this claim. He argues that in their non-literal approach to their source texts the three translations are similar. He writes, "Indessen sieht er die Aufgabe einer Uebersetzung nicht in der wörtlichen Wiedergabe des Originals, sondern vielmehr in gutgriechischen Ausdruck, der für poetische texte in der Tat besonders erforderlich war, und im Allgemeinen entfernt er sich dabei vom Original kaum weiter als die Uebersetzer der Proverbien und des Hiob. Oft genug kommt er aber auch über wörtliche Unbeholfenheit nicht hinaus."

CHAPTER 3: NOTES

[1]Smend, LXIII, writes, "Ohne Zweifel war er imstande, die im Ganzen sehr sorgfältig gearbeitete LXX zum Pentateuch und zu den historischen Büchern mit dem hebräischen Text zu vergleichen; öfter hat sie ihm als Wörterbuch gedient." In his footnote, Smend gives nine examples from the Pentateuch, one from Samuel, and one from Malachi. As we shall see, this does not compare to the number of places where the grandson departs from the usage of the OG, even in places where one might reasonably expect him to use it.

[2]Reiterer, 242-249.

[3]For the background on these discoveries, see, Chapter 1 above and the literature cited therein.

[4]See especially, Schechter and Taylor, The Wisdom of Ben Sira; A. Eberharter, Der Kanon des Alten Testament zur Zeit des Ben Sira, ATAbh (Münster i. W.: Aschendorff, 1911). Also see, the notes in Box and Oesterley; Smend; Peters; Lévi; Segal; as well as others, where references to the Bible abound.

[5]Schechter and Taylor, <u>The Wisdom of Ben Sira</u>,
12. See, J. G. Snaith's critique of this remark in
"Biblical Quotations in the Hebrew of Ecclesiasticus," <u>JTS</u> 18 (1967) 1-12.

[6]Schechter and Taylor, <u>The Wisdom of Ben Sira</u>,
13.

[7]Another example is the phrase זהב אופר, which
occurs in Sir 7.18 and in 1 Kgs 10.11, 1 Chr 29.4,
and 2 Chr 9.10. Cf. also, 1 Kgs 9.28 and 22.48.

[8]Certainly the commonality of traditions, the
oral circulation of this material, and its
transmission in school contexts make this option
likely. For more general discussion of wisdom
literature in the Ancient Near East, see the
appropriate sections and bibliography, especially
James Crenshaw's article on wisdom literature, in
Douglas A. Knight and Gene M. Tucker, eds., <u>The
Hebrew Bible and its Modern Interpreters</u> (Chico:
Scholars, 1985).

[9]Snaith, "Biblical Quotations, 11."

[10]Box and Oesterley, 279.

[11]See Box and Oesterley, 370-371, where they
note the difference in the Greek in a note. They
often give preference to the Hebrew as can be seen
in their translation of the Hebrew in the text and
the relegation of the Greek text to the notes. Many
times as well, the Hebrew on which they depend is
Smend's reconstructed Hebrew text; so, frequently,
in their textual notes.

[12]See above n. 5.

[13]Snaith, "Biblical Quotations," 3.

[14]See above, Chapter 2, n. 7. The main aim of
Middendorp's work is to argue that Ben Sira was
intended to be a school book. His discussion of the
influence of the Hebrew Bible is part of this
larger concern. On the general reception of this
idea, see especially the reviews by M. Hengel, <u>JSJ</u>
5 (1974) 83-87, and J. Marböck, <u>VT</u> 24 (1974) 510-
513.

[15]Middendorp, 37, writes, "Da ich G für eine
getreue Wiedergabe seiner Vorlage halte, nehme ich
an, V habe היש ר לי י enthalten."

[16] Snaith, "Biblical Quotations," 3.

[17] Eberharter, Der Kanon, 6.

[18] See, for example, Gen 32.5; 33.8, 15; Exod 33.13; 34.9; Deut 24.1; Judg 5.17; 1 Sam 27.5; 2 Sam 14.22.

[19] Snaith, "Biblical Quotations," 4.

[20] The division of the books in the prologue follows at least two of the traditional divisions of the Hebrew Bible, the Law, and the Prophets. The third group, the Writings, is not referred to as such. For detailed discussion of the problems of the canonization of the Hebrew Bible, see Sid Z. Leiman, The Canonization of Hebrew Scripture: The Talmudic and Midrashic Evidence, Transactions of the Connecticut Academy of Arts and Sciences 47 (Hamden, Conn.: Archon Books, 1976). For discussions of Ben Sira and the canon, see especially J. L. Koole, "Die Bibel des Ben Sira," OTS 14 (1965) 374-396.

[21] Sir 49.8 is one of the earliest uses of the term מרכבה as a description of what Ezekiel saw in his vision. For an excellent treatment of early Merkavah literature, see the introduction to 3 Enoch by P. Alexander in James Charlesworth, ed., The Pseudepigrapha of the Old Testament, vol. 1 (Garden City, N.Y.: Doubleday, 1983), and the literature cited therein.

[22] The discovery of the complete book of Isaiah found at Qumran (1QIsa^a) provides evidence for the existence of the entire book in one Hebrew scroll at the time of the grandson. The exact date of the Greek translation of the book remains problematic, but if Ben Sira's grandson used it, this provides evidence for a date of 117 BCE or earlier.

[23] On this issue, see Leiman, Canonization, Chapter I.

[24] Schechter and Taylor, The Wisdom of Ben Sira, 12.

[25] D. Michaelis ("Das Buch Jesus Sirach als typischer Ausdruck für das Gottesverhältnis des

nachalt-testamentliche Menschen," <u>TLZ</u> 83 [1958]
601-602 [cited in Snaith, 5]) has calculated that
over 96 percent of the Hebrew words in the Geniza
fragments also appear in the Bible. His study,
however, takes the entire Hebrew Bible into
account, and it does not divide the books according
to their canonical divisions.

[26]Some possible examples might be כל בשר
ימרו (16.1); בבני עולה (14.15); ליודי גורל (8.19);
(41.2) פיו (39.31); נוחו על משכב (40.5); ועבד תקוה
מצא חן בעיני (42.1); אנשי חיל (44.6).

[27]See, for example, בברכת יי (4.13); יי נלחם
(45.3); ויצוהו אל (41.11); אך שם לא יכרת (4.28); לך
הפרכת (50.5); ארץ זבח חלב ודבש (46.8); קדוש ישראל (50.17); מבית
הפרכת (50.5).

[28]Snaith, "Biblical Quotations," 5-6.

[29]Ibid., 3.

[30]See, as an example, the quotation from
Middendorp, 37, cited above.

[31]See, for example, the statements by Box and
Oesterley, 280, and Smend, LXIII, cited above.

[32]Reiterer deals with this issue sporadically,
but it is not a central focus of his work. See, for
example, below under κλώθω.

[33]The Hebrew הכתוב in Sir 48.10 is often
referred to as a quotation formula. I think that it
is not a citation, but a reference to Elijah being
"appointed" by God. For a detailed discussion, see
below, section 3.4.2.1.

[34]Although the section on the Hebrew of Ben
Sira was not so detailed, the different models
outlined here for the grandson's exposure to the OG
translations may also be relevant to an understanding of what the possibilities are for the ways
in which Ben Sira himself could have known the
Hebrew scriptural traditions. These models attempt
to take into account the complicated ways in which
these types of materials would have been communicated in Judaism at the time of Ben Sira and his
grandson. The situation appears much more complicated than someone sitting and copying from some
other works, whether or not they are scriptural.

[35]This use is somewhat different from the use
of the phrase "lexical equivalent" in Chapter 2.
There the phrase refers to the Hebrew and Greek
terms that positionally correspond to each other.
The Hebrew may not be the term which was in the
parent text, but in the present form of the text it
stands over against the Greek. For a longer
discussion of the concept of formal equivalence,
see above Chapter 1 and the literature cited there.

[36]For a summary of the attempts by P. Kahle,
H. St. John Thackeray, M. Gaster, and F. X. Wutz to
explain the origins and chronology of the OG, see
Jellicoe, The Septuagint and Modern Study, 59-73,
as well as work on specific books of the OG listed
in Brock, Fritsch, and Jellicoe, A Classified
Bibliography of the Septuagint.

[37]G. B. Caird, "Ben Sira and the Dating of the
Septuagint," in Studia Evangelica, VII: Papers
Presented to the Fifth International Congress on
Biblical Studies Held at Oxford, 1973, ed. E. A.
Livingstone, TU 126 (Berlin: Akademie, 1982) 95-
100.

[38]Ibid., 96, although he is largely dependent
on H. B. Swete, The Old Testament in Greek, 369-
370, for this judgment.

[39]Ibid., 97. See Thackeray's arguments in The
Septuagint and Jewish Worship, 2d ed. (London:
Published for the British Academy by H. Milford,
1923) and his article "Septuagint," in The
International Standard Bible Encyclopedia, ed.
James Orr (Chicago: Howard-Severance, 1915) 2722-
2732. Jellicoe has a shorter summary of Thackeray's
views in The Septuagint and Modern Study, 64-70.

[40]Caird, "Ben Sira and the Dating of the
Septuagint," 97.

[41]The large numbers of biblical references
given in the commentaries on Ben Sira are
indicative of this mindset. A good example is
Snaith's comment in "Biblical Quotations," 3, that
Ben Sira may have "quoted" from literature no
longer extant. The very notion of quoting from a
source, as he uses the word, seems to assume a
written form.

⁴²This is not, however, to assume that the בית
מדרש referred to in Ben Sira (51.23) and its later
rabbinic form are the same, although it probably
refers to a school of instruction. Skehan and Di
Lella, 578, argue for בית מוסר here rather than בית
מדרש, based on the use of παιδεία in the Greek and
a play on words involving the use of the verb מוסר
at the beginning of the stanza, a reading reconstructed by Smend to fit the acrostic poem [Die
Weisheit des Jesus Sirach hebräisch und deutsch
(Berlin: Georg Reimer, 1906) 61 (Hebrew section)].
They also refer to a similar situation in Sir 6.22.
On Jewish education in the Second Temple Period,
see S. Safrai, "Education and the Study of the
Torah," in S. Safrai, et al., eds., Compendia Rerum
Judicarum ad Novum Testamentum, Section One, The
Jewish People in the First Century, vol. 2, ed. S.
Safrai and M. Stern in Cooperation with D. Flusser
and W. C. van Unik (Philadelphia: Fortress, 1983)
945-970.

Although the Prologue 4-6 does not say that
Ben Sira or his grandson learned through oral
instruction, the reference to such instruction
seems clear. καὶ ὡς οὐ μόνον αὐτοὺς τοὺς
ἀναγινώσκοντας δέον ἐστὶν ἐπιστήμονας γίνεσθαι
ἀλλὰ καὶ τοῖς ἐκτὸς δύνασθαι τοὺς φιλομαθοῦντας
χρησίμους εἶναι καὶ λέγοντας καὶ γράφοντας;
"And they must understand [the truths given through
the Law and the Prophets] not only read them, but
also they, being lovers of learning, need to be of
benefit to those who are without [the truths], both
in speech and in writing."

⁴³Jack T. Sanders, Ben Sira and Demotic
Wisdom, SBL Monograph Series 28 (Chico: Scholars,
1983) 27.

⁴⁴For bibliography on Schechter and Taylor,
Eberharter, and Middendorp, see above note 5 and
Chapt. 2, n. 7. J. K. Gasser, Die Bedeuting der
Sprüche Jesu Ben Sira für die Datierung des
althebräischen Spruchbuches untersucht, Beiträge
zur Forderung christlicher Theologie, Jhrg. 8 Hft.
2, 3 (Gütersloh: Bertelsmann, 1904).

⁴⁵The works of Caird ("The Dating of the
Septuagint") and Snaith ("Biblical Quotations")
have been used primarily, along with the major
commentaries.

⁴⁶C. J. Ball, The Ecclesiastical or Deutero-
canonical Books of the Old Testament Commonly

<u>Called the Apocrypha</u> (London: Eyre and Spottis-
woode, n.d.). The commentaries of O. F. Fritzsche,
<u>Die Weisheit Jesus Sirach erklärt und Übersetzt</u>,
Kurzgefasstes Exegetisches Handbuch zu den Apokryphen des Alten Testamentes, vol. 5 (Lipsia: S.
Hirzel, 1859), and V. Ryssel, "Die Sprüche Jesus',
des Sohnes Sirachs," in <u>Die Apokryphen und</u>
<u>Pseudepigraphen des Alten Testaments</u>, I, ed., E.
Kautzsch (Tübingen: Mohr, 1921) were used primarily.

[47]Both Eberharter (<u>Der Kanon</u>) and Gasser (<u>Die</u>
<u>Bedeutung</u>) divide their passages into categories
depending on how close to the biblical wording the
passages are. I have combined them into one large
group because I have found what I consider to be
genuine examples of textual dependence by Ben Sira
in all of their groups. These findings support
their inclusion together. The last line of the
chart, called "Total Number of Different Texts,"
represents the number of specific passages found in
these authors, since many of the same passages are
cited by more than one of them. Column A in the
last line is blank because of the difficulty of
collating the total number of specific passages
found in all four authors. That number is not as
important as the numbers in columns B and C.

[48]P. C. Beentjes, <u>Jesus Sirach en Tanach</u>
(Nieuwegein: published by the author, 1981), 51,
cites this phrase from D. Patte, (<u>Early Jewish</u>
<u>Hermeneutic in Palestine</u>, SBLDS 22 [Missoula:
Scholars, 1975]). In his work, Patte uses the
phrase in order to try to understand how
apocalyptic literature uses "scripture." For the
term "anthological" applied to Ben Sira, see J. G.
Snaith, "Ben Sira's Supposed Love of Liturgy," <u>VT</u>
25 (1975) 167-174.

[49]A question mark appears with a passage for
which there is some ambiguity as to its relationship with its biblical tradition. In this category,
for example, there is some ambiguity concerning
whether the passage in the Hebrew of Sir really
reflects the Hebrew Bible.

[50]Skehan and Di Lella, 431, make the same
point.

[51]The Hebrew here is וְיִרֵשׁ (niphal), which
has the negative connotation "to be dispossessed"

(BDB, 434). The Greek translator has evidently read the hiphil יוֹרִשׁ "cause to inherit" and inter- preted the verse to mean that the nations will inherit God's wrath.

[52]BDB, 1052.

[53]Snaith, "Biblical Quotations," 8.

[54]Smend, 363, Peters, 167, Box and Oesterley, 458, Segal, 264, and Skehan and Di Lella, 457, all see Ps 107.34, ארץ פרי למלחה, as playing into the Hebrew here with למלחה having the sense of "waste- land." The Greek for למלחה, εἰς ἅλμην, is also used in Greek Sir here, but this could easily be a case of incidental agreement. In my opinion, the literary tie is closer to Gen 13.10 through the unusual use of משׁקה.

[55]Skehan and Di Lella, 461, argue that the Hebrew is an allusion to the Leviticus passage.

[56]See, for example, below under Sir 40.9. Sir 48.15 directs punishments at Israel that are also given against Israel in Deut 28.63. Beentjes (Jesus Sirach en Tanach, 135-136) argues that the punishments used in Ben Sira come from lists of punishments and not directly from the Hebrew Bible. In support of this argument he cites G. von Rad, "Hiob 38 und die altägyptische Weisheit," SVT 3 (1955) 293-301. Von Rad, however, is first of all speaking of the "Schöpfungshymnus" in Sir 43.1-33 and not of Sir 39, which seems to me to be of a different type of material. Second, for Sir 43, von Rad notes that the general scheme of the Egyptian Onomastikon of Amenemope is paralleled. He further says, "Es kann natürlich keine Rede davon sein, dass die beiden hebräischen Texte [Job 38 and Sir 43] direkt im literarischen Sinn von einem ägyptischen Onomastikon abhängig sind" (295). Beentjes's contention, then, does not appear to be substantiated for this text.

[57]According to the textual apparatus in John Wevers's Göttingen edition of Leviticus, there is no variant ῥομφαία in the OG tradition. Ziegler (Sapientia Iesu Filii Sirach), in his apparatus, shows no variant μάχαιρα for ῥομφαία in Sir 39.30.

[58]ῥομφαία only occurs here in 39.30 with a Hebrew equivalent in Sir. In 21.3, 22.21, and

26.28, there is no extant Hebrew. In 40.9,
ῥομφαία = חֹרֶב (drought). μάχαιρα, its synonym,
occurs in 28.18 where there is no extant Hebrew.

[59]The OG translation at this point could have
had a parent text different from the MT. Ben Sira's
Hebrew would be different from that text and could
be taken as reflecting the MT form of Deuteronomy.
This is all the more probable because the Greek of
Sir seems to presuppose the extant Hebrew as its
parent text. The Greek of Sir, in any case, does
not appear to depend on the preserved OG of
Deuteronomy here.

[60]In the second half of the colon, the Hebrew
and Greek do not preserve the same word order.
Middendorp, 43, argues, I think correctly, that the
Hebrew has been influenced in transmission by Isa
51.19, which has three of the same nouns (if in Sir
רעה is corrupted from רעב as seems likely). The
Greek probably preserves the proper order, that is,
the one which does not equal the MT of Isaiah.

[61]εἰσέρχομαι corresponds to נגש only in Exod
20.21 in the OG. נגש in the qal is rendered most
often by ἐγγίζω and in the hiphil by προσάγω
(cf. Sir 45.16).

[62]Reiterer, 175, also argues for the
grandson's independence from the OG here. כליל
appears two other places in Sir, but it is rendered
by different words, συντέλειαν in 45.8 and
ἐνδελεχῶς in 37.18. S. Daniel (Recherches sur le
vocabulaire du culte dans la Septante, Etudes et
Commentaires 61 [Paris: Librairie C. Klincksieck,
1965] 172) discusses this passage, but says that
ὁλοκαρπωθήσονται is a translation of מנחה. This
is clearly not the case. The Hebrew of 45.14 begins
מנחתו with the corresponding Greek θυσίαι αὐτοῦ.
כליל תקטר corresponds to ὁλοκαρπωθήσεται. On p.
257, she notes the difference from the Greek of Sir
and Leviticus on this verse. On the general use of
cultic vocabulary in Ben Sira, see pp. 375-379.

[63]MS B frequently uses triple ' as an
abbreviation for the Tetragrammaton rather than the
more usual two, as in MSS A, C, and E.

[64]Beentjes, Jesus Sirach en Tanach, 116.

[65]On the use of אישׁי in the OG, see Daniel, Recherches, 155-174.

[66]11.19; 30.19; 31.19; 36.20 = φάγομαι; 6.3 = κατεσθίω; 15.3 = ψωμιέω; 45.19 = καταναλίσκω.

[67]On this verse, see Reiterer, 208-210, and Beentjes, Jesus Sirach en Tanach, 116, especially for the use of θυσία and אישׁי. See also, Smend, 435, and N. Peters (Der jüngst wiederaufgefundene hebräische Text des Buches Ecclesiasticus: untersucht, herausgegeben, übersetzt und mit kritischen Noten versehen [Freiburg i. B.: Herdersche Verlagshandlung, 1902], 245 [Peters, Text]), who argue that the present stichometric order of the Hebrew is incorrect, although the Greek follows the extant order. Eberharter (Der Kanon, 11) refers to Lev 2.10, 5.12, and 7.35 for this verse.

[68]Middendorp, 47, argues that the Hebrew parent text read משׁנה. This argument reflects his view of "errors cause by memory" discussed above. The possibility of a genuine piece of exegesis on the part of the Greek translator makes me reluctant to agree with Middendorp on this issue.

[69]On the Hebrew text-critical problems connected with this verse, see especially Yadin, The Masada Scroll, 28; Strugnell, "Notes and Queries in the Ben Sira Scroll from Masada," 117; G. Prato, Il problema della teodica in Ben Sira, AnBib 65 (Rome: Pontifical Biblical Institute, 1975) 127-128; Segal, 293; Smend, 400; Peters, Text, 208; Lévi, 62.

[70]Yadin's reconstruction of the situation in 44.16 adequately explains this problem. As he argues, the lack of this verse in Syriac and in the Masada text testifies to its absence in the earliest forms of Sir. At some later point, parts of 49.14-16 were displaced before the account of Noah in order to restore Enoch to his rightful chronological position. Yadin (The Masada Scroll, 38) reconstructs the Enoch section as follows:

49.14a מעט נוצר על הארץ כחנוך / οὐ δὲ εἷς
ἐκτίσθη οἷος ἐνὼχ
τοιοῦτος ἐπὶ τῆς γῆς
44.16a אות דעת לדור דור / ὑπόδειγμα μετανοίας
ταῖς γενεαῖς

44.16b ויהתהלך עם אדני / καὶ εὐηρέστησεν κυρίῳ
49.14b וגם הוא נלקח פנים / καὶ γὰρ αὐτὸς
                                           ἀνελήμφθη ἀπὸ τῆς γῆς

G. Bickell ("Ein alphabetisches Lied Jesus
Sirach's," ZKT 16 [1882] 319-333) argued that the
Greek was misplaced and should be taken out of its
present position in chapter 44.

[71]Box and Oesterley, 482; Lévi, 88; Peters,
230; Segal, 207; Smend, 421.

[72]There are some other problems with the verse
that should be outlined here. Colon a ends with
ונלקח in MS B, which corresponds to μετετέθη. This
is the Greek word used for לקח in Gen 5.24. Smend,
422, however, sees this word as overloading the
poetic structure of the verse and as repeating
material from 49.14b. He has thus removed this word
from his text, a removal with which Yadin concurs.
This addition may be an early harmonization to the
Hebrew Genesis account, which seems to have
presented itself to the translator, although it
probably has little claim to be authentic to Ben
Sira. For the problems connected with colon b, see
Reiterer, 84-85, and the literature cited there.

[73]Peters, 381. Reiterer, 95, seems to concur
with Peters on this issue.

[74]Segal, 308, suggests something close to this
when he argues that the name אברהם was divided into
אב רם and corrupted to אב רב, which the grandson
rendered. He seems to suggest, however, that this
etymology was in the Hebrew parent text. I am not
so sure on this point. It may just as well be the
product of the grandson. A further suggestion might
be that μέγας is actually a doublet of המון
applied to Abraham himself. For an excellent
treatment of Philo's etymologies, see Lester L.
Grabbe, Etymology in Early Jewish Interpretation:
The Hebrew Names in Philo, Brown Judaic Studies 115
(Atlanta: Scholars, 1988).

[75]Skehan and Di Lella, 505, call these
similarities to Gen 22.16-18 "echoes."

[76]On this verse see especially Reiterer, 102-
103; Smend, 424; Segal, 308; Peters, Text, 232. For
a detailed discussion of v 21c, d, which are
missing in Hebrew due to parablepsis, see Reiterer,
103-106.

[77]See Box and Oesterley, 341, who do not
recognize the allusion here and reconstruct לב in
the missing part of v 27. Peters Text, 34, argues
that a transposition of לב and נפש did occur
although, interestingly, neither Peters, Smend, nor
Segal refer to Deut 6.5 as the background for Sir
7.27-30. Skehan and Di Lella, 206, do. See also,
Josef Haspecker, Gottesfurcht bei Jesus Sirach:
Ihre religiöse Struktur und ihre literarische und
doktrinäre Bedeutung, AnBib 30 (Rome: Pontifical
Biblical Institute, 1967) 301-304.

[78]This would only necessitate a change of א
and ר, י and ו. The י and ו problem is a common one
due to the orthography of the Masada manuscript.
For a complete discussion of the orthography of the
Masada scroll, see Yadin, The Masada Scroll, 13
(Hebrew section). The commentators almost
unanimously read ברית here (see especially,
Reiterer, 60-61). The Syriac has מומתא "oath,"
which could allow for ברית in its parent text.

[79]Reiterer, 60-61.

[80]A second, but more remote, possibility, that
באות עולם actually belongs here, is suggested by
Lévi, but without much conviction. The use of אות
in Gen 9.12, 13 is cited by him. As he further
notes, this makes the transitive verb לכרת lack an
object. The verb כרת is used in a technical sense
with ברית as an object often in the Hebrew Bible.
In this verse, MS B has the niphal, which further
indicates that ברית, and not באות, was the Hebrew
reading. MS B(mg) corrects to כרת. The Greek,
unfortunately, does not really help on this issue.
The translator, who read ברית עולם as the subject,
translated ἐτέθησαν. This could be entirely
independent of MS B, where a copyist might have
read the text the same way as the Greek translator.
On the other hand, the Greek could have read נכרת.
This raises some questions concerning the use of
the OG as a basis for the argument that כרת is the
proper reading. It could just as easily be a
harmonization to the biblical passage.

[81]ἐξαλείφω occurs elsewhere in Sir in 41.11
with a Hebrew parent text of כרת; in 49.13b it
corresponds to מחה.

[82]Reiterer, 93-94. Lévi, 89, and Peters, Text, 231, incorrectly call the addition of κατακλυσμός "commentary." Smend, 423, sees the addition of the word as conditioned by the translation of ἐξαλειφθῆ in the passive voice.

[83]זרע is usually the equivalent of σπέρμα in Sir. See, for example, 10.19; 44.11, 12, 13; 45.15, 21, 24; 46.9.

[84]Of course, the quandry is whether זרע or יצוע is the Hebrew parent text. Middendorp, 46, Peters, 407, and Box and Oesterley, 498, argue that זרע is the parent text. Smend, 455, Peters, Text, 268, Segal, 228, and Lévi, 130, believe יצועיך to be the parent text, although for different reasons. It is quite impossible to be sure. If יצועיך is the parent text, the case that the Greek used Lev 21.15 seems more secure.

[85]Liddell and Scott, 660. Henrico Stephanus (ed., Thesaurus Graecae Linguae [Paris: Ambrosius Firmin Didot, 1835]) cites its usage in a sermon of Ps-Chrysostom, Eustathius, Nicet. Man. Comm, and Eudocia.

[86]Eberharter, Der Kanon, 6.

[87]On the phrase חק עולם, see below, section 3.2.2.1b. On the phrase גוע יגועו, Box and Oesterley, 368, and Smend, 136, refer to Gen 2.17, but they provide no discussion of the connection.

[88]See Smend, 325; Peters, 299; Segal, 234.

[89]Skehan and Di Lella, 427.

[90]Middendorp, 43, seems to suggest (2) although he does not make this explicit. He does not suggest a parent text כנגדו and may even want to argue that the Syriac has been influenced by the Greek here.

[91]Skehan and Di Lella, 270, argue that Ben Sira's use of נמיכי קדם is actually a conscious avoidance of the mythological overtones of Genesis.

[92]This reference is presumably to Canaan. See the longer text of Codex Sinaiticus(c,a) where this identification is explicit. Box and Oesterley, 372.

[93]See Reiterer, 196, who says that
ἐπισυνέστησαν is "kontextensprechund," which I do
not think is adequate. The verb likely became part
of the oral tradition of this event, perhaps
originating in the OG translation. The question
here, however, is whether it provides good evidence
for a textual dependence of the Greek of Sir on the
OG. It probably does not.

[94]See below under the entry for συναγωγή.

[95]At this point, the Greek of Sir adds the
phrase ἐν φόβῳ, which is not in the OG tradition
about Phinehas, nor is it in the Hebrew of MS B.
The "fear of the Lord" is an important theme in
Sir. See, for example, 9.16, 10.22, 40.26, 27 for
the phrase יראת אלהים, which may be the parent text
here. See also, Haspecker, Gottesfurcht.

[96]For διαθήκη, see below, under the entry for
this term. For כפר, see, 3.30, 45.16.

[97]The work of W. Fuss would probably shed
considerable light on this issue. His unpublished
dissertation, "Tradition und Komposition im Buche
Jesus Sirach" (Ph.D. diss., University of Tübingen,
1963), however, was unavailable to me.

[98]See the grandson's comment in his prologue
(5-6) cited above. Note especially his statement
that in Egypt he found "opportunity for no little
instruction." Box and Oesterley, 317, argue that
this instruction took place in the synagogues. This
text, however, is beset by textual difficulties.
The text accepted by Box and Oesterley has the word
ἀφορμήν, in spite of its inferior attestation in
the manuscript tradition. Ziegler's text, which is
followed by Skehan and Di Lella, reads with the
majority tradition, ἀφόμοιον. This changes the
thrust of the text to mean "finding no little
difference of culture (παιδείας)." This textual
difficulty makes Box and Oesterley's argument shaky
at best, and the better text on which to rely is
the prologue 5-6, which mentions oral instruction.

[99]Besides the commentaries, see Di Lella, The
Hebrew Text of Sirach, 119-125; J. B. Bauer, "Der

priesterliche Schöpfungshymnus in Gen. 1 [Sir
15,14]," _TZ_ 20 (1964) 1-9; idem, "Sir. 15,14 et
Gen. 1,1," _VD_ 41 (1963) 243-244; F. Vattioni,
"Genesi 1,1 ed Eccli. 15,14," _Augustinianum_ 4
(1964) 105-108.

[100]Di Lella, _The Hebrew Text of Sirach_, 121.
He also argues that the first two words of MS A
appear to have been retroverted from Syriac. See H.
P. Rüger, _Text und Textform im hebräischen Sirach:_
Untersuchungen zur Textgeschichte und Textkritik
der hebräischen Sirachfragmente aus der Kairoer
Geniza, BZAW 112 (Berlin: Walter de Gruyter, 1970)
77-78, who, although he does not approach the
problem from the point of view of retroversion from
Syriac, agrees that MS B is the older and better
form of the Hebrew.

[101]The Syriac evidence for the verse is
divided. Walton and Mosul begin with הו which
agrees with הוא of MS B and αὐτὸς. Codex
Ambrosianus and Lagarde's text begin the colon with
אלהא. The Syriac also has ברישׁיח מן which may
reflect a text like that of MS A.

[102]See Middendorp, 42. Segal, 227, suggests
that for the first word of the verse השׁבח, the
translator, who rendered σύντριψον, read שׁבר. He
refers to Ps 74.13 where this equivalence occurs
(see also Smend, 320). The Syriac בטל, however,
seems to presume השׁבח as its parent text (Smend,
321). Also the use of συντρίβω as a translation of
שׁבח is not necessarily ruled out. The translator
may well have wanted to intensify the meaning of
the Hebrew verb. Smend's suggestion that the phrase
κεφαλὰς ἀρχόντων ἐχθρῶν is derived from the OG
of Deut 32.42 seems unlikely to me, since the Greek
is a satisfactory translation of the text of MS B
as it stands.

[103]Smend, 429; Box and Oesterley, 486; Skehan
and Di Lella, 509.

[104]Reiterer, 150.

[105]This passage could perhaps be explained
using Middendorp's idea of "errors caused by

memory." On this idea, see above in this chapter
and Middendorp, 36-37.

[106]The Hebrew has an additional two words,
וילבישה פעמונים (MS B[mg] תועפה in place of
פעמונים), which neither the Greek nor Syriac
attest. Although these words are viewed as
secondary by all the major commentators except
Lévi, it does not seem to have been suggested that
perhaps this is an explanatory doublet for ויאזרהו
תועפות ראם. Lévi, 97, argues that this is, in fact,
the Hebrew for καὶ περιέζωσεν αὐτὸν περιστολὴν
δόξης, and that . . .ואזרהו is rendered by
ἐμακάρισεν αὐτὸν ἐν εὐκοσμίᾳ, and finally that
וישרתהו בכבודו is left untranslated by Greek and
Syriac. This argument presumes that חואר is the
correct Hebrew rather than ראם, and it also makes
more difficult the equivalence ראזר/μακαρίζω, which
can be explained above as a misreading or corruption of ישרתהו. Although Lévi's idea is creative, I
think he is wrong here.

[107]Reiterer, 242-249; Caird, "Ben Sira and the
Dating of the Septuagint," 97, cited above.

[108]Emanuel Tov, "The Impact of the LXX
Translation of the Pentateuch on the Translation of
the Later Books," in Mélanges Dominique Barthélemy,
ed. P. Cassetti, O. Keel, and A. Schenker, OBO 38
(Fribourg-Göttingen: Editions Universitaires-
Vandenhoeck & Ruprecht, 1981) 577-592.

[109]Smend, 488, argues that a transposition has
occurred with the words לשרת and משפטיו, and that
the translator read מזבח as אל or אח ''. Neither
Segal nor Peters offers any explanation for the
problem, only a retroversion from the existing
Greek.

[110]BDB, 726; Jastrow, 1045. According to HR,
עדן only occurs once as the sole equivalent of
παράδεισος in OG, that is in Isa 51.3. Of course,
the same exegetical principle may be operative
there as here in Sir.

[111]On the problem, see Yadin, The Masada
Scroll, 15, who argues on the basis of Greek and
Syriac (בערנא) that the translations were
influenced by 40.27, but the reading was made
easier by the presence of בעד in the Hebrew text.

This confirms the reconstruction of those
commentators who did not know the Masada text.

[112]Cf. Exod 33.3, 5; 34.9; and Deut 9.6.

[113]Those passages not treated here are 11.33,
which has ברית, although Segal, 77, argues that it
is a corruption of מביתך. In any case, a different
parent text is likely here. On this passage, see
also Smend, 113, and Peters, 104. ברית also occurs
in 50.14 with no corresponding Greek. διαθῆκαι as
an equivalent of באות in 44.18 has been treated
above.

[114]The Greek attests a different sequence from
the Hebrew. This involves a transposition of ברכה
(v 22) and ברית (v 23). This passage may be an
allusion to a tradition found in Gen 28.4, which
speaks of Isaac receiving the blessing of Abraham.
This interchange is also supported by the Syriac,
which has בורכתא דכל קדמיא. On this verse, see
Rüger, Text und Textform, 110-111; Segal, 309;
Smend, 425.

[115]Lévi, 90. Smend accepts this judgment, and
it is also reflected in Box and Oesterley's
translation. See also Rüger, Text und Textform, 99.
The phrase ברת חק does not occur at all in the
Hebrew scriptures. It could be suggested that an
original ברית was changed to חק at some point in
the textual transmission, but חק makes sense here,
and I would see no clear reason to change it.

[116]Cf. 2 Sam 23.5; Jer 33.21; Isa 55.3; 2 Chr
13.15; Ps 89.4 for the covenant with David.

[117]Smend, 459; Box and Oesterley, 489.

[118]The Greek, however, may represent a bit of
exegesis. The Hebrew (missing in MS B, but
recovered in Masada) has ברית in the singular as
does the Syriac, which indicates one more or less
overarching covenant made by God with his people.
The Greek, on the other hand, has the plural
διαθήκαις, probably referring collectively to the
covenants made with individual fathers. An
interesting parallel occurs in Rom 9.4 where Paul
uses the plural αἱ διαθῆκαι when speaking about
the Jews. An early papyrus (p[46]), along with other
uncials, attests the singular.

[119]For פרר ברית, see Isa 33.8, 1 Kgs 15.19.
The entire section is a series of things of which
to be ashamed. Only Masada contains the beginning
of the phrase מהפר אלה וברית. The Greek translator
read אלה as אלוה and rendered θεοῦ. This seems to
be the fundamental problem here; see Yadin, <u>The
Masada Scroll</u>, 21. The מהפר of Masada rendered the
reconstructions of Smend, 386, and Peters, 351,
unnecessary. Yadin (<u>The Masada Scroll</u>, 21) as did
Segal, 281, and Peters, 351, before him, notes that
ἀπὸ ἀληθείας of the Greek may be an inner-Greek
corruption of ἀπὸ λήθης.

[120]BDB, 349.

[121]The second half of the verse confirms the
meaning of "task." It reads ובמלאבכתך החישׁן, "and
grow old in your work." Here מלאכה is parallel to
חק. Skehan and Di Lella, 236, translate חוקך as
"your duty."

[122]On this verse, see Reiterer, 146. For the
sake of completeness, David is given a חק ממלכה,
which is rendered, possibly under the influence of
45.25, διαθήκην βασιλέων.

[123]One other place in Greek Sir where Hebrew
is extant reads νόμος ὑψίστου. In Sir 9.15, the
Hebrew בינוחם should probably be תורת ʏʏ or תורה
עליון. The Syriac here has באורחחא דמריא ("in the
way of the Lord"). See Smend, 88. 46.14 reads ἐν
νόμῳ κυρίου where there is a small lacuna in MS
B. Smend, 445, Peters, 398, and Box and Oesterley,
493, reconstruct במצוה on the basis of the main
verb צוה, the Syriac בנמומה, and the parallel
passage in 44.20. Segal, 322, notes that the Greek
presupposes תורה ʏʏ. For the phrase "keep the
commandments," see, for example, Gen 26.5; Lev
22.31; Deut 4.2; 5.8; 7.11; 8.1, 2, 6, 11; 10.13;
11.8; 13.5, 19; 15.5; 26.18; 27.1; 28.1, 15, 45;
30.10, plus numerous places outside the Pentateuch.
For a more complete list, see Reiterer, 98. νόμος
does translate מצוה in the phrase שמר מצוה in Prov
29.8, where the verb is φυλάσσω.

[124]This suggestion is also made by Segal, 209.

[125]On this verse, see Reiterer, 194; Smend,
434. 35.18 has תורה as part of a doublet that
Smend, 293, and Segal, 208, call the parent text of

the Greek. חורה (MS B; MS B(mg) = מצוה), however,
may be a corruption of מורא.

[126] See Smend, 293; Peters, 268; Segal, 208.

[127] See Smend, 382; Peters, 346; Segal, 276.

[128] Box and Oesterley, 470; Segal, 276; Lévi,
53, suggest πυλῶν. Smend, 393, reads πόλει. With
the parallel in Sir 7.7, I would incline toward a
form of πόλις.

[129] Smend, 274; Peters, 852; Segal, 190. Skehan
and Di Lella, 380, argue for לקבץ based on the
Syriac.

[130] Box and Oesterley, 458; Lévi, 7; Segal,
263; Smend, 362.

[131] For יאר as the Nile, see Gen 41.1, 2, 3;
Exod 1.22; 2. 3, 4, etc. For נהר as the Euphrates,
see Gen 15.18.

[132] See Segal, 269, and Smend, 372, who do not
suggest a parent text of מבול, but also do not
suggest the possibility of a transposition here.
Box and Oesterley, 462, hint at the possibility of
a transposition, and Lévi, 19, says that he
believes the translator read מבול in this place.
For the problem of חמוש in this verse, see the
commentators and H. P. Rüger ("Zum Text Sir 40.10
und Ex 10.21," ZAW 82 [1970] 103-109) who argues
for the meaning of "arrive" for this verb.

[133] Elmar Camilo Dos Santos, An Expanded Index
for the Hatch-Redpath Concordance to the Septuagint
(Jerusalem: Dugith, n.d) 96.

[134] Smend, 429-430. See Peters cited in Box and
Oesterley, 486 (who follow Peters and Smend).
Against this, see Reiterer, 155-156, who argues
forcefully that the Greek translator did not have a
different parent text.

[135] Peters, 401; Lévi, 121; Segal, 324.

[136] Smend, 448.

[137] BDB, 873. The word, however, does not seem
to be used of sacrifices per se in the Hebrew Bible.

[138] Reiterer, 243-247.

[139]See Box and Oesterley, 406, and Smend, 244.

[140]Liddell and Scott, 347.

[141]BDB, 715.

[142]על החשׁן in this verse was correctly identified by Smend (431) as a gloss. This position was accepted by Box and Oesterley. It has no Greek equivalent and, as Smend notes, this phrase is used in Exodus 28 with reference to the ephod and the waistband, which are mentioned in Sir 45.10. See also, Reiterer, 164.

[143]Reiterer, 163.

[144]Snaith, "Biblical Quotations," 10. The other use of κλῶσμα in the OG is in Judg 16.9 (A text) where it renders פתיל. The B text has στρέμμα. Further evidence for a direct use of Num 15.38 by the translator is that of the ten times where פתיל is used in the Hebrew biblical traditions only these two, Numbers and Judges, are rendered κλῶσμα. One use of פתיל, in Exod 28.37(33), is rendered by the verb κλώθω.

[145]Liddell and Scott, 1676.

[146]In this verse the Syriac reads חגר, which according to Box and Oesterley, 346, presumes a Hebrew of חמסך. Further, Sanhedrin 100b and Yebamoth 63b also have למסוך in a rather loose citation of this verse. Smend, 86, writes that the Greek could be taken from the Hebrew of MS A. Skehan and Di Lella, 218, and Segal, 57, read חסבא, as does G. Kuhn ("Beiträge zur Eklärung des Buches Jesus Sira," ZAW 47 [1929] 293). Peters, 83, suggests חרב for חסב. In any case, none of these possibilities reflects the OG equivalence. On this verse in its larger context, see Warren C. Trenchard, Ben Sira's View of Women: A Literary Analysis, Brown Judaica Series 38 (Chico: Scholars, 1983) 108-115.

[147]Smend, 172.

[148]Smend, 280; Segal, 196.

[149]BDB, 1036.

[150] Segal, 114.

[151] An examination of the facsimiles leaves the possibility of 'ש or 'מ. Cowley and Neubauer (The Original Hebrew of a Portion of Ecclesiasticus, 12) read 'ש and are followed by Box and Oesterley, and Segal. Lévi, Smend, Vattioni, and the Hebrew Language Academy read 'מ.

[152] Box and Osterley, 470, in reading 'ש in MS B(mg), want to restore the Hebrew שמצה based on the Exodus passage. The use of ἐπίχαρμα in Sir makes שמחה appear to be a much better possibility.

[153] Peters, 136, writes that "die Uebersetzung durch VII I mit seinem σκληροτράχηλος veranlasst." This seems unlikely in that the grandson would be seen as having translated v 11 and then v 10. I have not been able to illustrate this technique in Sir as yet, nor does Peters attempt to establish such a method of operation.

[154] See Leiman, Chapter I, on the issue of canon.

[155] The manner in which Middendorp discussed these passages makes it difficult to arrive at a total number of passages. This number, however, is not the most crucial issue here.

[156] The differences from Samuel involve the use of the passive voice and a preposition. Skehan and Di Lella, 233, also note the similarity to Ps 113.8a.

[157] Ps 113.8 נדיב = ἀρχόντων, but the context is similar to Sir.

[158] Could it be Israel? See Beentjes, Jesus Sirach en Tanach, 146-47; Prato, Problema della Teodicea, 252-254.

[159] Peters, Text, 185. Only Segal, 273, retains וכן here, although he notes that the Greek and Syr read ועל. Skehan and Di Lella, 467, read ועל.

[160] He probably read חִפָּחָה or חִפָּתָה. Most of the commentators point this out. See Smend, 379; Segal, 273; Peters, Text, 185; Lévi, 30; Beentjes, Jesus Sirach en Tanach, 32, 38.

[161]In fact, the commentators do point out the parallel, but do not note the possibility of connecting this phrase with the section on Elijah, which comes immediately after it. Skehan and Di Lella, 529, in their strophic arrangement position this verse with the following section about Elijah.

[162]This equivalence occurs a number of times in Isaiah. See 28.6; 30.15; 33.13; 63.15.

[163]The facsimile of MS B only shows [..]הל, and most of the commentators reconstruct להשׁיב here. See especially Lévi and Smend.

[164]That להרם is a gloss is noted by Segal, 338, Smend, 470, Peters, Text, 282, and Skehan and Di Lella, 541.

[165]Beentjes (Jesus Sirach en Tanach, 57) argues that for this reason [להשׁיב] is authentic. The two cola of the verse would then have ל..ו..ל with accompanying infinitives. He does not try to account for the absence of an equivalent in the Greek.

[166]Greek MS 705 has ἀνασκάπτων, which perhaps represents a harmonization in this manuscript to the Jeremiah passage.

[167]Smend, 420; Segal, 338; Box and Oesterley, 505.

[168]See Smend, 471, who says, "wahrscheinlich hat Sirach Jer 1.10 das לבנות ולנטוע gelesen. . . während der Enkel es vermutlich auch in der OG las."

[169]Sometimes the issue hangs on one particular word, In this instance on πλήν as a translation of תולח. The only other occurrence of תולח is in Sir 36.12, and it is rendered πλήν. The proximity of the two occurrences, however, diminishes the importance of the evidence. Did the grandson use 2 Sam 7.22 or 1 Chr 17.20? I cannot say for sure.

[170]The phrase יבשׁ עץ also appears two times with reference to actual trees (Ezek 17.24; 21.3). In both cases the Greek translation is the same as Sir.

[171]Unfortunately, the adjective ξηρός only occurs here in Sir.

172Isa 50.9 יבלו כבגד כלם הן; Isa 51.6 והארץ
כבגד חבלה.

173The phrase is also used in this manner in
Ps 102.26.

174The instances of בגד in Sir are almost
evenly split between στολή and ἱμάτιον. This is
the only case of בלה in Sir. παλαιόω = ישׁן in 9.10
and 11.20.

175Snaith, "Biblical Quotations," 9. The
prayer, however, could have been a synogogue
prayer, which Ben Sira used but did not compose
himself. See, for example, M. R. Lehmann, "Ben Sira
and the Qumran Literature," RevQ 3 (1961) 106-107,
who compares this prayer with a battle prayer from
1QM.

176In Hebrew Sir, אף is the most commmon word,
but see 16.6 where חמה = ὀργή.

177Smend, 442, and Peters, 396, regard להדריכם
as an error and refer to the use of להביאם in v 8
for its origin. ἐπιβῆναι αὐτόν, however, supports
הדריכם as its parent text. Further, some of the
commentators note the connection between 46.9 and
Amos and Micah. Most want to break up the phrase,
and they point to Deuteronomy and Joshua for the
להדריכם/ἐπιβῆναι pair.

178See also 51.15 for this pair. καταλαμβάνω
is used in 15.1, 7 for דרך in the hiphil.

179An almost identical phrase ידרכנ׳ במוח׳ ועל
appears in Hab 3.19, but here the Greek uses τὰ
ὑψηλά for במוח׳ rather than ἰσχύς.

180See Box and Oesterley, 500, Lévi, 137, and
Skehan and Di Lella, 530, who translate, "as it is
written," and Smend, 46, who seems to assume this
meaning. Also Middendorp, 134, who says, "הכחוב
weist im übrigen auf ein bestimmtes Verständnis der
nahen Schriften hin, es verleint diesen schon fast
kanonisches wurde."

181Beentjes, Jesus Sirach en Tanach, 39-40.

182For כחב in the qal passive participle
meaning "appoint, enroll" see, BDB, 507. Cf. also

the use of כחוב in eschatological and predictive
passages in Jer 22.30; Isa 4.3; Dan 12.1.

[183]The existence of a variant form of the
Malachi passage may be strengthened by a citation
of Mal 3.23 in Luke 1.17. Luke's form shares the
verb ἐπιστρέψαι with Sir, but it has καρδία in
the plural, and instead of πρὸς υἱόν like
Malachi and Sir, it has ἐπὶ τέκνα. For a brief
note on Malachi-Sir-Luke, see, Turner, "The
Relation of Luke I and II to the Hebraic Sources,"
101. For colon b, some of the commentators take
מפני [..]מפני as parallel to Mal 3.23 בוא לפני
יום יקים. There may be a conceptual parallel here,
but certainly not a textual dependence.

[184]Prato, Problema della Teodicea, 128;
Peters, Text, 148. Smend, 329, notes this
possibility, but rejects it in favor of an Arabic
root meaning "an untrustworthy guide." For a
detailed look at the Latin and Syriac, see Skehan
and Di Lella, 429.

[185]1 Macc 7.41, οἱ παρὰ τοῦ βασιλέως ὅτε
ἐδυσφήμησαν, ἐξῆλθεν ἄγγελός σου καὶ ἐπάταξεν
ἐν αὐτοῖς ἑκατὸν ὀγδοήκοντα πέντε χιλιάδες.
2 Macc 8.19 καὶ τὴν ἐπὶ Σενναχηρειμ, ἑκατὸν
ὀγδοήκοντα πέντε χιλιάδες ὡς ἀπώλοντο.

[186]This is the opinion of most of the
commentators. See, for example, Smend, 467, and
Peters, Text. The same position is implied by
Skehan and Di Lella, 537.

[187]Box and Oesterley, 503.

[188]Jastrow, 730.

[189]See above on the relationship between 47.20
and Genesis. Although in 47.18 the language is
close to 1 Kgs 10.27, different metals are referred
to, and the general tradition most likely is
reflected here rather than any specific text.

[190]Smend, 150; Peters Text, 93; Segal, 101.

[191]Rüger, Text und Textform, 1-11.

[192]See above in Chapter 2 under "Quantitative
Representation" for more detail on this issue.

[193]In this case, the Greek bears no resemblance to the Psalms text.

[194]Schechter and Taylor, The Wisdom of Ben Sira, 469; Smend, 390; Peters Text, 197; Segal, 283. On the Masada reading, see Yadin, The Masada Scroll, 23.

[195]Liddell and Scott, 66. HR shows the term occurring in Mal 1.7, 12 and Dan 1.8.

[196]BDB, 146.

[197]In the OG אגל = ἀπολυτρόω, μολύνω, συμμολύνομαι; ליגל = βδελλύσσω, ἀπωθέω, ἀφίστημι, μισέω, προσοχθίζω, ὠμοτοκέω. See Dos Santos, An Expanded Hebrew Index.

[198]BDB, 865. Most of the commentators note this sense as well.

[199]ἀντίζηλος is also found in the same sense in 26.6, but no Hebrew is extant for this verse.

[200]Dos Santos, An Expanded Hebrew Index, 183.

[201]For a discussion of the textual problems of the remainder of the verse, see A. A. Di Lella, "Sirach 10.19-11.6," 157-164; idem, The Hebrew Text of Sirach, 60-63; Prato, Problema della Teodicea, 372.

[202]Jer 14.6 and Ps 104.4 = פרא; Dan(θ') 5.21 = ערד.

[203]See Job 6.5, 39.5; Isa 32.14; Jer 14.6.

[204]The same pair, σπινθήρ and נצץ, occurs in Ezek 1.7.

[205]Yadin, The Masada Scroll, 27 (English).

[206]Strugnell, "Notes and Queries," 117.

[207]Prato, Problema della Teodicea, 126; Strugnell, "Notes and Queries," 117, n. 17.

[208]BDB, 840; Jastrow, 1257.

[209]Lévi, 64.

[210]לפם occurs a number of times in the MT represented by a number of different Greek words: ἀποκακέω(?): ἐμφυσάω; ἐκφυσάω; καίω; ὑποκαίω; ἄκαυστος.

[211]On the verse as a whole and its difficulties, see Lévi, 64; Box and Oesterley, 474; Prato, Problema della Teodicea, 129-130; Peters Text, 209-210; Smend, 401; Segal, 294; Skehan and Di Lella, 488.

[212]Sir 30.11; 42.9; 47.4; 47.14; 51.15. In 7.23 the Hebrew has ושא להם נשים בנעוריהם, but the Greek has nothing to do with sexual relations - καὶ κάμψον ἐκ νεότητος τὸν τράχηλον αὐτῶν. In fact, the Greek seems to presuppose a different parent text altogether.

[213]καρτερέω is used in Job 2.9, but there it renders חזק in the hiphil meaning "keep hold of."

[214]It means "blister, boil." BDB, 101.

[215]Smend, 131; Peters, Text, 78; Prato, Problema della Teodicea, 250.

[216]See 11.27; 14.16; 18.32; 37.29.

[217]See 44.19; 45.9; 50.18.

[218]λάκκος ὡσεὶ θαλάσσης suggests that the Hebrew read אשיד כים where the extant Hebrew has אשיח בם.

[219]Peters, Text, 258. "τὸ περίμετρον des Gr. ist nüchterne Erklärung des hyberbolischen בהמונו."

[220]On the issue of these other wisdom books and Ben Sira's possible knowledge of them, see Eberharter, Der Kanon; Koole. "Die Bibel des Ben Sira;" Skehan and Di Lella. For Qoheleth in particular, see N. Peters, "Ekklesiastes und Ekklesiastikus," BZ 1 (1903) 129-150.

[221]Reiterer, 242-249.

[222]C. Larcher, Études sur le livre de la Sagesse, EBib (Paris: Librairie Lecoffre, 1969) 101-102. He writes, "Résumons maintenant les traits dominants de cette utilisation des sources bibliques en Sag. Si elle est abondante et révèle

un auteur familiarisé avec la langue de la Bible
grecque, les citations implicites sont exception-
nelles et très peu de textes sont repris
littéralement. En règle générale, l'auteur traite
ses sources avec une assez grande liberté et
l'expression de sa pensée reste partout person-
nelle: il n'a pas voulu composer une mosaïque
astucieuse de mots et d'expressions biblique. . . ."

CHAPTER 4: NOTES

[1]See the introductory sections to the
commentaries by Smend, Peters, and Skehan and Di
Lella.

[2]Reiterer's study of 44.16-45.26.

[3]Segal, 54.

[4]Work on the Syriac is hindered by the fact
that no good critical edition of the text exists.
It is scheduled to be done in the Leiden Peshitta
series by M. M. Winter. Winter has published a
concordance to the Syriac version (A Concordance to
the Peshitta Version of Ben Sira, Monographs of the
Peshitta Institute - Leiden vol. II [Leiden: E. J.
Brill, 1976]) based primarily on the editions of
Codex Ambrosianus by A. M. Ceriani (Translatio Syra
Pescitto Veteris Testamenti ex codice Ambrosiano
sec. fere VI photolithographice edita, 2.4 [Milan,
1878]), and British Library Add. 12142, published
by P. A. de Lagarde (Libri Veteris Testamenti
apocryphi syriace [Leipzig-London: F. A. Brockel-
haus-Williams & Norgate, 1861]). A critical edition
does exist for the Latin. Biblia Sacra iuxta
latinam Vulgatam versionem, 12 Sapientia Salomonis,
Liber Hiesu Filii Sirach (Rome: Typis Polyglottis
Vaticanis, 1964).

[5]See above, 2.4.3.2 for these problems.

[6]For problems of reconstructing elements such
as the definite article, certain prepositions,
possessive pronouns, see Tov, The Text-Critical Use
of the Septuagint, 218-228. For those elements not
routinely retroverted in the CATSS data base see,
Tov, Computer Data Base, 102-103.

[7]Patrick W. Skehan, "Structures in Poems on
Wisdom: Proverbs 8 and Sirach 24," CBQ 41 (1979)
365-379.

[8]Skehan (Skehan and Di Lella, 330) remarks that the primary purpose of the reconstruction is to demonstrate the poetic structure. In his reconstruction, he gives little detail concerning his approach, but it appears as if he is relying primarily on the Greek text as a basis for the Hebrew reconstruction, although he depended heavily on the Syriac as well, especially when the Greek did not enable a clear decision to be made.

[9]Skehan, "Structures in Poems on Wisdom," 377, n. 31. In this note, which concerns his claim that vv 5-7 contain much alliteration, Skehan remarks that he is not forgetting that he is "working from a retroversion: vocabulary choices that might misrepresent the original Ben Sira have nothing to do with a sequence such as בכל. . .בכל. . .בגלי. בנחלת מי. . .בכל."

[10]The hithpael of פאר is found in 11.4; 38.25; 48.4; 50.20. 24.1, 2; 30.2; and 39.8 have no Hebrew available. Skehan's reconstruction is almost certainly based on the Syriac. At the end of v 1 Syriac has חתיקר, and at the end of v 2, תשחבה. Since Syriac שבח often renders הלל, the reconstruction at the end of v 2 is clear. The Syriac verb יקר renders פאר twice in Sir in contexts of praise. Thus, the use of יקר and καυχάομαι could have convinced Skehan that פאר was the Hebrew at the end of v 1.

[11]The Syriac does not have anything that corresponds to 24.8b, and thus, Skehan's reconstruction appears to be based primarily on the Greek text.

[12]κτίζω has three primary Hebrew equivalents in Sir; ברא, יצר, and חלק. For the participial use of ποιέω to render participial עשה plus a pronomial object, see 10.12; 32.17; 33.14; 38.15; 43.5, 11; 47.8. For this phrase, Otto Rickenbacher argues for בורא on the basis of the Greek Sir and Isa 42.5, even though the Syriac has מרא here (corrupt for מריא?). Rickenbacher, however, follows a method I have criticized above in Chapter 3. He argues against following the Syriac here because the Hebrew phrases יהוה הכל and אדני הכל do not occur in the Hebrew scriptures. See, Otto Rickenbacher, Weisheitsperikopen bei Ben Sira, OBO

308   SIRACH AND ITS PARENT TEXT

1 (Freiburg-Göttingen: Universitätsverlag-Vandenhoeck & Ruprecht, 1973) 121.

[13]The Syriac here has עבדני. עבד in Syriac almost always translates either עשׂה or עבד.

[14]The Syriac has ואתרבית, "and I increased."

[15]The Syriac for this colon does not provide any assistance, and one must rely on the Greek.

[16]For example, 3.11 - אמו = μήτηρ; 3.12 - בני = τέκνον; 3.16 - אביו = πατέρα; 5.12 - רעך = τῷ πλησίον; 8.17 - סודך = λόγον. These are just a few examples of a widespread problem in Sir.

[17]The Syriac does not have the possessive pronoun here.

[18]One additional text may qualify as evidence in this discussion. In 9.15, where MS A has בינוחם, the Greek translation has ἐν νόμῳ ὑψίστου. Is this a bit of translational exegesis on the part of the grandson or did he have בתורת עליון in his source text? Skehan and Di Lella, 218, and Smend, 88, accept the alternative Hebrew based on the Greek and the Syriac, which has באוריחה דמריא. For the phrase under consideration, the Syriac only has מריא, which usually does not render עליון. In two places (Sir 46.5 and 48.20), אל עליון is rendered into Syriac as מריא only, which raises the possibility that there were two names in the Hebrew of Sir 24.23.

[19]Smend, 224, hints that he thinks this to be the case when he quotes the Latin text as I have above. He quotes only the Latin, however, and does not explicitly give an inner-Greek corruption as a likelihood.

[20]Although γάρ almost always represents כי in Sir, there are 19 cases where γάρ has no Hebrew equivalent at all. γάρ represents conjunctive ו only a few times (2.18?; 3.22; 11.29?; 14.17; 16.17; 43.28; 47.7?; 49.4, 5, 9, 14; 51.12).

[21]24.31a has μου τὸν κῆπον for which Skehan has reconstructed גני, and 24.31b has μου τὴν πρασιάν for which Skehan has ערוגתי.

[22]On the poetry of Ben Sira, see the section in Skehan and Di Lella entitled "The Poetry of Ben

Sira" and the literature cited therein. The Syriac
may be of great assistance in this regard.

[23]The Syriac has the same parallelism that
Skehan has reconstructed for the Hebrew.

[24]For detailed studies of Sirach 24, see M.
Gilbert, "L'Éloge de la Sagesse (Siracide 24)," RTL
5 (1974) 326-348; J. Marböck, Weisheit im Wandel:
Untersuchungen zur Weisheitstheologie bei Ben Sira,
BBB 37 (Bonn: Peter Hanstein, 1971); Rickenbacher,
Wiesheitsperikopen. Rickenbacher, Weisheitsperikopen, 111-172, has an extended discussion of
this chapter. No attempt has been made here
thoroughly to integrate his discussions since
Skehan's reconstruction is being used as a means of
illustrating the general difficulties of reconstructing the Hebrew Sir.

[25]Skehan, "Structures in Poems on Wisdom,"
377.

[26]Skehan, "Structures in Poems on Wisdom,"
378. There are two names for plants used in Sir
24.13 and 14 that do have equivalents elsewhere in
the book and that are different from those chosen
by Skehan. In 24.13, Skehan reconstructs ברוש as
the parent text of κυπάρισσος. The same Greek word
occurs in 50.10 where its formal equivalent is אך
שמן (MS B). Skehan and Di Lella, 549, take the
Hebrew phrase differently from the Greek; they
argue that MS B and the Syriac have the correct
text, and that the image in the Greek is borrowed
from 24.13. The Syriac does seem to reflect אך שמן,
but it is not clear to me why κυπάρισσος is not an
adequate translation of the phrase.
     In 24.14, the Greek ῥόδου is reconstructed
as ורד, whereas in 50.8, the phrase ὡς ἄνθος
ῥόδων most likely has כנץ בעני׳פ as its parent
text (the Hebrew of MS B has כנץעפני׳פ). Whether
this equivalent should have any bearing on this
verse is not clear.

APPENDIX: NOTES

[1]For a more detailed discussion of the
limitations of some of these tools, see Tov, Text-
Critical Use of the Septuagint, 142-154.

[2]The Thesaurus Linguae Graecae (TLG) project
at the University of California at Irvine, for

example, has as its goal the encoding of all Greek
literature through the sixth century CE, while the
Packard Humanities Institute (PHI) (directed by
David Packard) has a similar goal for Latin texts.
The Center for the Computer Analysis of Texts
(CCAT) at the University of Pennsylvania is also
involved in expanding this data bank and in
facilitating the use of computer materials for
scholarly purposes. Each of these projects, TLG,
PHI, and CCAT, currently have put their textual
material onto CD-ROMs.

[3]For detailed descriptions of the history of
the project, see R. A. Kraft, "Lexicon Project:
Progress Report," BIOSCS 12 (1979) 14-16; Kraft and
Emanuel Tov, "Computer Assisted Tools for Septua-
gint Studies," BIOSCS 14 (1981) 22-40; John R.
Abercrombie, William Adler, R. A. Kraft, and
Emanuel Tov, Computer Assisted Tools for Septuagint
Studies: Volume 1, Ruth, SCS 20 (Atlanta: Scholars,
1986) 1-18.

[4]Kraft and Tov, "Computer Assisted Tools," 24.

[5]CATSS is also cooperating on a fourth aspect
of the data bank, the morphological analysis of the
MT. This work is being done at Westminster Theological Seminary in Chestnut Hill, Pennsylvania,
under the direction of Alan Groves.

[6]For a description of how Packard's program
works and a more general discussion of this aspect
of the data files, see the chapter on morphological
analysis by William Adler in Abercrombie, et al.,
Computer Assisted Tools; also published separately
as William Adler, "Computer Assisted Morphological
Analysis of the Septuagint," Textus 11 (1984) 1-16.

[7]For a description of this program and the
problems of aligning these two texts automatically,
see the chapter entitled "Computer Aspects of the
Alignment" by John R. Abercrombie in Abercrombie,
et al., Computer Assisted Tools; also published
separately as John R. Abercrombie, "Computer
Assisted Alignment of the Greek and Hebrew Biblical
Texts -- Programming Background," Textus 11 (1984)
125-139.

[8]A complete description of the system of
notation is impossible here. For a complete

description of the parallel alignment, the philosophy behind it, and the system of notation, see Tov, A Computerized Data Base for Septuagint Studies.

[9]Except for the new manuscript identified as F by A. A. Di Lella, which will be a part of the next update of the CATSS data bank now available on CD-ROM. Fr. Di Lella kindly allowed me to see a pre-publication transcription of the text (31.24-32.7 and 32.12-33.8), which has appeared with plates in Biblica. For a short discussion of the fragment, originally identified by A. Scheiber as part of MS D, see Chapter 1, n. 7 above.

[10]Historical Dictionary of the Hebrew Language, The Book of Ben Sira: Text, Concordance and an Analysis of the Vocabulary (Jerusalem: The Academy of the Hebrew Language and the Shrine of the Book, 1973).

[11]See Tov, Computerized Data Base.

[12]Two good examples of programs that enable the personal computer user to do sophisticated searching and concording of texts are the Oxford Concordance Program (OCP), Oxford Electronic Publishing, Oxford; and LBase, Silver Mountain Software, Winona Lake, Indiana. For excellent reviews of currently available software of this kind, see John Hughes, Bits, Bytes, and Biblical Studies: A Resource Guide for the Use of the Computer in Biblical and Classical Studies (Grand Rapids: Zondervan, 1987).

WORKS CONSULTED

(The entries for works specifically treating the book of Ben Sira are preceded by an asterisk.)

Abercrombie, John. R. "Computer Assisted Alignment of the Greek and Hebrew Biblical Texts -- Programming Background." Textus 11 (1984) 125-139.

Abercrombie, John R., William Adler, R. A. Kraft, and Emanuel Tov. Computer Assisted Tools for Septuagint Studies: Volume 1, Ruth. SCS 20. Atlanta: Scholars, 1986.

*Adler, E. N. "Some Missing Chapters of Ben Sira [7,29-12,1]." JQR 12 (1899-1900) 466-480.

Adler, William. "Computer Assisted Morphological Analysis of the Septuagint." Textus 11 (1984) 1-16.

Aejmelaus, Anneli. Parataxis in the Septuagint: A Study in the Renderings of the Hebrew Coordinate Clauses in the Greek Pentateuch. AASF 31. Helsinki: Suomalainen Tiedeakatemia, 1982.

Aejmelaus, Annelli, and Raija Sollamo, eds. Ilmari Soisalon-Soininen: Studien zur Septuaginta-Syntax. AASF B 237. Helsinki: Suomalainen Tiedeakatemia, 1987.

Alexander, P. "3 (Hebrew Apocalypse of) Enoch," in The Old Testament Pseudepigrapha, vol 1. Ed. James H. Charlesworth, 223-316. Garden City: Doubleday, 1984.

*Alonso Schökel, L. "The Vision of Man in Sirach 16:24-17:14," in Israelite Wisdom: Theological and Literary Essays in Honor of Samuel Terrien. Ed. John G. Gamme, et al., 135-145. Missoula, Montana: Scholars, 1978.

*Auvray, P. "Notes on the Prologue de l'Ecclésiastique," in Mélanges bibliques rédigés en l'honneur de André Robert. Paris: Bloud & Gay, 1957, 281-287.

*Bacher, W. "Notes on the Cambridge Fragments of Ecclesiasticus." JQR 12 (1899-1900) 272-290.

*Baillet, M., J. T. Milik, and R. de Vaux. Les
"Petites Grottes" de Qumrân. DJD 3. Oxford:
Clarendon, 1962.

Ball, C. J. The Ecclesiastical or Deutero-canonical
Books of the Old Testament Commonly Called the
Apocrypha. London: Eyre and Spottiswoode, n.d.

Barr, James. The Typology of Literalism in Ancient
Biblical Translations. NAWG, I. phil.-hist.
Kl. Göttingen: Vandenhoeck & Ruprecht, 1979.

Barthélemy, Dominique. Les devanciers d'Aquila.
VTSup 10. Leiden: E. J. Brill, 1963.

*Barthélemy, Dominique, and O. Rickenbacher.
Konkordanz zum hebräischen Sirach mit syrisch-
hebräischen Index. Göttingen: Vandenhoeck &
Ruprecht, 1973.

*Bauckmann, E. G. "Die Proverbien und die Sprüche
des Jesus Sirach: Eine Untersuchung zum
Strukturwandel der israelitischen Sirach." ZAW
72 (1960) 33-63.

*Bauer, J. B. "Der priesterliche Schöpfungshymnus
in Gen 1 [Sir 15:14]." TZ 20 (1964) 1-9.

*_____. "Sir. 15,14 et Gen. 1,1." VD 41 (1963)
243-244.

*Baumgarten, J. M. "Some Notes on the Ben Sira
Scroll from Masada." JQR 58 (1968) 323-327.

*Baumgartner, W. "Die literarische Gattungen in der
Weisheit des Jesus Sirach." ZAW 34 (1914) 161-
198.

*Beentjes, P. C. Jesus Sirach en Tanach. Nieu-
wegein: printed privately, 1981.

*_____. "Jesus Sirach 38:1-15: Problemen rondom
een symbool." BTFT 41 (1980) 260-265.

*_____. "Recent Publications on the Wisdom of
Jesus Ben Sira (Ecclesiasticus)." BTFT 43
(1982) 188-198.

*_____. "Some Misplaced Words in the Hebrew
Manuscript C of the Book of Ben Sira." Bib 67
(1986) 397-401.

*Biblia sacra iuxta latinam Vulgatam versionem, 12:
Sapientia Salomonis, Liber Hiesu Filii Sirach.
Rome, Typis Polyglottis Vaticanis, 1964.

*Biblia sacra juxta simplicem quae dicitur Pschitta,
2. Beirut: Imprimerie Catholique, 1951.
(Referred to as the Mosul edition). Sirach,
pp. 204-255.

*Bickell, G. "Ein alphabetisches Lied Jesus
Sirach's." ZKT 6 (1882) 319-333.

Bickerman, E. J. "The Septuagint as a Translation."
PAAJR 28 (1959) 1-39.

*Boer, P. A. H. de. "זרעם עמד בבריחם Sirach xliv
12a." VTSup 16 (1967) 25-29.

*Box, G. H., and W. O. E. Oesterley. "Sirach," in
APOT 1. Ed. R. H. Charles, 268-517. Oxford:
Clarendon, 1913.

Brock, Sebastian. "Aspects of Translation Technique
in Antiquity." GRBS 20 (1979) 67-87.

_____. "The Phenomenon of the Septuagint." OTS 7
(1972) 11-36.

Brock, Sebastian, Charles Fritsch, and Sidney
Jellicoe. A Classified Bibliography of the
Septuagint. Arbeiten zur Literatur und
Geschichte des hellenistischen Judentums 6.
Leiden: E. J. Brill, 1973.

Brooke, A. E., N. McLean, and H. St. John Thackeray
(vol. II,1 onwards), eds. The Old Testament in
Greek according to the Text of Codex
Vaticanus, Supplemented from Other Uncial
Manuscripts with a Critical Apparatus
Containing the Variants of the Chief Ancient
Authorities for the Text of the LXX.
Cambridge: Cambridge, 1897-1940.

Brown, F., S. R. Driver, and C. A. Briggs. A Hebrew
and English Lexicon of the Old Testament.
Oxford: Clarendon, 1907.

*Cadbury, H. J. "The Grandson of Ben Sira." HTR 48
(1955) 219-225.

*Caird, G. B. "Ben Sira and the Dating of the
    Septuagint," in Studia Evangelica, vol VII:
    Papers Presented to the 5th International
    Congress on Biblical Studies Held at Oxford,
    1973. Ed. E. A. Livingstone, 95-100. Berlin:
    Akademie, 1982.

*Carmignac, J. "Les Rapports entre l'Ecclésiastique
    et Qumrân." RevQ 3 (1961) 209-218.

*Celada, B. "El velo del templo [Sir 50]." Cultura
    Biblica 15 (1958) 109-112.

*Ceriani, A. M. Translatio Syra Pescitto Veteris
    Testamenti ex codice Ambrosiano sec. fere VI
    photolithographice edita, 2.4. Milan:
    Pogliani, 1878.

Charles, R. H., ed. The Apocrypha and Pseudepi-
    grapha of the Old Testament. 2 vols. Oxford:
    Clarendon, 1913.

Charlesworth, James. The Old Testament Pseudepi-
    grapha. 2 vols. Garden City: Doubleday, 1983,
    1985.

Colson, F. H. and G. H. Whitaker. Philo. Loeb
    Classical Library - Philo I and III.
    Cambridge: Harvard University, 1929, 1930.

*Conzelmann, H. "Die Mutter der Weisheit [Sir 24:3-
    7]," in Festschrift R. Bultmann, vol 2, 225-
    234. Tübingen: Mohr, 1964.

*Cowley, A. E., and A. Neubauer, eds. The Original
    Hebrew of a Portion of Ecclesiasticus. Oxford:
    Clarendon, 1897.

*Crenshaw, J. L. "The Problem of Theodicy in
    Sirach: On Human Bondage." JBL 94 (1975) 47-
    64.

Daniel, S. Recherches sur le vocabulaire du culte
    dans la Septante. Études et Commentaires 61.
    Paris: Librairie C. Klincksieck, 1965.

*De Bruyne, D. "Étude sur le texte latin de
    l'Ecclésiastique." RBén 40 (1928) 5-48.

*Delcor, M. "Le texte hebreu du cantique de
    Siracide 51.13 et ss et les anciennes
    versions." Textus 6 (1968) 27-47.

*_____. Review of Die Stellung Jesu ben Siras zwischen Judentum und Hellenismus, by Th. Middendorp. In BLE 76 (1975) 67.

*Di Lella, A. A. "Authenticity of the Geniza Fragments of Sirach." Bib 44 (1963) 171-200.

*_____. "Conservative and Progressive Theology: Sirach and Wisdom." CBQ 28 (1966) 139-154.

*_____. The Hebrew Text of Sirach: A Text-Critical and Historical Study. Studies in Classical Literature 1. The Hague: Mouton, 1966.

_____. "The Poetry of Ben Sira." Eretz Israel 16 (1982) 26-33*.

*_____. "Qumran and the Geniza Fragments of Sirach." CBQ 24 (1962) 245-267.

*_____. "The Recently Identified Leaves of Sirach in Hebrew." Bib 45 (1964) 153-167.

*_____. Review of Sapientia Iesu Filii Sirach, ed. Joseph Ziegler. In CBQ 28 (1966) 539-541.

*_____. "Sirach 10:19-11:6: Text Criticism, Poetic Analysis, and Exegesis," in The Word of the Lord Shall Go Forth: Essays in Honor of David Noel Freedman in Celebration of His Sixtieth Birthday. Ed. C. L. Meyers and M. O'Connor, 157-164. Winona Lake, Ind.: ASOR-Eisenbrauns, 1982.

*_____. "Sirach 51:1-12: Poetic Structure and Analysis of Ben Sira's Psalm." CBQ 48 (1986) 395-407.

*_____. "The Newly Discovered Sixth Manuscript of Ben Sira from the Cairo Geniza." Bib 69 (1988), 226-238.

Dos Santos, Elmar Camilo. An Expanded Hebrew Index for the Hatch-Redpath Concordance to the Septuagint. Jerusalem: Dugith, n.d. [ca. 1968].

*Driver, G. R. "Ben Sira XXXIII, 4." JJS 5 (1954) 177.

*_____. "Hebrew Notes on the Wisdom of Jesus Ben Sirach." JBL 53 (1934) 273-290.

*Duesberg, H. "La dignité de l'homme: Siracide 16,24-17,14." BVC 82 (1968) 15-21.

*_____. "Il est le tout, Siracide 43, 27-33." BVC 54 (1963) 29-32.

*_____. "Le médecin, un sage (Ecclésiastique 38,1-15)." BVC 38 (1961) 43-48.

*Duhaime, J. L. "El elogio de los Padres de Ben Sira y el Cántico de Moisés (Sir 44-50 y Dt 32)." EstBib 35 (1976) 223-229.

*Eberharter, A. "Exegetische Bemerkungen zu Ekkli. 16,1-5." Der Katholik 4te Folge 37 (1908) 386-389.

*_____. Der Kanon des Alten Testaments zur Zeit des Ben Sira. ATAbh 3.3. Münster i.W.: Aschendorff, 1911.

*_____. "KSL in Ps 105,3 und Ekkli 14,9." BZ 6 (1908) 155-161.

*_____. "Zu Ekkli 16,14." BZ 6 (1908) 162-163.

Elliger, K., and W. Rudolph, eds. Biblia Hebraica Stuttgartensia. Stuttgart: Deutsche Bibelgesellschaft, 1983.

Even-Shoshan, Abraham. A New Concordance of the Bible: Thesaurus of the Language of the Bible, Hebrew and Aramaic Roots, Words, Proper Names, Phrases, and Synonyms. Jerusalem: Kiryat Sepher, 1983.

*Facsimiles of the Fragments Hitherto Recovered of the Book of Ecclesiasticus in Hebrew. Oxford-Cambridge: Oxford and Cambridge University, 1901.

*Fang Che-yong, M. "Ben Sira de novissimis hominis." VD 41 (1963) 21-38.

*_____. "Sir 7,36 (Vulg 7,40) iuxta hebraicam veritatem." VD 40 (1962) 18-26.

*_____. "Usus nominis divini in Sirach." VD 42 (1964) 153-168.

*Fransen, I. "Les oeuvres de Dieu (Sir 42,1-50,20)." BVC 81 (1968) 26-35.

*Fritzsche, O. F. Die Weisheit Jesus Sirach erklärt und überstezt. Kurzgefasstes Exegetisches Handbuch zu den Apokryphen des Alten Testamentes, vol. 5. Lipsia: S. Hirzel, 1859.

*Gasser, J. K. Die Bedeutung der Sprüche Jesu Ben Sira für die Datierung des althebräischen Spruchbuches untersucht. Beiträge zur Forderung christlicher Theologie, Jhrg. 8. Hft. 2, 3. Gütersloh: Bertelsmann, 1904.

*Gaster, M. "A New Fragment of Ben Sira [parts of chaps. 18, 19, and 20]." JQR 12 (1899-1900) 688-702.

*Gilbert, M. "L'Éloge de la Sagesse (Siracide 24)." RTL 5 (1974) 426-442.

*Ginsberg, H. L. "The Original Hebrew of Ben Sira 12 10-14." JBL 74 (1955) 93-95.

Grabbe, Lester L. Etymology in Early Jewish Interpretation: The Hebrew Names in Philo. Brown Judaic Studies 115. Atlanta: Scholars, 1988.

*Gray, G. B. "A Note on the Text and Interpretation of Ecclus. XLI. 19." JQR 9 (1896-1897) 567-572.

*Hadot, J. Penchant mauvais et volonté libre dans Sagesse de Ben Sira. Brussels: Presses Universitaires, 1970.

*Hart, J. H. A. Ecclesiasticus: The Greek text of Codex 248. Cambridge: Cambridge University, 1909.

*_____. "[Note on] Sir xlviii 17a,b." JTS 4 (1902-1903) 591-592.

*_____. "Primitive Exegesis as a Factor in the Corruption of Texts of Scripture Illustrated from the Versions of Ben Sira." JQR 15 (1902-1903) 627-631.

*Haspecker, Josef. Gottesfurcht bei Jesus Sirach:
Ihre religiöse Struktur und ihre literarische
und doktrinäre Bedeutung. AnBib 30. Rome:
Pontifical Biblical Institute, 1967.

*Hatch, E. "On the Text of Ecclesiasticus," in
Essays in Biblical Greek. Oxford: Clarendon,
1889, 246-282.

Hatch, E., and Henry A. Redpath. A Concordance to
the Septuagint and the Other Versions of the
Old Testament. Oxford: Clarendon, 1897; repr.
Graz: Akademisches Druck- U. Verlagsanstalt,
1954.

Hengel, M. Judaism and Hellenism. Philadelphia:
Fortress, 1974.

*_____. Review of Die Stellung Jesu ben Siras
zwischen Judentum und Hellenismus, by Th.
Middendorp. In JSJ 5 (1974) 83-87.

*Historical Dictionary of the Hebrew Language. The
Book of Ben Sira: Text, Concordance and an
Analysis of the Vocabulary. Jerusalem: Academy
of the Hebrew Language and Shrine of the Book,
1973 [Hebrew].

Hughes, John. Bits, Bytes, and Biblical Studies: A
Resource Guide for the Use of the Computer in
Biblical and Classical Studies. Grand Rapids:
Zondervan, 1987.

Jastrow, M. A Dictionary of the Targumim, The
Talmud Babli and Yerushalmi, and the Midrashic
Literature. New York: Judaica, 1971.

Jellicoe, Sidney. The Septuagint and Modern Study.
Oxford: Clarendon, 1968.

*Kearns, C. "The Expanded Text of Ecclesiasticus:
Its Teaching on the Future Life as a Clue to
Its Origin." S.S.D. diss., The Pontifical
Biblical Commission, Rome, 1961.

*_____. "Ecclesiasticus," in New Catholic
Commentary on Holy Scripture. Ed. R. D.
Fuller, et al., 541-562. New York: McGraw-
Hill, 1969.

*Knabenbauer, I. Textus Ecclesiastici Hebraeus.
    Appendix to Commentarius in Ecclesiasticum.
    Cursus Scripturae Sacrae 6. Paris:
    Lethielleux, 1902.

Knight, Douglas A., and Gene M. Tucker, eds. The
    Hebrew Bible and Its Modern Interpreters.
    Chico: Scholars, 1985.

*Koole, J. L. "Die Bibel des Ben Sira." OTS 14
    (1965) 374-396.

Kraft, R. A. "Lexicon Project: Progress Report."
    BIOSCS 12 (1979) 14-16.

_____. "Septuagint," in The Interpreter's
    Dictionary of the Bible: Supplementary Volume,
    807-815. Nashville: Abingdon, 1976.

Kraft, R. A., and G. W. E. Nickelsberg, eds. Early
    Judaism and Its Modern Interpreters. Atlanta:
    Scholars, 1986.

Kraft, R. A., and Emanuel Tov. "Computer Assisted
    Tools for Septuagint Studies." BIOSCS 14
    (1981) 22-40.

*Krinetzki, G. "Die Freundschaftperikope Sir 6,5-17
    in traditionsgeschichtlicher Sicht." BZ 23
    (1979) 212-233.

*Kuhn, G. "Beiträge zur Erklärung des Buches Jesus
    Sira." ZAW 47 (1929) 289-296; 48 (1930) 100-
    121.

*Lagarde, P. A. de. Libri Veteris Testamenti
    apochryphi syriace. Leipzig-London: F. A.
    Brockhaus-Williams & Norgate, 1861.

Larcher, C. Études sur le livre de la Sagesse.
    EBib. Paris: Librairie Lecoffre, 1969.

*Lee, Thomas R. Studies in the Form of Sirach 44-
    50. SBLDS 75. Atlanta: Scholars, 1986.

*Lehmann, M. R. "Ben Sira and the Qumran
    Literature." RevQ 3 (1961) 103-116.

*_____. "'Yom Kippur' in Qumran [and Ben Sira]."
    RevQ 3 (1961) 117-124.

322   SIRACH AND ITS PARENT TEXT

Leiman, Sid Z. The Canonization of Hebrew
    Scripture: The Talmudic and Midrashic
    Evidence. Transactions of the Connecticut
    Academy of Arts and Sciences 47. Hamden,
    Conn.: Archon Books, 1976.

*Lévi, I. "Le Chapitre III de Ben Sira," in
    Festschrift zu Ehren des Dr. A. Harkavy. Ed.
    D. v. Günzburg and I. Markon, 1-5. St.
    Petersburg, 1908.

*_____. "Découverte d'un fragment d'une version
    hébraïque de l'Ecclésiastique de Jésus, fils
    de Sirach." REJ 32 (1896) 303-304.

*_____. "Fragments de deux nouveaux manuscrits
    hébreux de l'Ecclésiastique." REJ 40 (1900) 1-
    30.

*_____. The Hebrew Text of the Book of Ecclesi-
    asticus. SSS 3. Leiden: E. J. Brill, 1904.

*_____. L'Ecclésiastique ou la Sagesse de Jésus,
    fils de Sira. 2 parts. Paris: Leroux, 1898,
    1901.

*_____. "Notes sur les ch. VII.29-XII.1 de Ben
    Sira édités par M. Elkan Adler." JQR 13 (1900-
    1901) 1-17.

*_____. "Notes sur les nouveaux fragments de Ben
    Sira. II. III." REJ 40 (1900) 355-257.

*_____. "Un nouveau fragment de Ben Sira." REJ
    92 (1932) 136-145.

*_____. "Les nouveaux fragments hébreux de
    l'Ecclésiastique de Jésus fils de Sira." REJ
    39 (1899) 1-15; 177-190.

*_____. "La Sagesse de Jésus, fils de Sirach:
    découverte d'un fragment de l'original
    hébreu." REJ 34 (1897) 1-50.

Liddell, H. G., Robert Scott, Henry Stuart Jones,
    and Roderick McKenzie. A Greek-English
    Lexicon. 9th ed. Oxford: Clarendon, 1940.

*Lührmann, D. "Aber auch dem Artzt gibt Raum (Sir
    38,1-15)." WDienst 15 (1979) 35-78.

*Mack, Burton L. Wisdom and the Hebrew Epic: Ben Sira's Hymn in Praise of the Fathers. Chicago Studies in the History of Judaism. Chicago: University of Chicago, 1985.

*Maertens, T. "L'éloge des Pères [Sir 44-50]." Lumière et vie 74 (1955) 1-6.

*Marböck, J. "Das Gebet um Rettung Zions Sir 36,1-22 (G:33,1-13a; 26,16b-22) im Zusammenhang der Geschichtsschau Ben Siras," in Memoria Jerusalem. Ed. J. B. Bauer, 93-116. Jerusalem/Graz: Akademische Druck- und Verlagsanstalt, 1977.

*_____. "Gesetz und Weisheit: Zum Verständnis des Gesetzes bei Jesus Sira." BZ N.F. 20 (1976) 1-21.

*_____. "Henoch--Adam--der Thronwagen: Zu frühjüdischen pseudepigraphischen Traditionen bei Ben Sira." BZ N.F. 25 (1981) 103-111.

*_____. Review of Die Stellung Jesu ben Siras zwischen Judentum und Hellenismus, by Th. Middendorp. In VT 24 (1974) 510-513.

*_____. "Sir 38,24-39,11: Der schriftgelehrte Weise. Ein Beitrag zu Gestalt und Werk Ben Siras," in La Sagesse de L'Ancien Testament. Ed. M. Gilbert, 293-316. BETL 51. Gembloux/Louvain: Duclot/University, 1979.

*_____. "Sirachliteratur seit 1966: Ein Überblick." TRu 71 (1975) 177-184.

*_____. Weisheit im Wandel: Untersuchungen zur Weisheitstheologie bei Ben Sira. BBB 37. Bonn: Peter Hanstein, 1971.

*Marcus, J. The Newly Discovered Original Hebrew of Ben Sira (Ecclesiasticus xxxii, 16-xxxiv, 1): The Fifth Manuscript and a Prosodic Version of Ben Sira (Ecclesiasticus xxii, 22-xxiii, 9). Philadelphia: Dropsie College, 1931.

*Margoliouth, D. S. "The Destruction of the Original of Ecclesiasticus." ExpTim 16 (1904-1905) 26-29.

*_____. "Observations on the Fragment of the
     Original of Ecclesiasticus Edited by Mr.
     Schechter." Expositor 5th series 4 (1896) 140-
     151.

*_____. The Origin of the "Original Hebrew" of
     Ecclesiasticus. London: Parker, 1899.

*Margoliouth, G. "The Original Hebrew of
     Ecclesiasticus XXXI.12-31, and XXXVI.22-
     XXXVII.26." JQR 12 (1899-1900) 1-33.

*Margolis, M. L. "Ecclus. 3, 27." ZAW 25 (1905)
     199-200.

*_____. "Ecclus. 6, 4." ZAW 25 (1905) 320-322.

*_____. "Ecclus. 7, 6d." ZAW 25 (1905) 323.

*_____. "Mr. Hart's 'Ecclesiasticus.'" JQR n.s.
     1 (1910-1911) 403-418.

*_____. "A Passage in Ecclesiasticus [34, 16-
     17]." ZAW 21 (1901) 271-272.

Marquis, Galen. "Consistency of Lexical Equivalents
     as a Criterion for the Evaluation of
     Translation Technique as Exemplified in the
     LXX of Ezekiel," in VIth Congress of the
     International Organization for Septuagint and
     Cognate Studies - Jerusalem. Ed. Claude E.
     Cox, 405-424. SCS 23. Atlanta: Scholars, 1987.

_____. "Word Order as a Criterion for the
     Evaluation of Translation Technique in the LXX
     and the Evaluation of Word-Order Variants as
     Exemplified in LXX-Ezekiel." Textus 13 (1986)
     59-84.

Martin, Raymond. Syntactical Evidence of Semitic
     Sources in Greek Documents. SCS 3. Cambridge,
     Mass.: Society of Biblical Literature, 1974.

McGregor, Leslie John. The Greek Text of Ezekiel:
     An Examination of Its Homogeneity. SCS 18.
     Atlanta: Scholars, 1985.

*McRae, C. A. The Hebrew Text of Ben Sira [39,15-
     43,33]. Ph.D. diss., University of Toronto,
     1910.

*Michaelis, D. "Das Buch Jesus Sirach als typischer
    Ausdruck für das Gottesverhältnis des nachalt-
    testamentlichen Menschen." TLZ 83 (1958) 601-
    608.

*Middendorp, Th. Die Stellung Jesu ben Siras
    zwischen Judentum un Hellenismus. Leiden: E.
    J. Brill, 1973.

*Milik, J. T. "Un fragment mal placé dans l'édition
    du Siracide de Masada." Bib 47 (1966) 425-426.

*Nebe, G. W. "Sirach 42.5c." ZAW 82 (1970) 283-286.

*Nelson, Milward Douglas. "The Syriac Version of
    the Wisdom of Ben Sira Compared to the Greek
    and Hebrew Materials." Ph.D. diss., UCLA,
    1981.

*Nestle, E. "Zum Prolog des Ecclesiasticus." ZAW 17
    (1897) 123-134.

Nida, E. Towards a Science of Translating. Leiden:
    E. J. Brill, 1964.

*Nöldeke, T. "Bemerkungen zum hebräischen Ben
    Sira." ZAW 29 (1900) 81-94.

*Oesterley, W. O. E. The Wisdom of Jesus the Son of
    Sirach or Ecclesiasticus. Cambridge: Cambridge
    University, 1912.

Orlinsky, H. M. "The Septuagint as Holy Writ and
    the Philosophy of the Translators." HUCA 46
    (1975) 103-114.

Patte, D. Early Jewish Hermeneutic in Palestine.
    SBLDS 22. Missoula: Scholars, 1975.

*Patteson, Roy K. Jr. "A Study of the Hebrew Text
    of Sir 39:27-41:24." Ph.D. diss., Duke
    University, 1967.

*Payne, Ph. B. "A Critical Note on Eccl. 44.21's
    Commentary on the Abrahamic Covenant." JETS 15
    (1972) 186-187.

*Penar, T. Northwest Semitic Philology and the
    Hebrew Fragments of Ben Sira. BibOr 28. Rome:
    Pontifical Biblical Institute, 1975.

*Peters, N. Das Buch Jesus Sirach oder
Ecclesiasticus. EHAT 25. Münster i.W.:
Aschendorff, 1913.

*_____. Ekklesiastes und Ekklesiastikus." BZ 1
(1903) 47-54, 129-150.

*_____. Der jüngst wiederaufgefundene hebräische
Text des Buches Ecclesiasticus: untersucht,
herausgegeben, übersetzt und mit kritischen
Noten versehen. Freiburg i.B.: Herder, 1902.

*_____. Liber Jesu filii Sirach sive
Ecclesiasticus hebraice. Freiburg i.B.:
Herder, 1905.

*Pietersma, A. "The 'Lost' Folio of the Chester
Beatty Ecclesiasticus." VT 25 (1975) 497-499.

*Prato, G. Il problema della teodica in Ben Sira.
AnBib 65. Rome: Pontifical Biblical Institute,
1975.

*Priest, J. "Ben Sira 45, 25 in the Light of the
Qumran Literature." RevQ 17 (1964) 111-118.

*Purvis, James D. Review of The Hebrew Text of
Sirach: A Text-Critical and Historical Study,
by A. A. Di Lella. In JNES 27 (1968) 157-160.

Rabin, C. "The Translation Process and the Character of the Septuagint." Textus 6 (1968) 1-26.

*Rabinowitz, I. "The Qumran Original of Ben Sira's
Concluding Acrostic on Wisdom." HUCA 42 (1971)
173-184.

Rad, G. von. "Hiob 38 und die altägyptische
Weisheit." SVT 3 (1955) 293-301.

*_____. "Die Weisheit des Jesus Sirach." EvT 29
(1969) 113-133.

Rahlfs, A., ed. Septuaginta. 5th ed. Stuttgart:
Württembergische Bibelanstalt, 1952.

*Reiterer, Franz Vinzenz. "Urtext" und
Übersetzungen: Sprachstudie über Sir 44,16-
45,26 als Beitrag zur Siraforschung. Arbeiten
zu Text und Sprache im Alten Testament 12. St.
Ottilien: EOS, 1980.

*Rickenbacher, Otto. Weisheitsperikopen bei Ben Sira. OBO 1. Freiburg-Göttingen: Universitäts-verlag-Vandenhoeck & Ruprecht, 1973.

Rife, J. M. "The Mechanics of Translation Greek." JBL 52 (1933) 244-252.

*Rivkin, E. "Ben Sira--The Bridge Between Aaronide and Pharisaic Revolutions." Eretz Israel 12 (1975) 95-103.

*Roth, W. "The Lord's Glory Fills Creation: A Study of Sirach's Praise of God's Words (42:15-50:24)." Explor 6 (1981) 85-95.

*_____. "On the Gnomic-Discursive Wisdom of Jesus Ben Sirach." Semeia 17 (1980) 59-79.

*Rüger, H. P. Text und Texform im hebräischen Sirach: Untersuchungen zur Textgeschichte und Textkritik der hebräischen Sirachfragmente aus der Kairoer Geniza. BZAW 112. Berlin: De Gruyter, 1970.

*_____. "Zum Text von Sir. 40.10 und Ex. 10.21." ZAW 82 (1970) 103-109.

*Ryssel, V. "Die Sprüche Jesus', des Sohnes Sirachs," in Die Apokryphen und Pseudepigraphen des Alten Testaments 1. Ed. E. Kautzsch, 230-475. Tübingen: Mohr, 1921.

Safrai, S. "Education and the Study of the Torah," in Compendia Rerum Judicarum ad Novum Testamentum, Section One, The Jewish People in the First Century. Vol 2. Ed. S. Safrai and M. Stern in Cooperation with D. Flusser and W. C. van Unnik, 945-970. Philadelphia: Fortress, 1983.

*Sanders, J. A. The Dead Sea Psalms Scroll. Ithaca, N. Y.: Cornell University, 1967.

*_____. The Psalms Scroll of Qumrân Cave 11 (11QPs^a). DJD 4. Oxford: Clarendon, 1965.

*Sanders, Jack T. Ben Sira and Demotic Wisdom. SBL Monograph Series 28. Chico: Scholars, 1983.

*Schechter, Solomon. "A Fragment of the Original
    Text of Ecclesiasticus." Expositor 5th Ser. 4
    (1896) 1-15.

*_____. "A Further Fragment of Ben Sira [MS C:
    parts of chaps. 4, 5, 25, and 26]." JQR 12
    (1899-1900) 456-465.

*_____. "Genizah Specimens: Ecclesiasticus
    [original text of 49:12-50:22]." JQR 10 (1897-
    1898) 197-206.

*_____. "The Quotations from Ecclesiasticus in
    Rabbinic Literature." JQR 3 (1890-1891) 682-
    706.

*Schechter, Solomon, and C. Taylor. The Wisdom of
    Ben Sira: Portions of the Book of
    Ecclesiasticus from Hebrew Manuscripts in the
    Cairo Genizah Collection Presented to the
    University of Cambridge by the Editors.
    Cambridge: Cambridge University, 1899.

*Schiffer, S. "Le Paragraphe 40, 13-17 de
    l'Ecclésiastique de Ben Sira," in Oriental
    Studies Dedicated to Paul Haupt, 106-110.
    Baltimore: Johns Hopkins, 1926.

*Schirmann, J. "דף חדש מתוך ספר בן-סירא העברי".
    Tarbiz 27 (1957-1958) 440-443.

*_____. "דפים נוספים מתוך ספר 'בן-סירא'." Tarbiz
    29 (1959-1960) 125-134.

*Segal, M. H. "The Evolution of the Hebrew Text of
    Ben Sira." JQR n.s. 25 (1934-1935) 91-149.

*_____. ספר בן-סירא השלם. 2d ed. Jerusalem:
    Bialik Institute, 1958.

*Selmer, C. "A Study of Ecclus. 12:10-19." CBQ 8
    (1946) 306-314.

*Siebenbeck, R. T. "May Their Bones Return to
    Life!-- Sirach's Praise of the Fathers." CBQ
    21 (1959) 411-428.

*Skehan, Patrick W. "The Acrostic Poem in Sirach
    51:13-30." HTR 64 (1971) 387-400.

*_____. "Didache 1,6 and Sirach 12,1." Bib 44
    (1963) 533-536.

*_____. "The Divine Name at Qumran, in the Masada Scroll, and in the Septuagint." BIOSCS 13 (1980) 14-44.

*_____. Review of Il problemo della teodica in Ben Sira, by G. Prato. In Bib 57 (1976) 271-274.

*_____. Review of Text und Textform im hebräischen Sirach, by H. P. Rüger. In Bib 52 (1971) 273-275.

*_____. "Sirach 30:12 and Related Texts." CBQ 36 (1974) 535-542.

*_____. "Sirach 40,11-17." CBQ 30 (1968) 570-572.

*_____. "Staves, Nails and Scribal Slips (Ben Sira 44:2-5)." BASOR 200 (1970) 66-71.

*_____. "Structures in Poems on Wisdom: Proverbs 8 and Sirach 24." CBQ (1979) 365-379.

*_____. "They Shall Not be Found in Parables (Sirach 38,33)." CBQ 23 (1961) 40.

*Skehan, Patrick W., and A. A. Di Lella. The Wisdom of Ben Sira. Anchor Bible 39. Garden City: Doubleday, 1987.

*Smend, Rudolph. Griechisch-syrisch-hebräischer Index zur Weisheit Jesus Sirach. Berlin: Georg Reimer, 1907.

*_____. Die Weisheit des Jesus Sirach erklärt. Berlin: Georg Reimer, 1906.

*_____. Die Weisheit des Jesus Sirach, hebräisch und deutsch. Berlin: Georg Reimer, 1906.

*Snaith, J. G. "Ben Sira's Supposed Love of Liturgy." VT 25 (1975) 167-174.

*_____. "Biblical Quotations in the Hebrew of Ecclesiasticus." JTS 18 (1967) 1-12.

Soisalon-Soininen, I. Die Infinitive in der Septuaginta. AASF B 132,1. Helsinki: Suomalainen Tiedakatemia, 1965.

_____. "Methodologische Fragen der Erforschung der Septuaginta-Syntax," in VIth Congress of the International Organization for Septuagint and Cognate Studies - Jerusalem. Ed. Claude E. Cox, 425-444. SCS 23. Atlanta: Scholars, 1987.

_____. "The Rendering of the Hebrew Relative Clause in the Greek Pentateuch." Proceedings of the Sixth World Congress of Jewish Studies. I. Ed. Avigdor Shinan, 401-406. Jerusalem: World Union of Jewish Studies, 1977.

Sollamo, Raija. Renderings of Hebrew Semiprepositions in the Septuagint. AASF 19. Helsinki: Suomalainen Tiedeakatemia, 1979.

Stephanus, H., ed. Thesaurus Graecae Linguae. Paris: Ambrosius Firmin Didot, 1835.

*Stöger, A. "Der Arzt nach Jesus Sirach (38,1-15)." Arzt und Christ 11 (1965) 3-11.

*Stone, M. E. "Apocryphal Notes and Readings 1, 2 Ben Sira xlii 1, 3." IsOrSt (1971) 123-125.

*Strugnell, John. "Notes and Queries on 'The Ben Sira Scroll from Masada.'" in W. F. Albright Volume, ed A. Malamat. Eretz Israel 9 (1969) 109-119.

*_____. "'Of Cabbages and Kings'--or Queans: Notes on Ben Sira 36:18-21," in The Use of the OT and Other Essays: Studies in Honor of W. E. Stinespring. Ed. James M. Elford, 204-209. Durham: Duke University, 1972.

*_____. Review of The Hebrew Text of Sirach: A Text-Critical and Historical Study, by A. A. Di Lella. In CBQ 30 (1968) 88-91.

Swete, H. B. An Introduction to the Old Testament in Greek. 3rd ed. Cambridge: Cambridge University, 1907.

Talmon, Shemaryahu. "The Textual Study of the Bible - A New Outlook," in Qumran and the History of the Biblical Text. Ed. F. M. Cross and S. Talmon, 321-400. Cambridge: Harvard University, 1975.

Thackeray, H. St. John. A Grammar of the Old
Testament in Greek According to the Septuagint. I, Introduction, Orthography, and Accidence. Cambridge: Cambridge University, 1909.

_____. "The Greek Translators of the Four Books
of Kings." JTS 8 (1907) 262-278.

_____. "Septuagint," in The International
Standard Bible Encyclopedia. Ed. James Orr,
2722-2732. Chicago: Howard-Severance, 1915.

_____. The Septuagint and Jewish Worship. 2d ed.
London: Published for the British Academy by
H. Milford, 1923.

*Thomas, D. W. "The LXX's Rendering of שׁנוח לב טוב
in Ecclus. XXXIII 13." VT 10 (1960) 456.

*Torrey, C. C "The Hebrew of the Geniza Sirach," in
Alexander Marx Jubilee Volume, 585-602. New
York: Jewish Theological Seminary of America,
1950.

Tov, Emanuel. A Classified Bibliography of Lexical
and Grammatical Studies on the Language of the
Septuagint and Its Revisions. Jerusalem:
Akademon, 1982.

_____. "Computer Assisted Alignment of the
Greek-Hebrew Equivalents of the Masoretic Text
and the Septuagint," in La Septuaginta en la
Investigacion Contempoanea (V Congreso de la
IOSCS). Ed. Natalio Fernandez Marcos, 221-249.
Consejo Superior de Investigaciones Cientif-
icas. Madrid: Textos y Estudios "Cardenal
Cisneros" de la Biblia Poliglota Matritense
Instituto "Arias Montano" C.S.I.C., 1985.

_____. A Computerized Data Base for Septuagint
Studies: The Parallel Aligned Text of the
Greek and Hebrew Bible. CATSS 2. Journal of
Northwest Semitic Language Supplementary
Series 1. Stellenbosch: Journal of Northwest
Semitic Languages, 1986.

_____. "The Impact of the LXX Translation of the
Pentateuch on the Translation of the Other
Books," in Mélanges Dominique Barthélemy. Ed.
P. Cassetti, O. Keel, and A. Schenker, 577-
592. OBO 38. Freiburg-Göttingen: Editions
Universitaires-Vandenhoeck & Ruprecht, 1981.

_____. "The Nature and Study of the Translation Technique of the LXX in the Past and Present," in VIth Congress of the International Organization for Septuagint and Cognate Studies - Jerusalem. Ed. Claude E. Cox, 337-359. SCS 23. Atlanta: Scholars, 1987.

_____. "The Representation of the Causative Aspects of the Hiph'il in the LXX - A Study in Translation Technique." Bib 63 (1982) 417-424.

_____. The Text-Critical Use of the Septuagint in Biblical Research. Jerusalem Biblical Studies 3. Jerusalem: Simor, 1981.

Tov, Emanuel, and Benjamin G. Wright. "Computer-Assisted Study of the Criteria for Assessing the Literalness of Translation Units in the LXX." Textus 12 (1985) 149-187.

*Trenchard, Warren C. Ben Sira's View of Women: A Literary Analysis. Brown Judaic Studies 38. Chico.: Scholars, 1982.

Turner, N. A Grammar of New Testament Greek, III, Syntax. Edinburgh: T & T Clark, 1963.

_____. "The Relation of Luke I and II to the Hebraic Sources and to the Rest of Luke-Acts." NTS 2 (1955-1956) 100-109.

*Vaccari, A. "Ecclesiastico, 37, 10.11: critica ed esegesi." EstEcl 34 (1960) 705-713.

*Vattioni, F. Ecclesiastico: Testo ebraico con apparato critico e versioni greca, latine e siriaca. Pubblicazioni del Seminario di Semitistica, Testi 1. Naples: Istituto Orientale di Napoli, 1968.

*_____. "Genesi 1,1 ed Eccli. 15,14." Augustinianum 4 (1964) 105-108.

Vetus Testamentum Graecum Auctoritate Academiae Scientiarum Gottingensis editum. Göttingen: Vandenhoeck & Ruprecht, 1931-.

    Hanhart, Robert. Esther, 1966
    Kappler, W. Maccabaeorum I, 1936, 1967[2].

Kappler, W. and Robert Hanhart. <u>Maccabaeorum</u>
    <u>II</u>, 1959.
Rahlfs, Alfred. <u>Psalmi cum Odis</u>, 1931, 1967²,
    1979³.
Wevers, John. <u>Genesis</u>, 1974.
_____. <u>Deuteronomium</u>, 1977.
_____. <u>Numeri</u>, 1982.
_____. <u>Leviticus</u>, 1986.
Ziegler, Joseph. <u>Isaias</u>, 1939, 1967².
_____. <u>Duodecim Prophetae</u>, 1943, 1967².
_____. <u>Ezechiel</u>, 1952, 1967².
_____. <u>Susanna, Daniel, Bel et Draco</u>, 1954.
_____. <u>Ieremias, Baruch, Threni, Epistula</u>
    <u>Ieremiae</u>, 1957.
_____. <u>Sapientia Salomonis</u>, 1962.
*_____. <u>Sapientia Iesu Filii Sirach</u>, 1965.

*Vogt, E. "Einige hebräischen Wortbedeutungen." <u>Bib</u>
    48 (1967) 57-74.

*_____. "Novi textus hebraici libri Sira." <u>Bib</u>
    41 (1960) 184-190.

*_____. "Novum folium hebr. Sir 15,1-16,7 MS B."
    <u>Bib</u> 40 (1959) 1060-1062.

Walton, B. <u>Biblia sacra polyglotta</u>, 4. London:
    Thomas Roycroft, 1657.

*Winter, M. M. <u>A Concordance to the Peshitta</u>
    <u>Version of Ben Sira</u>. Monographs of the
    Peshitta Institute - Leiden 2. Leiden: E. J.
    Brill, 1976.

*_____. "The Origins of Ben Sira in Syriac." <u>VT</u>
    27 (1977) 237-253, 494-507.

*Wright, Benjamin G. "Ben Sira 43.11b - 'To What
    Does the Greek Correspond?'" <u>Textus</u> 13 (1986)
    111-116.

*_____. "The Hebrew-Greek Parallel Alignment of
    the Wisdom of Ben Sira." in <u>PHI Demonstration</u>
    <u>CD ROM #1</u>. Packard Humanities Institute, 1987.

_____. "A Note on the Statistical Analysis of
    Septuagintal Syntax." <u>JBL</u> 104 (1985) 111-114.

_____. "The Quantitative Representation of
    Elements: Evaluating 'Literalism' in the LXX,"
    in <u>VIth Congress of the International</u>

Organization for Septuagint and Cognate
Studies - Jerusalem. Ed. Claude E. Cox, 311-
335. SCS 23. Atlanta: Scholars, 1987.

*_____. Review of "Urtext" und Übersetzungen:
Sprachstudie über Sir 44,16-45,26 als Beitrag
zur Siraforschung, by Franz Vinzenz Reiterer.
In JQR 75 (1984) 182-185.

*Yadin, Yigael. The Ben Sira Scroll from Masada.
Jerusalem: Israel Exploration Society, 1965.

*Ziegler, Joseph. "Hat Lukian den griechischen
Sirach rezensiert?" Bib 40 (1959) 210-229.

*_____. "Die hexaplarische Bearbeitung des
griechischen Sirach." BZ N.F. 4 (1960) 174-
185.

*_____. "Ursprüngliche Lesarten im griechischen
Sirach," in Mélanges Eugène Tisserant, 1, 461-
487. Studi e testi 231. Vatican: Biblioteca
Apostolica Vaticana, 1964.

*_____. "Die Vokabel-Varianten der O-Rezension
im griechischen Sirach," in Hebrew and Semitic
Studies Presented to Godfrey Rolles Driver.
Ed. D. Winton Thomas, 172-190. Oxford:
Clarendon, 1963.

*_____. "Zum Wortschatz des griechischen
Sirach." ZAW 77 (1958) 274-287.

*_____. "Zwei Beiträge zu Sirach." BZ N.F. 8
(1964) 277-284.

INDEX OF AUTHORS

INDEX OF SUBJECTS

(Due to the frequency of their occurrence, the following subjects have not been included in this index: Ben Sira, Ben Sira's grandson, Greek Sir, Hebrew scriptures [MT], Hebrew Sir, Jewish-Greek [OG] translations, parent text, source text.)

ROBERT A. KRAFT (editor)
Septuagintal Lexicography (1975)
Code: 06 04 01
Not Available

ROBERT A KRAFT (editor)
1972 Proceedings: Septuagint and Pseudepigrapha Seminars (1973)
Code: 06 04 02
Not Available

RAYMOND A. MARTIN
Syntactical Evidence of Semitic Studies in Greek Documents (1974)
Code: 06 04 03
Not Available

GEORGE W. E. NICKELSBURG, JR. (editor)
Studies on the *Testament of Moses* (1973)
Code: 06 04 04
Not Available

GEORGE W.E. NICKELSBURG, JR. (editor)
Studies on the *Testament of Joseph* (1975)
Code: 06 04 05
Not Available

GEORGE W.E. NICKELSBURG, JR. (editor)
Studies on the *Testament of Abraham* (1976)
Code: 06 04 06

JAMES H. CHARLESWORTH
Pseudepigrapha and Modern Research (1976)
Code: 06 04 07
Not Available

JAMES H. CHARLESWORTH
Pseudepigrapha and Modern Research with a Supplement (1981)
Code: 06 04 07 S

JOHN W. OLLEY
"Righteousness" in the Septuagint of Isaiah: A Contextual Study (1979)
Code: 06 04 08

MELVIN K. H. PETERS
An Analysis of the Textual Character of the Bohairic of Deuteronomy (1980)
Code: 06 04 09
Not Available

DAVID G. BURKE
The Poetry of Baruch (1982)
Code: 06 04 10

JOSEPH L. TRAFTON
Syriac Version of the Psalms of Solomon (1985)
Code: 06 04 11

(Continued on previous page)

JOHN COLLINS, GEORGE NICKELSBURG
Ideal Figures in Ancient Judaism: Profiles and Paradigms (1980)
Code: 06 04 12

ROBERT HANN
The Manuscript History of the Psalms of Solomon (1982)
Code: 06 04 13

J.A.L. LEE
A Lexical Study of the Septuagint Version of the Pentateuch (1983)
Code: 06 04 14

MELVIN K. H. PETERS
A Critical Edition of the Coptic (Bohairic) Pentateuch
Vol. 5: Deuteronomy (1983)
Code: 06 04 15

T. MURAOKA
A Greek-Hebrew/Aramaic Index to I Esdras (1984)
Code: 06 04 16

JOHN RUSSIANO MILES
Retroversion and Text Criticism:
The Predictability of Syntax in An Ancient Translation
from Greek to Ethiopic (1985)
Code: 06 04 17

LESLIE J. MCGREGOR
The Greek Text of Ezekiel (1985)
Code: 06 04 18

MELVIN K.H. PETERS
A Critical Edition of the Coptic (Bohairic) Pentateuch,
Vol. 1: Genesis (1985)
Code: 06 04 19

ROBERT A. KRAFT AND EMANUEL TOV (project directors)
Computer Assisted Tools for Septuagint Studies
Vol 1: Ruth (1986)
Code: 06 04 20

CLAUDE E. COX
Hexaplaric Materials Preserved in the Armenian Version (1986)
Code: 06 04 21

MELVIN K.H. PETERS
A Critical Edition of the Coptic (Bohairic) Pentateuch
Vol. 2: Exodus (1986)
Code: 06 04 22

(Continued on previous page)

CLAUDE E. COX (editor)
VI Congress of the International Organization for Septuagint
and Cognate Studies: Jerusalem 1986
Code: 06 04 23

JOHN KAMPEN
The Hasideans and the Origin of Pharisaism:
A Study of 1 and 2 Maccabees
Code: 06 04 24

Order from:

Scholars Press Customer Services
P.O. Box 6525
Ithaca, NY 14851
1-800-666-2211